THE ENGLISH CAROL

THE ENGLISH CAROL

THE
ENGLISH CAROL

By
ERIK ROUTLEY

GREENWOOD PRESS, PUBLISHERS
WESTPORT, CONNECTICUT

Library of Congress Cataloging in Publication Data

Routley, Erik.
    The English carol.

    Reprint of the 1959 ed. published by Oxford Univer-
sity Press, New York.
    Bibliography: p.
    1. Carols--History and criticism. 2. Hymns,
English--History and criticism. I. Title.
[ML2881.E5R7 1973]   783.6   73-9129
ISBN 0-8371-6989-5

Originally published in 1959 by Oxford University Press,
New York

Reprinted with the permission of Barrie & Jenkins,
Publishers

Reprinted in 1973 by Greenwood Press,
a division of Congressional Information Service, Inc.
88 Post Road West, Westport, Connecticut 06881

Library of Congress catalog card number 73-9129
ISBN 0-8371-6989-5

Printed in the United States of America

10 9 8 7 6 5 4 3

CYRILLO VINCENTIO TAYLOR

Ecclesiæ Anglicanæ Sacerdoti
Scholæ Regiæ Sanctæ Musicæ olim Custodi
Amico adjutori præceptori
  dedicatum

Preface

I DO not know that there could be a more delightful task than that which the publisher invited me to undertake in preparing this book about carols. Apart from the limitations which it unavoidably derives from those of its author, the book does not venture beyond a discussion of English carol singing. To go thoroughly into the religious folk-song of all the countries where carols are sung would be at this stage both premature and beyond your present author's capacity. The work there is still being done, notably by such authorities as Dr. Laurence Picken of Cambridge, whose discoveries of Asiatic folk-song have so enriched the first volume of the *New Oxford History of Music*. But in any case, such a work would require many volumes, and is not only beyond my capacity, but, I think, beyond my brief.

On English carols, as the opening pages of this book acknowledge, a certain amount of close scholarly work has been done since the last general history of our carols was published. And at the present time collections of carols, designed for users of varying degrees of seriousness, are being published in great numbers. My own purpose is to tell the story of carol-singing, and place it over against church history, in much the same way which I have ventured to adopt with hymns and their tunes.

The difficulty with a book of this kind, which is designed to be read for pleasure as well as to be in some sense a work of reference, is to keep the citation of examples within a reasonable compass and also within the reader's reasonable reach. There is one English collection of carols which eclipses all the others in catholicity and comprehensiveness; that is, of course, *The Oxford Book of Carols*. That is the one collection which can quite easily be used as a book of reference. All the others, by comparison, are specialised or incomplete. The reader is advised to have a copy of this book at his elbow. Most of what it contains is mentioned here, and the printer will be saved a great deal of music-type if the reader can refer to it for music examples.

I have now to acknowledge the help of a large number of people to whom the reader is indebted for what he reads here. If we removed from the book everything that is not directly owed to this group of friendly people and institutions, it would at once lose whatever distinction it may claim. First, I must thank the Warden of the Royal School of Church Music, the Reverend Cyril Taylor, for a great deal of help. Had he written this book I verily believe the reader would have been better served; but he has helped me in all manner of ways. I have been made free of the Colles Library at the Royal School of Church Music, a library which no serious music student can afford to pass by; and I am particularly grateful for his presenting me with all the important clues to the truth about the Service of Nine Lessons and Carols. The facts recorded in the penultimate section of this book are in the first place owed to him.

In the same connection I record my gratitude to the Provost and Fellows of King's College, Cambridge, for allowing me to reproduce certain orders of service in the Appendix, and especially to the Dean, Dr. A. R. Vidler, and the organist, Mr. David Willcocks, for their practical help. Equally I am grateful to the Dean of York, Dr. E. A. Milner-White, for permission to reproduce his statement about the King's College Festival, and for other help in correspondence.

The Vicar of Addington (the Reverend Canon F. W. Greenaway), the organist of Addington, Mr. W. H. Still, and Canon F. W. B. Bullock, formerly of Truro, have very kindly furnished further information on the same matter, and Mr. W. A. J. Davey, M.B.E., T.D., of the *West Briton*, Truro, has most kindly furnished me with press-cuttings and other information about the Truro service.

At other points I gratefully acknowledge help from the following people: From Mrs. Peter Scott for the use of her hitherto unpublished carol on p. 218; from Miss Maud Karpeles for permission to reprint Examples 22, 26, 27, 30, 31 and 39; from the Executors of the late Walter de la Mare and Miss Violet Barton for permission to print Walter de la Mare's poem, "A Ballad of Christmas" on pp. 224–225; from the Executors of the late A. A. Milne and Messrs. Curtis Brown for permission to print the verse from Mr. Milne's carol on pp. 222–223; from Messrs. Novello, Ltd., for permission to print Ex. 49; from Dr. Vaughan Williams for Ex. 12, from Miss Imogen Holst for Ex. 48, and from Messrs. A. R. Mowbray & Co. Ltd., for the quotation from a carol by Selwyn Image on p. 223. Certain other music examples are taken from the *Oxford Book of Carols*, and I am glad to acknowledge the co-operation of the Oxford Press in allowing me to reproduce material from that book, to which at each place detailed reference is made. The Royal Musical Association and Messrs. Stainer & Bell,

Ltd., have kindly allowed me the use of Exx. 1 and 2, from the fourth volume of *Musica Britannica*. I am indebted to the Ryerson Press, Toronto, and to the compilers of *Traditional Songs from Novia Scotia* for the quotation on page 90.

Most of the illustrations are acknowledged in their place, but I should especially wish to thank the Vicar of Horspath, near Oxford, for permission to reproduce the picture of the Copcot Window (facing page 65), and to my friends Dr. G. D. Parkes and Mr. A. D. Parkes for taking the photograph.

I reproduce the order of service in Appendix II with the knowledge and kind consent of the Principal of Mansfield College, Oxford. The arrangement of the tune in Ex. 44 is the present author's copyright.

They will hardly expect to find their names here, but I cannot forbear to record my debt to certain minstrels of my acquaintance, among them the Reverend Derek Jones, now of Maun, Bechuanaland, Mr. David Allen and Mr. Norman Hart, for their part in introducing me to that form of minstrelsy which I mention on my closing pages; Mr. Hart in particular has allowed me to plague him with correspondence.

Very little, then, of the present work is really my own. I must hasten, however, to absolve my friends and authorities from any share in the imperfections of this work; these at any rate I confidently claim for myself alone. I must also say that if I have inadvertently infringed any rights of which I was not aware, I apologise at once, and shall have such matters corrected in any future edition.

Oxford   E.R.

Contents

List of Illustrations

Abbreviations

These are kept to a minimum in this book. The only abbreviations which do not appear on the same page as the first mention of the full titles they denote are these:

Hymns A. & M. = Hymns Ancient and Modern, Revised edition (1950); where the Standard edition (1922) is intended, the sign (S) is added.

E.H. = *English Hymnal* (Oxford University Press, 1933).

G. with a number following = R. L. Greene, *The Early English Carol* (Clarendon Press, 1935); the number indicates the serial number of the carol in the main section of the book.

M.B. = *Musica Britannica* (ed. J. Stevens), Vol. IV (Stainer & Bell, 1952).

Oxford = *The Oxford Book of Carols* (Oxford University Press, 1928). Similarly: *Cowley* and *Cambridge* implying in each case, "Carol Book".

S.P. = *Songs of Praise* (Oxford University Press, enlarged edition, 1931).

U.C.B. = University Carol Books (E. H. Freeman, Brighton): publication of the small books, each containing about six carols, was begun in 1923. At the time of writing twenty-four books have been published.

My own book, *The Music of Christian Hymnody* (Independent Press, 1957), to which of necessity fairly frequent reference has to be made, is indicated by the abbreviation *M.C.H.*

A Note to the Reader

With wise judgment, and with an eye to your convenience and pleasure, the publisher has asked me to avoid all footnotes. Material that would have appeared in footnotes, chiefly bibliographical, will be found in the section beginning on p. 257 and headed "Annotated Bibliography". Your eye will not be caught by any direct references to these notes in the text; but they are designed to answer the questions which might well arise in your mind as you read, concerning the sources of my information, the identity of the less celebrated characters in the story, and clues to the further study of points which may interest you but which are treated insufficiently for your taste in the text. Each note is preceded by a page number and, where necessary, a clue-word.

Introduction

"THE genius of the present age," wrote William Sandys in the
year 1833, "requires work and not play." The reader who
perseveres to the end of this book will perhaps feel that what
I here write is chiefly an exposition of that text from Sandys. That,
indeed, is what I feel I ought to do. Much learned work has been done
during the past generation or two by way of establishing the sources
and editing the manuscripts of our earliest carols, not to mention the
discoveries that have been made since about 1880 in the field of the
folk-carol, and there would be nothing gained by going over that
ground again. My purpose is to tell the story of the carol, which story
I owe entirely to the learned writers and researchers whom I am about
to name; but as the story unfolds itself I hope to show what comment
it offers on the developing social and religious life of our country over
a period of half a thousand years.

The two learned treatises to which we stand chiefly in debt for our
knowledge of the earliest carols (if indeed they are the earliest) are
Dr. R. L. Greene's *The Early English Carols* and the fourth volume,
edited by Mr. John Stevens, of *Musica Britannica*, entitled *Medieval
Carols*. Dr. Greene's book, which at the time of writing is almost
impossible to obtain outside the libraries, is a close study of those
medieval carols which survived in manuscripts dated before 1550,
preceded by an introduction of 145 pages, which remains the classic
work on the subject. The body of the book contains the texts of 474
medieval carols, critically edited, with explanatory notes following.
The *Musica Britannica* volume is a similarly critical edition of such
music associated with these medieval carols as has survived in manuscripts of the same period. Here we have 135 musical settings, mostly
polyphonic, but a few monodic, with all the necessary critical apparatus
added, and a brief but important introduction. A comparison of the
474 with the 135 shows at once that about seventy per cent of the music
of these carols has perished.

But these two works deal with the carol only in a specialised and limited sense. If the reader who is at the moment unfamiliar with the curious lore of the subject looks at Greene he will see scarcely anything that he recognises as a carol: this is because these scholars define the word "carol" in a special sense that excludes much that in our popular speech is called by that name. The story of this larger and more loosely-styled class of verse and music is accessibly told only in such places as the Preface to *The Oxford Book of Carols*, or in similar introductions to other collections. The first complete edition (about 1877) of Bramley and Stainer's famous Collection, *Christmas Carols New and Old*, has an excellent introduction by Bramley. Chope's *Carols for Use in Church* (edition of 1894) has an equally interesting one by Sabine Baring-Gould. Sandys's book, which we have already mentioned, has an introduction by its author of 136 pages, containing a great deal of material about primitive Christmas customs as well as important conjectures on the origins of folk-carols. But few of these are easily come by at the present time. Another book which has long gone out of print is *The Story of the Carol*, by Edmundstone Duncan of Sale, Cheshire, published in 1911; agreeable and informative though that book is at many points, it suffers from the double disadvantage of being in itself a singularly disorganised composition, badly indexed and useless as a book of reference, and of having been written at a time when certain theories about the origin of the carol were current which are now seriously doubted, and when modern conventions of scholarship governing the transcription of ancient music had not yet become fully established.

All modern carol books have some kind of an introduction: a particularly good one of the briefer kind is that of the Rev. Cyril V. Taylor in the Batsford book of *Christmas Carols*. And of course there are many carol-books in circulation now to which we shall have to refer. But in the end the book which forms the handiest work of reference for examples is *The Oxford Book of Carols*, to which we shall hereinafter refer simply as *Oxford*. The 197 carols included in that book form the most comprehensive and representative collection of carols in English, and while at certain points the editing of the book is open to criticism of a kind which is none of our business in this present book, it is the obvious source-book for contemporary English practice. If the reader has that book at hand, he will be able to refer often to words and music which we shall not need to quote in full. Of other collections, we shall frequently refer to the late G. R. Woodward's *Cambridge* and *Cowley* Carol Books, using simply the names *Cambridge* and *Cowley* for our references.

But we are going to be concerned with something slightly different from what the authors of the existing histories have been saying. You could put it thus: writing 125 years ago, Sandys, a London solicitor, produced a collection of carols, with a little music appended, which he had to go to Devon and Cornwall to collect. Why did he have to travel so far? Why to what was then (and remained until the advent of the motor-car) the remotest part of England? It was because in the great cities, where English culture was advancing most rapidly, something was going "underground" which in the depths of the country was still discernible "on the surface". We may approach this situation by considering one or two parallels.

When Sir Richard Terry rambled round the docks of Tyneside to look for authentic sea-shanties, he knew that time was short. The sea-shanty, he tells us, is primarily a "labour-song", and the screw-steamer was, when he was collecting some fifty years ago, abolishing the kind of labour without which the sea-shanty had no meaning. Shanties are songs that need a context, and the movement of civilisation was driving the sea-shanty underground, or driving it into an embalmed retirement in Sir Richard's editions. We shall never again sing shanties in the conditions which gave them birth, because we have carefully and on principle done away with the conditions. The rhythmical discipline of the capstan and the long haul of the great sail produced song as naturally as marching produced song; but no genius has yet arisen to offer us a minstrelsy appropriate to the filling of the tank with diesel-oil, or the replacement of the nuclear power-unit.

It is somewhat the same with folk-songs. One recalls Miss Lucy Broadwood's words about the collecting of folk-songs:

> In all parts of the country, the difficulty of getting the old-fashioned songs out of the people is steadily on the increase, and those who would undertake the task of collecting them . . . should lose no time in setting to work.

The great folk-song revival at the turn of the present century, in which Miss Broadwood was a leading figure, had a sense of urgency about it simply because the folk-songs were disappearing, and because, in the absence of those social circumstances in which they flourished, people who did remember them were disinclined to sing them. Returning to Terry, we remember his story of the old Irishwoman who, asked to give a demonstration of "keening", replied, "But how can I keen without a body?"—that is, without a palpable corpse and a genuine grief, "keening" makes nonsense. Similarly the sailors said, "How can we sing a shanty without having our hands on the rope".

So, as we read in the *Journal of the Folk-Song Society* of the results of the researches of folk-song collectors, chiefly in the decade immediately preceding the first World War, we see again and again how they are noted down from the singing of very elderly people who learnt them from their seniors by oral tradition; and while we are left to make a fairly easy guess as to the techniques of persuasion, it is made quite clear that the songs were not easily come by.

And so it is, at bottom, with the carol. Our modern carols—that is to say, the carols that are now sung in however formal or informal conditions—are all sung from books and papers, and what is written on the papers is in almost every case (apart from hymns) the result of diligent research. The exceptions to this are carols composed during the past century or so. The words of "Good King Wenceslas", for example, are little more than a hundred years old. The words and tune of "In the bleak midwinter" date from a little before, and a little after, the year 1900. But the exceptions are few. Most of the carols that we now sing are carols that "went underground" and were rescued at the last minute from running away altogether into the sand.

All this we shall have to discuss in greater detail as we go on; the point at present is that carols belong natively to a civilisation, an outlook, a religious habit, which at certain points is in controversy with the civilisation, outlook and religious habit of present-day protestant England. One way of putting this is Sandys's way: the genius of 1833 required "work and not play", and carols belonged then, and belong now, to "play". The carol is a strictly medieval technique that has obstinately survived in modern English popular use. I shall not at once substantiate this in detail, but an obvious confirmation of that statement is in the fact that during the age—let us say the period 1880–1950—when large numbers of people were (and remain) exceedingly doubtful about the Virgin Birth and the Annunciation, reserving these traditions to a place well away from the centre of their faith and in some circles excluding references to them from their hymn books, there were very few, if any, who were unwilling at Christmas time to sing the praises of Mary and the story of Gabriel in their carols.

In this there was, and is, no sense of anachronism or insincerity. It is just that carols are a survival of a religious habit that in other contexts has been superseded; the imagery of the carol brings a picture not only of what is written in its verses but of that goodwill and hospitality,

both of substance and also of mind, which Christmas as a whole
insists upon.

But none the less the controversy is there, and at other levels we shall
encounter it. It will be our business, then, first to examine the medieval
manuscript carols, then to look at the ballad-carols which are today
much more familiar, and, following that, to trace the carol through
the Puritan ages to modern times. Our concern is chiefly with the
carol as a comment on English culture, but nowadays we are familiar
with almost as many carols from non-English sources as carols from
our own home ground, and of these also we shall have to take notice.
As we go, we shall perhaps see what moved Sandys to make his
distempered observation.

PART ONE

THE SINGING AGES

The Medieval Manuscript Carols

What is a Carol?

As soon as we seek to define the carol, we are involved in one of those acts of historical self-adjustment which are constantly demanded by a study of these agreeable anachronisms. Most readers, I take it, would find little to quarrel with in that description of carols which opens the Preface to *The Oxford Book of Carols*:

> Carols are songs with a religious impulse that are simple, hilarious, popular and modern.

That, though offered as a definition, is nothing of the kind. It was characteristic of Dr. Percy Dearmer that, promising a definition, he should offer us a highly provocative description. Dearmer was a trenchant critic of English Edwardian religion (as a reading of his early work, *A Parson's Handbook*, confirms), and everything that he detested in it is conveniently summarised in the opposites of the four adjectives he applies to carols: to him most of it was, fairly exactly, confused, lugubrious, bourgeois and antiquated. When he says that carols are "modern" he means, "set in such language as shall express the manner in which the ordinary man at his best understands the ideas of his age, and bring the traditional conservative religion up to date".

Few, I say, will feel that, though provocative, that is an unfair description. And if we turn to the dictionaries, most of them lay stress on the notion of popularity, and lead us to expect something that is certainly religious, certainly "of the people", and certainly distinguishable from a hymn. In some places the notion of Christmas is included in the definition, thus:

> *Concise Oxford Dictionary:* "Joyous song, human or of birds, esp. Christmas hymn."
> *Oxford Companion to Music* (P. A. Scholes): "A religious seasonal song, of joyful character, in the vernacular and sung by the common people."
> *Everyman's Dictionary of Music* (E. Blom, Dent, 1946): "A Christmas song, dating from the fourteenth and fifteenth centuries in England, but older on the Continent."

International Cyclopaedia of Music and Musicians (O. Thompson, Dent, 1942): "A traditional song for the celebration of Christmas."

That is all very well, but once we consider the derivation of the word "carol", we see that something must be added to, and something else subtracted from, the popular definition.

Bramley quotes one the Reverend Arthur Bedford (sometime incumbent of the Temple Church) as saying that carols are so called because they were popular during the reign of King Charles I, *Carolus* being the Latin form of the name Charles. That is a pleasant fancy, and as we shall see, in the early years of Charles I carols of a kind were indeed exceedingly popular. But of course that definition cannot be taken seriously by anybody who knows that carols are a medieval technique. The word "carol" appears in many places in medieval English literature, as we may read in the first section of Dr. Greene's Introduction. A source dated about 1300, the *Cursor Mundi*, uses the word "carol" (spelt as we now spell it) in the sense of a round dance, taking it direct from the French; and from then on we find "carole", "karolle" and "caral" in English sources, and in a French source, "kyrielle", which last caused some ecclesiastically-minded persons to derive the word from the liturgical formula *Kyrie eleison*.

But it is generally held now that Bramley was right to derive the word from the Greek *choros*, meaning a dance, and perhaps from the associated word *choraules*, which means one who accompanies the dance on an hautboy. "Dance" is at the heart of it. Therefore, dismissing all sentimental derivations and interpretations, Dr. Greene gives us this definition: "A song on any subject, composed of uniform stanzas and provided with a burden."

That definition covers everything that Dr. Greene has included in his book and transcribed from medieval manuscripts. It will be observed that what has been subtracted is the use of anything corresponding to the word "religious" in the definition, and anything corresponding to "popular"; indeed, all adjectives have disappeared from it. What has been added is, in the implication of the words *burden* and *stanza*, the notion of the dance. Now it may appear to some that it is a fantastic pedantry to try to claim that a carol is not what everybody now thinks it is, but something different. Two things could be said in reply to that. One is that, while it is fair enough to forget at this time of day that a "carol" is strictly a dance-form, and that there is nothing in its definition to suggest either religion or joy, it is certainly unfair and improper to follow popular opinion so far as to confine all carols to

Christmas, which on certain definitions we are obliged to do; to that extent we must beware of being impatient of precision. But we may also say that, even if we say that to all general purposes today a carol is a cheerful seasonal song appropriate to a popular festive occasion, we ignore at our peril the continuing implications of the fact that it began as a dance. Its dance-content is its most anti-puritan, anti-"work" element, and we shall never understand its extraordinary history if we forget that it began not as a pious religious gesture but as a dance.

The Form of the medieval manuscript Carol

The two component parts of the medieval carol-form are the *burden* and the *stanza*. The stanza is what we should call the "verse", but the burden is not quite what we should call the "refrain", although it is repeated at each change of stanza. The difference is that the "burden" comes first of all, as well as after each stanza, and that its simple form of words usually expresses a summary of the thought of what follows in the stanzas.

The simplest example of "burden" in a modern song familiar to everybody today is in the hymn, "All things bright and beautiful". Here the first quatrain, verbally and musically self-contained, gives you the sense of the whole, and becomes a chorus after each verse. "Onward, Christian soldiers" is almost, but not quite, in "burden" form, since the first quatrain is part of verse 1, and not separate from it. But the "Hail thee, Festival Day" series in the *English Hymnal* (624, 628, 630, 634) are all, in words and music, faithful to the form.

This form survives in practice in very few English carols in modern use. *Oxford* has altogether thirteen, and in some the traces of the form can still be seen. Take for example, No. 62, "Nowell sing we both all and some" (G. 29, M.B. 7). The melody is faithfully preserved, though harmonised according to modern convention in four parts. The "burden" is the first two lines—

> Nowell sing we both all and some
> Now *rex pacificus* is come,

and if it be sung at the beginning, after each stanza, and at the end, you have the original burden form. Similarly No. 23, "Make we joy now in this feast" (G. 31, M.B. 26 and 97) is correctly marked to be sung with its burden beginning and ending. "A babe is born of high nature", No. 40 (G. 117, M.B. 27), with a magnificent tune credibly ascribed to Dunstable, is again correctly marked, and No. 36, "Tidings true" (G. 239, M.B. 4A) would be so if a *dal segno* mark were inserted at the sixth bar. "Dieu vous garde", 21 (*G*. 6, *M.B.* 80) is, on the other hand, deformed by its arranger, since originally "verses" 1 and 2 were all part of the burden, thus:

> Nowell, Nowell, Nowell, Nowell,
> Who is there that singeth so, Nowell, Nowell?
> *I am here, Sir Christemass.*
> Welcome, my Lord, Sir Christemass,
> Welcome to us all both more and less,
> Come near, Nowell!

A modern setting of a medieval carol which preserves the "burden" form exactly is Gustav Holst's "Lullay my liking" (182, *G.* 143). Here the burden is unchanging, and sung in its proper place, even though the music of the other verses changes each time. Other medieval carols set by modern composers are to be found near the end of *Oxford* at Nos. 169, 172, 174, 177, 178, and 184, all of which are in Greene. No. 173, "The Golden Carol", is a medieval carol of the same kind, whose burden has disappeared (*G.* 25).

Now this burden-stanza form comes direct from the medieval processional dance. Greene illustrates this from the practice that survives in the Padstow May-dances. In these the "burden" is a chorus sung by the spectators over and over again while the dancers swing through the street; the stanza is sung by a leader while the dancers pause for breath. "Burden" originally is a "theme" or "song": it survives in this sense in the Authorised Version of the Bible (see the opening verses of Isaiah 15, 17, 19, 21, 22, 23, and other places), and it survives in the musical term "fa-burden". "Stanza" comes from the Latin *stare* "to stand", and *stantes*, "people standing", and therefore naturally refers to the halting, or the marking time, of the dance-pattern.

It is not, of course, to be supposed that these medieval carols were designed to be danced to. The most we can say is that they take their form from the form that developed through dancing, and that they shared it with the traditional processional dances.

Indeed, "traditional" is not the right word for these carols at all. Dr. Greene's special contention is that the carol in this period was composed by literate, learned and probably clerical authors, to be "one weapon of the Church in her long struggle with the survivals of paganism and with the fondness of her people for unedifying entertainment". It is not in any sense folk-song, even if there are signs here and there— turns of phrase, rhythmical tricks and so forth—that indicate that folk-song is in the back of its writer's mind. But the very fact of their being written down at once is the best evidence that they are not folk-song. Among all the 474 carols collected from manuscripts by Dr. Greene there is only one which has survived in folk-song form. This is a carol which Greene found in manuscript, in burden-stanza form, which also a collector heard quite independently in Derbyshire at the end of the nineteenth century, received by the singer by oral tradition and sung with a refrain. As it happens, this is one of the most remarkable of all surviving carols, and it will engage our attention a little later (G. 322, compare *Oxford* 61 and 184). But its solitariness is impressive testimony to the rightness of Dr. Greene's thesis.

It was, then, a phase of the familiar controversy, summed up in the aphorism, attributed to more than one religious reformer, "Why should the devil have all the good tunes?" The dance could be trivial, but the church would spiritualise it. Feasting could be orgiastic, but the church would balance it with fasting. Joy could be selfish and frantic, but the church would make it sane. Dr. Greene sums it all up by saying that while the medieval carols of his collection were not popular by origin, they were "popular by destination". They were composed by literate men for the people at large to sing. The words would be transmitted among the people by oral tradition, but there was a written text by which those who could read and were interested enough could check them. The names of the authors and composers of these carols have almost all been lost. Richard Smert, Rector of Plymtree, Exeter, from 1435 to 1477, is mentioned several times in *M.B.* Two other names have survived, Childe and Trouloffe, but nothing is known about either. One carol (which is mentioned again below) is attributed to John Dunstable on the evidence of the initials J.D. against the tune.

The following is a carol of the simpler kind from one of these manuscript sources. Every one of the tunes, except only one (*M.B.* 86) employs triple time, but this is one of the shorter and less elaborate tunes. In the manuscript it is harmonised in two parts, the counterpoint running above the melody as here given:

For in this rose contained was
Heaven and earth in little space,
   Res miranda.

The angels sang the shepherds to:
Gloria in excelsis Deo,
   Gaudeamus.

By that rose we may well see
That he is God in persons three,
   Pari forma.

Leave we all this worldly mirth
And follow we this joyful birth;
   Transeamus.

The tune may be found harmonised in two parts, as in the original, at
M.B. 14. The original form of the words is at *G.* 173. See also Terry, *A
Medieval Carol Book* (Curwen, no date), p. 56. Translations of the Latin
phrases: v. 2, "A wonderful thing"; v. 3, "Of like form"; v. 4, "Glory
to God in the highest, let us rejoice"; v. 5, "Let us pass over" (*sc.* from
this world to the other).

This is one of the simplest of these carols, both in words and music.
It could easily have been popularly sung. We shall discuss later (p. 32)
the interposition of Latin words among the English. The reader will
note in this example the juxtaposition of pure orthodox theology with
a single strong element of imagery—that of "the rose". This figure is
often used in medieval literature of our Lord, or of our Lady; we may
compare the well known German carol:

> Es ist ein' Ros' entsprungen
> Aus einer Wurzel zart,   (*Oxford,* 76)

which itself goes back to Isaiah xi, "There shall come forth a shoot
out of the stock of Jesse".

That is the texture of all medieval religious carols—imagery, strong
and memorable because not overdone, along with a light-hearted
acceptance of the theological profundities. How fond they were of
singing of the mysterious Trinity! One recalls how in *Piers Plowman*
one hears such lines as these:

> Every bishop who bears the cross is thereby commanded
> To pass through his provinces, to bring the people to him,
> To tell them of the Trinity, to teach them faithfully.

"To tell them of the Trinity" means simply "to teach them the
Christian Faith", and thus it was accepted in those days, when the
metaphysics of doctrine came to the common man through images
rather than through concepts. What you do not get in the medieval
carol is what we now call the "Christmas card" imagery—self-conscious

references to snow and cold weather, detailed pictures of Bethlehem, and so forth. Their images are simpler, and more Biblical.

Many of the religious carols were in this way simple. Their words were always simple. But often their music was more elaborate. Many examples of elaborate and learned music, harmonised sometimes in three-part polyphony, can be read in *Musica Britannica*. The indications in such cases are that although the words were "popular by destination", the musical setting ensured that they would only be performed by capable choirs, probably as adornments of the Rites and Offices of the church. While it is still fair to describe the carol in this form as

"popular by destination", it must be understood that where the music was as elaborate as this the common people did not themselves perform it, but only listened to it. I choose the next example, which is of this kind, for the limpid beauty of its melody. It will be seen that it has a double burden, and the editor of *Musica Britannica* IV suggests that the first burden was sung only at the very beginning, while the second burden was sung immediately after the first, and also after each stanza. Here again we have a development that leaves the immediate context of the dance well behind. In the original the melody is written

on the lowest line; the second burden and the bars marked with abtie
are harmonised in three parts in the original, the rest in two. The
original is in British Museum Add. Mss. 5665, and the carol bears
the name (presumably as composer) of Richard Smert (G. 59,
M.B. 119).

It is in the words, rather than the music, of these carols that one
can most easily see the force of the description "popular by destination". They were designed to be improving and also attractive.
Therefore their teaching of theology was wrapped up in a lyrical, and
here and there even in a dramatic form—as in the carol mentioned
above (p. 28), "I am here, Sir Christemass". The pattern of the
messenger bringing good news, or more simply of the narrator telling
a story, is very often encountered in these pieces; you can see it in
"A babe is born" (*Oxford* 40):

> *What tidings bringest thou, messenger,*
> *Of Christes birth this jolly day?*
> A babe is born of high nature,
> The Prince of peace that ever shall be. . . .

The "narrative" style appears in such carols as "I will you sing with
all my might" (173), "I saw a fair maiden sitten and sing" (182), and
"I sing of a maiden that is makeless" (183). It is possible to doubt, in
these cases where the "burden" consists of a question answered in the
stanzas, whether in fact the burden was in performance repeated at
the end; if it was, the sense of the words was corrupted; but in the
strict burden form, of course, the burden should be self-contained, and
not rely on the stanzas for the completion of its sense, and we can
therefore suppose that the notion of making the stanzas answer the
burden was a later invention, from a time when the dance-associations
of the style were becoming forgotten.

Another agent of popularity must have been the conscious use in
the carols of the metre of the earliest Christian Latin hymns, and the
liberal use in them of quotations from such hymns. Many of the
religious carols are written (the burden apart) in those eight-syllable
lines which are the metre of the Ambrosian Office hymns (preserved
usually in the translations of such hymns in modern hymn books). In
the hymns you normally find four-line verses of regular form, while
in the carols more commonly you find two or three rhyming octosyllables and a short line following.

A good example of the use of hymns to tie the carol into the religious
habits of the people is in "Make we joy now in this feast" (*Oxford* 23).

Here we have the strict Ambrosian metre (called in modern books "Long Metre"), with quotations from hymns of the English breviaries. We will set it out with references to current hymn books where these apply:

Make we joy now in this feast
In qua Christus natus est

A patre unigenitus   (*A. & M. (S)*) 486)
Through a maiden is come to us:
Sing we of him and say, "Welcome",
Veni Redemptor gentium.   (*E.H.* 14)

Agnoscat omne saeculum
A bright star made three Kinges come
For to seek with their presents
Verbum supernum prodiens.   (*E.H.* 2)

A solis ortus cardine   (*E.H.* 18)
So mighty a Lord was none but he:
He on our kind his peace has set
Adam parens quod polluit.

Maria ventre concipit,
The Holy Ghost was ay her with;
In Bethlehem yborn he is
Consors paterni luminis.

O lux beata Trinitas!   (*E.H.* 164)
He lay between an ox and ass,
And by his mother, maiden free
Gloria tibi, domine!   (*A. & M. (S)* 486,
                                                      doxology)

The Latin lines (except the last) are the opening lines of well known medieval office-hymns. The references against most of them will show how they have been translated in English use. Those beginning *Agnoscat, Adam,* and *Maria* all come from the same hymn in the York Breviary—a hymn, that is, probably of English origin and familiar to Englishmen—and that beginning *Consors* comes from another hymn in the same source: neither of these survives in modern English use. It will be seen that the sense of the carol runs straight through the Latin lines, and that it is obviously an ingenious composition by an ecclesiastic designed for the edifying of the common people.

There is another form of Latin interlineation, with which we may as well deal here, although it belongs as much to other kinds of carol as to those we are considering. The most familiar example is "In dulci jubilo" (*Oxford* 86: see below, p. 192). This form, where Latin phrases which are not necessarily quotations, but which carry on the sense of the vernacular words, are interpolated with the vernacular, is called the *macaronic* style. In the English version of "In dulci jubilo" we have:

> *In dulci jubilo*
> Now sing with hearts aglow;
> Our delight and pleasure
> Lies *in praesepio.*

The original, of course, has German lines where we have English. This is less self-consciously pedagogic than the ecclesiastical form, whose chief object was always to anchor down the dance-form and the familiar narrative to the church's teaching. By slipping in Latin tags whose sense matched fairly well the sense of the narrative, they would superimpose on the popular image, the image of the church of the faithful.

Another kind of Latin-tagged carol is exemplified in *Oxford* 62. Here it is not the monastic hymns but the Scriptures which are recalled by tags from Vulgate passages associated with the Christmas season.

> Nowell sing we both all and some
> Now *Rex pacificus* is come.   (Zech. 9.9)
>
> *Exortum est* in love and lysse   (Isa. 60.1)
> Now Christ his gree he gan us gysse
> And with his body brought to bliss
>   Both all and some.
>
> *De fructu ventris* of Mary bright   (Luke, 1.42)
> Both God and man in her alight,
> Out of disease he did us dight
>   Both all and some.
>
> *Puer natus* to us was sent   (Isa. 9.6)
> To bliss us bought, fro bale us blent,
> And else to woe we had ywent
>   Both all and some.
>
> *Lux fulgebit* with love and light   (Isa. 9.2)
> In Mary mild his pennon pight,
> In Mary took kind with manly might
>   Both all and some.

Lysse = "joy"; *gan us gysse* = "*gave us his favour*"; *fro bael us blent* = "delivered us from woe"; *his pennon pight* = "pitched his tent" (cf. "Behold the *tabernacle* (i.e. *tent*) of the Lord is with men"—Rev. 21. 3).

It is not that the singers were expected to be bilingual. Few among "the people" knew Latin. But the words were familiar, and they brought with them an image, and that was what the churchmen who composed the carols were counting on. The whole enterprise was strategy against the devil on a typically systematic medieval scale.

Carols on Secular Subjects

But the medieval manuscript carol, although most of the time it is of a religious cast, is not always on a religious subject. Dr. Greene notes that of his 474, only 77 have neither religious nor didactic sense— that is, about one-sixth. But of the five-sixths that are religious, not much more than half (less than half of the total) deal with the Nativity. That is the answer if we add together the carols of the seasons from Advent to Candlemas, and the carols about Mary and Joseph. Many others deal with the non-religious aspects of Christmas, such as (chiefly) hospitality. But there are the 77 that while preserving the carol-form and coming from manuscripts that contain religious pieces are entirely secular in their tone. Of these this is an example:

> My lady is a pretty one,
> A pretty, pretty, pretty one,
> My lady is a pretty one
>   As ever I saw.
>
> She is gentle and also wise,
> Over all other she beareth the prize,
>   That ever I saw.
>
> To hear her sing, to see her dance!
> She will the best herself advance
>   That ever I saw . . .   (G. 445)

A couple of examples of the tavern humour of the middle ages, preserved in carol form, lend point to our story here. One is a "lying song", the context being a game in which the winner was he who could tell the tallest story. Here are three verses, which we must quote in the original tongue:

> Hey, hey, hey, hey!
> I will have the whetstone and I may.

I saw a dog sething sowse,
And an ape thechyng an howse
And a podyng etyng a mowse;
    I will have the whetstone and I may!

I saw an urchin shape and sewe,
And another bake and brewe,
Scowre the pots as they were new,
    I will have the whetstone and I may!

I saw a codfysshe corn sowe
And a worm a whystyll blowe,
And a pye tredyng a crow,
    I will have the whetstone and I may!   (4 verses follow)

G. 471, from a ms. in Balliol College, Oxford. The Burden refers to the custom of tying a whetstone round the neck of a convicted perjurer in the pillory. *Sething sowse* = "pickling pork"; *urchin* = "hedgehog"; *pye* = "magpie".

This reminds us of a strange and amusing nursery-rhyme that runs thus:

I saw a fishpond all on fire
I saw a house bow to a squire
I saw a parson twelve feet high
I saw a cottage near the sky
I saw a balloon made of lead
I saw a coffin drop down dead
I saw two sparrows run a race
I saw two horses making lace
I saw a girl just like a cat,
I saw a kitten wear a hat,
I saw a man who saw these too,
And said though strange they all were true.

There is a development here, in that those lines are to be understood in two ways (i.e. they make sense if you begin each phrase in the middle of the line). But the origin may be in the "lying" game.

Then there is this rather agreeable verse from a carol on the general subject, "I'll trust a woman when the moon turns blue":

When thes thynges foloyng be done to our intent,
Then put women in trust and confydent:

When spawnys byld chyrchys on a hyth,
And wrenys cary sekkes on to the myll,

And curlews cary tymber, howses to dyth,
And semaus her butter to market to sell,
And woodcokes her woodknyfe carnis to kyll,
And green fynchys to goslings do obedyens,
Than put women in trust and confydens.

G. 402. The sense is:
When the following things are seen happening, trust women:
When frogs build a church on a hill,
When wrens carry sheaves to the mill,
When curlews carry timber to build their houses,
When seamews carry butter to market to sell,
When woodcocks take woodknives crows to kill,
When greenfinches take off their hats to geese,
Then trust women.

This is the fifth of seven verses.

A more serious note is struck by the immortal "Agincourt Song", which belongs to this general family, and is classed by Greene among "political carols".

O God, thy arm was here;
And not to us, but to thy arm alone
Ascribe we all!—when without stratagem,
But in plain shock and even play of battle,
Was ever known so great and little loss
On one part and on th' other? Take it, God,
For it is only thine! . . .

Come, go we in procession to the village:
And be it death proclaimed through our host
To boast of this, or take that praise from God
Which is his only. (*King Henry V*, V viii 107-117)

So does Shakespeare cause the religious King Henry the Fifth to celebrate the victory of Agincourt. Dr. Greene suggests that to a minstrel's defiance of the royal prohibition of personal praise a cleric added the burden, *Deo gracias*. It may be so, but in whatever form it originally was sung, you have here as fine and merry a popular song as ever came out of medieval England (*G. 426, M.B. 8*):

*Deo gracias Anglia
Redde pro victoria.*

Our King went forth to Normandy
With grace and might of chivalry;

Their God for him wrought marvellously
Wherefore England may call and cry
    Deo gracias!

He set a siege, the sooth for to say,
To Harfleur town with royal array;
That town he won and made a fray
That France shall rue till doomesday:
    Deo gracias!

Then went our King with all his host
Through France, for all the Frenshe boast;
He spared no dread of least or most
Till he came to Agincourt coast;
    Deo gracias!

Then, forsooth, that knight comely
In Agincourt field he fought manly;
Through grace of God most mighty
He had both the field and the victory.
    Deo gracias!

There dukes and earls, lord and baron,
Were taken and slain, and that well soon,
And some were led into London
With joy and mirth and great renown,
    Deo gracias!

Now gracious God he save our King,
His people and all his well-willing!
Give him good life and good ending,
That we with mirth may safely sing
    Deo gracias!

As for the celebrated tune, its history is as obscure as that of any folk-song; its appearance in several medieval sources shows that it was well known at the time. If indeed a minstrel originally sang the song as a ballad, then probably the original part of the tune is simply the stanza and its refrain, that mighty shout *Deo gracias!* It is not without interest to observe how closely some of the musical phrases of other carols of this period follow the line of the "Agincourt Song", as the following examples show. Dunstable's tune, the fourth in the example, must be read in the minor mode for the similarity to become apparent.

A Agincourt Song   Ex.3

De — o gra-ci-as

B Oxford 62

A pa-tre u-ni ge-ni-tus thro' a mai-den is come to us; sing

we to her and say: Wel-come Ve-ni re-demp-tor gen-ti-um.

C Oxford 23

In Beth-lem in that fair ci-ty a child was born of a mai-den free

that shall a lord and prin-ce be a so-lis or-tus car-di-ne.

D Oxford 40   ? Dunstable

A babe is born of high na-ture, the Prince of peace that e-ver shall be

of heav'n and earth he hath the care his lord-ship is e-ter-ni-ty.

Nobody can say, of course, whether the Agincourt Song was sung to an already popular tune, or whether its tune became popular because of the widespread use of the Song as a kind of National Anthem; but we have here an example of that community of tunes which we find to a much more marked degree in the ballad carols.

The other famous near-secular carol from the middle ages is the carol "The Boar's Head", which is still sung at Christmas dinner in The Queen's College, Oxford (*Oxford* 19; compare G. 132–5. The Queen's College version is G. 132c). By this carol, and others on the same subject, hangs an often told but excellent tale. It appears that at some time in the fifteenth century a man of learning was walking from the direction of Oxford towards Horspath village, where he proposed to attend Mass on Christmas morning. The old road from Oxford to London, from which you diverge a little to the south to reach Horspath, runs over Shotover Common, which is still an open space on (relatively) high ground. The scholar, whose name has come down to us as Copcot, was reading Aristotle while he was walking, and looked up to see a wild boar approaching him. He overcame the beast by stuffing his Aristotle down his throat—a triumphant victory of the academic over the brutish. With superb nonchalance he severed the head, carried it on his staff to church, left it in the church porch during the service, and took it back to College for dinner. Boars were a natural hazard in those parts at that time, as we remember from the name of Boar's Hill, which stands over against Shottover on the other side of the Isis river. The episode is commemorated in a window in the parish church of Horspath.

The Queen's College version is of venerable antiquity, having been first printed in 1521 by Wynkyn de Worde. It comes within the Christmas category for its last verse:

> Be gladde, Lordes, bothe more and lasse,
> For this hath ordeyned our stewarde
> To cheer you all this Christmasse,
> The Bores heed with mustarde.

But Oxford does not hold a monopoly of boar's head carols, as the presence of three others in Greene shows. Boar's head was in fact a familiar first course at Christmas dinner in those days. One version uses the boar's head in a somewhat grotesque conceit as a symbol of Christ:

> The boar's head that we bring here
> Betokeneth a Prince without peer,
> Is born this day to buy us dear,
> Nowell, Nowell. (G. 133)

A General View of Greene

These few examples give us some notion of the variety of material to be found in the medieval manuscripts. Indeed, the subject-headings in Greene, if drawn up in the form of a Table of Contents, suggest something very like a modern hymn book: or even more, one of those community song-books which contain both hymns and secular songs, like Mr. Sid Hedges' *Youth Sing Book* (1953). Among the headings we find "Convivial carols", "Satirical carols", "Picaresque Carols", "Amorous Carols" and "Humorous Carols", and we must admit that in a modern hymn book the picaresque, the convivial and the humorous find too little place, while the amorous, though much in evidence in the music, is there hardly by intention. Very broadly, however, there is some sense in saying that this carol repertory did for the medieval Christian what the hymn repertory does for the modern Christian. We shall say much at a later stage about the difference between carols and hymns: and that will make it clear how hazardous it is to build much on this proposition. But it was the design of their authors that these carols should become the folk song of the people, and should displace the less noble forms of folk song. If highly secular compositions found their way into those manuscript collections which are chiefly devoted to religious songs, this means no more than that if the clerks in holy orders did not write them down, nobody would, and that there was (as we shall continually be saying) less weight in the middle ages placed on that distinction between sacred and secular in such matters which is the chief characteristic of the puritan age.

By way of epilogue, here is one of the most beautiful of the Nativity carols preserved in these manuscripts. Wherever you touch them, indeed, you find this simple assured beauty that graciously disguises the didactic and controversial motive that lay behind their composition.

Ecce quod natura
Mutat sua jura:
Virgo partit pura
    Dei filium (1)

Both young and old, take heed to this:
The course of nature changed is;
A maid that never did amiss
    Hath borne our Saviour.

What time mankind had done amiss
And for his mys (2) was put from bliss,
A rose, a valiant flower, y-wis,
    Christ made springe of thorn.

Christ hath made spring out of a thorn
A Maid that him meekly hath born
Being both after and beforne
    As pure as lily flower.

As a sweet flower bear'th his odour
This maiden mild of great honour
Without maternal dolour
    Our Saviour hath borne.

Upon a night an angel bright
From bliss down light, saying full right,
"Through Goddes might a worthy wight
  Hath borne our Saviour."

Then kinges three from far country
In her degree came for to see
This King so free of majesty
  That in Bethlem was born.   (G. 65)

(1) "Lo, nature has changed its course. A pure Virgin gives birth to the
Son of God."
  (2) = sin.

The Ballad Carol

AT this point we enter waters which are both more familiar and less well-charted than those in which we have so far been travelling. For when we begin to treat of the carol as most modern Englishmen know it, the kind of carol which nowadays everybody sings, we are in the realm of folk-song. Dr. Greene condemned as "sentimental" the notion that carols (in his sense) were "a spontaneous product of the popular joy at the Christmas season", and that was, of course, justly said. But what we now know best as carols are the pieces which were not written in any manuscript, but were preserved until recently by oral tradition. It was this that "went underground" in the days of puritanism. The medieval manuscript carol did not "go underground"; it simply came to an end. The dance form in which it was cast became meaningless with the decline of the processional dance, and the ecclesiastical culture to which that kind of carol was committed was too clearly at variance with the culture of English Protestantism to remain in the popular mind when the lines of communication had been broken.

Dr. Greene can write of manuscripts and sources, but here we have neither. Nobody knows who composed the words or music of the folk-song carol, or, except very broadly, when. In matters of historical origin we can only generalise. "The word 'Traditional'," writes the editor of *Oxford*, "may cover any date or era from the fifteenth to the eighteenth century," and even though the same editor at another point suggests 1647, the date when Herrick was extruded from his benefice, as a fair date to use as a *terminus ad quem* for the traditional carol, he rightly admits that this is a purely conventional date.

Folk-song can be pressed as far back into history as you care to press it. It is what "the people" sing otherwise than when they are being instructed by the church or by the musically learned. Folk-song is like "Sing a Song of Sixpence" or "Three Blind Mice" or "John Brown's Body"—sung first and written down later. Folk-song is normally written down only when it becomes clear either that you

43

will forget it if it remains unwritten, or that you can sell it written.

As Dr. Greene warns us, we must not be sentimental. Although it is a tolerable hypothesis that men could, in a sense, sing before they could speak, it must be historically the case that people at large followed the lead of those who could sing a coherent melody and compose a witty verse. The Book of Genesis, with its shrewd and credible legends of the origins of civilisation, providing a theory of the first murderer, the first war-maker, and the first drunkard as well as of the first sinner, makes room for the first musician where it mentions Jubal "who was the father of all those who play the lyre and the pipe" (Gen. 4.21); and in any ethnic group there was, no doubt, some pioneer of the techniques of coherent song. If it was not Jubal, it was somebody else. Jubal is a possible name, and the name (as Genesis tacitly admits by never mentioning him again) does not matter two straws.

The point is not that Jubal was the originator of folk-song, but that it has no detectable origin apart from Jubal. Its origin is historically unknown, and does not matter. Folk-song is what we encounter among a people sufficiently far removed from its Jubal in history for its Jubal not to matter. And just as, I think, it is not improper to say that man was born singing, but was not born Christian, so it is proper to think of all ecclesiastical music and song as a development from, even when it is superficially a reaction against, folk-song. Father G. B. Chambers has given an impressive vindication of this view, with documents, in his most excellent and suggestive treatise, *Folksong-Plainsong*, in which he shows the relation between the ornate plainsong *melisma* and the uninhibited folk-song of a period of centuries, perhaps even thousands of years, before that which we regard as our English folk-song period. This must be set over against any tendency to exaggerate the ecclesiastical aspects of Dr. Greene's theory—and Dr. Greene is himself eminently fair about it. The medieval carol evolved from and is written in the form of the processional dance. It is merely in its intention that it differs from folk-song. Where folk-song is uninhibited, it is disciplined; where folk-song is narrative, it is didactic; where folk-song is uncritical, it is vigilant.

But English folk-song as we know it now is a fairly sophisticated musical form. Indeed, the music is more sophisticated than the words. As we have them, our folk-songs and carols not infrequently have rough and metrically unstable words, but almost always they have beautifully-proportioned tunes. I must insist on "as we have them", because what we have is what has been remembered by the country folk and transcribed by the researchers. It was inevitable that words

and music should be smoothed out, improved, altered or even forgotten and improvised, in the course of this oral transmission. True—
students of folklore agree in telling us that the ages of oral tradition
are ages of good memories, and that print has made us by comparison
careless and oblivious; and in the light of that fact it is possible to
judge that while words probably came down to us with small alteration,
apart from what was just forgotten and left out or what was inserted
as of local significance, tunes may well have suffered conventionalisation and alteration in the course of transmission. This would be because
more people can understand words critically and memorise them
accurately than can understand music critically and memorise it without
alteration. One has only to hear a modern congregation singing certain
well-known hymn tunes (such as AUSTRIA) which are almost invariably
sung neither as their composers wrote them nor as they are printed
in the book from which the congregation is singing, to be reminded
how easy it is for a person who enjoys singing to believe he is singing
what he has been taught to sing, when he is really singing it as he
himself thinks it should go.

But allowing for this, the melodies of the folk-songs that we have
are of surpassing beauty, coherence, and (usually) attractiveness to
the singer. The best, of course, have survived. The toughest have
proliferated. The others have gone. Oral tradition is a sterner judge
of the trivial and the second-rate than any manuscript, let alone any
printed book. We may with reasonable confidence say that when these
melodies—tunes like GOD REST YOU MERRY, which is a carol, or GREEN-
SLEEVES, which is not—are compared with the tunes of the Troubadours
preserved in learned books, we are looking at a musical development
of no earlier date, and probably rather later, than that of the medieval
religious carols. We are entering that "bridge period" between the
middle ages and modern times in which folk-song and carol alike
came to their highest excellence.

The Noel

So far as form goes, the familiar English ballad-carol can be traced
for its origin to the French *noël*. The *Noel* is by definition a Christmas
song written for popular enjoyment in any literary form, but probably
not in the first place for communal singing. *Noëls* have neither burden
nor, normally, refrain, and are to be found in France from about the
middle of the fifteenth century onwards. Later we shall attend to some
examples of *noels* which have come direct into the English repertory.
The *noël* itself (the word derives from the Latin *natalis* = "birthday")

is part of that nativity celebration which is traditionally ascribed to St. Francis of Assisi. The story is that St. Francis, in order to combat the kind of heresy and heathenism which denied the Incarnation, instituted the custom of the adoration of the crib. If the story is true, St. Francis is the progenitor of the ballad carol.

But more directly the *noel* is obviously a development of the kind of popular song associated with the Troubadours, whose stock-in-trade were narrative ballads and love-songs which provided the popular entertainment of medieval France. And it may well be true that, just as the English hymn-tune, derived from the puritan psalm-tune, has a French origin in the church of John Calvin, and was connected to the French psalm-tune by the dispersion of Protestants from England consequent upon the Marian persecution (see *M.C.H.* pp. 38ff.), so the English popular carol may owe its origin at least in part to the intercourse between English people of less than aristocratic class with people of the same class on the Continent in the course of the Crusades. If this be true then here is an origin older than St. Francis and more intimately associated with the Troubadours at their earliest stages.

We cannot get far in tracing origins in these medieval cultures which were so light-hearted about proprietorial values in the arts. But we can note that the Troubadours were the pioneers in Europe of organised popular song, and that their German cousins, the Meistersingers, had a discernible influence on the early German chorale. But folk-song remains an essentially anonymous, objective musical form. Wilfred Mellers wisely wrote recently that just as in the middle ages there was little of our modern distinction between the sacred and the secular, so there was little of our modern notion of the artist as a "person apart". That is the primary conditioning factor in the peculiar quality of all folk-song.

The Ballad

But the most immediate force bearing on the traditional English carol is the English ballad. Ballad (from a medieval dance-form, *ballata*) is defined in the *Concise Oxford English Dictionary* as "a simple poem in short stanzas in which some popular story is graphically narrated", and the *Oxford Companion to English Literature* says that it first arose in the later fifteenth century—that is, right in the middle of the "manuscript carol" period. Sir Arthur Quiller-Couch, in his delightful Preface to the *Oxford Book of Ballads* makes no attempt further to define the ballad; he simply quotes snatches, and says in effect, "This kind of thing is ballad". That is more or less the method I adopt here in presenting the ballad-carols. There is in the English ballad a freshness, a verve and a naturalness which have little to do with the canons by which we judge the poetry of later days. To say that is not to adopt a bucolic-sentimental attitude which exalts the ballads over all poetry; for what is natural is only one form of what is beautiful, and at its worst the natural can be crude and even repulsive. But it is the distinguishing feature of ballad that, in Sir Arthur Quiller-Couch's words, it "appealed to something young in the national mind", or, to put it in Sandys's category, that it is essentially "play" rather than "work".

The traditional form of the ballad runs to great length at times—as in the 456 stanzas of *Robin Hood and his Meiny*. Its normal metre is the "fourteener", a line of fourteen syllables with a marked caesura at the eighth, usually printed in two lines of eight and six, but not always or consistently rhyming at the eighth, thus:

> They sought her back, they sought her fore, they sought her up and down,
> They got her in the gude green wood nursing her bonny young son.

> He took the bonny boy in his arms and kist him tenderlie;
> Says, "though I would your father hang, your mother's dear to me."

In *Chevy Chase* we meet the occasional rhyme at the eighth syllable, but this is not consistent throughout the ballad:

> This began on a Monday at morn
> In Cheviot the hills so hye;
> That child may rue that is unborn,
> It was the more pitye.

> The drivers through the woodes went
> All for to raise the deer,
> Bowmen bickered upon the bent
> With their broad arrows clear.

Not infrequently the ballad is found in a triple rhythm which runs in equal lines with a pronounced stop at the end of each—Long Metre, as it were, in triple time:

> When captains courageous, whom death could not daunte,
> Did march to the siege of the city of Gaunte,
> They muster'd their soldiers by two and by three,
> And the foremost in battle was Mary Ambree.

A reading of the ballads in "fourteeners", soon shows of course, that you must read far before you find a couplet containing two lines of exactly fourteen syllables each; the tripping extra syllable and the tied syllable are an almost inalienable property of the ballad, as is the shifted accent. That, by the way, is what makes KINGSFOLD (*E.H.* 574) such a perfect ballad tune—its flexible melody allows the tripping syllables to take their place with perfect naturalness, and it is not surprising to learn that it was one of the most popular tunes of the ballad era.

It is here, of course, that the ballad provides a connection between the carol and the modern hymn. It was because the Groom of King Edward VI's Royal Wardrobe, Thomas Sternhold (d. 1549), invented the notion of putting the psalms into English ballad verse for the pleasure of the court (and no doubt to provide yet another weapon for the church against "unedifying entertainment") that the traditional "fourteener" became the archetypal English hymn metre, now called Common Metre. But nobody can read a page of Sternhold's psalms and mistake it for a page of ballad. They are terrible literature:

> My shepherd is the living Lord, nothing therefore I need,
> In pastures fair, near pleasant streams he setteth me to feed.
> He shall convert and glad my soul, and bring my mind in frame:
> To walk in paths of righteousness for his most holy name.

Part of the laboured and artificial effect of that comes, of course, from Sternhold's scrupulous avoidance of the tripping syllable. Those psalms in the complete English Metrical Psalter (commonly known as the *Old Version*) of 1562 which were written by later hands are worse than Sternhold's, because by 1558 the English psalm-tune had abandoned all pretence of modelling itself on the ballad-form, and had settled itself in a firmly syllabic and decorous habit.

The pious of the sixteenth century had little gift of disguising didactic purpose under gracious verse. An even more horrid example of pious doggerel is Christopher Tye's *Acts of the Apostles* of 1553, chiefly remembered now as the source of some uncommonly pleasant and simple church music, but from the literary point of view pure *Stuffed Owl* from end to end. It is entertaining to compare a verse from a ballad carol of St. Stephen with a verse from the relevant chapter of the *Acts* rendered by Tye. Here is the carol (*Oxford* 26):

> "But O," quoth he, "you wicked men!
>   Which of the prophets all
> Did not your fathers persecute
>   And keep in woeful thrall?"

> But when they heard him so to say
>   Upon him they all ran,
> And then without the city gates
>   They stoned this holy man.

How excellently that runs—with the largest emphasis of the whole stanza on "stoned", the word placed just where it will "tell" most. Here is the unspeakable Tye:

> Then sayde the chief priest, Is it so,
>   Ye men and eke bretherne
> And all ye fathers herke unto
>   My words and then discerne.
> There did appear to Abraham
>   The God of great glorye
> Before that he dwelt in Charran
>   In Mesopotamie.

Tye prints no inverted commas, but *prima facie* it appears either that Stephen is the chief priest or that the whole speech is made by the leader of the Sanhedrin. A fine way to write.

That, we may say, is what "work" does for the ballad. It is a heartening experience to spend years scratching the barren soil of the metrical psalms, as I have done, and then to turn, as I am now doing, to the ballad-carols. The puritans were short on poetry, but there were poets among the minstrels.

The Words of the Ballad-Carols

Minstrels! These are the men we have to thank for our ballad-carols. The excellent William Chappell wrote thus in the preface to his *Old English Ditties* (1861):

> Before the time of Cromwell every parish in town or country, if moderately populous, had its resident musicians, called waits, who were sometimes dignified by the name of minstrels. As there was scarcely a sport or festivity unaccompanied by music, these men found profitable employment. The evening dances on the village green were from Whitsuntide to Lammas day. Harvest was then close at hand, and with harvest came rejoicings from farm to farm. Christmas furnished its indoor amusements and dances; Easter, its holiday gambols. . . . Now, on the contrary, owing to an absurd piece of over-legislation in George the Second's time, the innkeeper cannot have musicians to sing or play in his house without the trouble and expense of annual application for a licence.

There is the immediate source of our ballad-carols. Their metre is that of the village dance, and their chief purpose is to tell a story.

Once again, we have a reinforcement of the Christmas-emphasis in carols, in that it is the Nativity which provides the simplest, homeliest and most dramatic of the stories connected with the Christian Faith.

The commonest kind of ballad carol, then, is that which simply re-tells the Nativity story, or a scene from it, in words that closely follow the Gospel narratives. But there are other kinds. There are some which tell the whole story of our Redemption, some that re-tell some non-Biblical legend associated with the nativity or infancy of Christ, and some which are primarily gnomic, didactic or hortatory. Beyond these again there are some which are associated simply with Christmas good cheer and hospitality, and some associated with village festivals of a secular kind. We will attend to a few examples that show their variety.

The Nativity

Two examples well known to everybody will be enough to show how ballad-carols told the story of the nativity. One is "God rest you merry", which is written in ballad-metre in stanzas of three lines instead of the normal two, and with a refrain. In its full version it ends with a hospitable verse calling for God's blessing on the master of the house (see *Oxford* 11 and 12). Its subject is the Nativity seen through the eyes of the Shepherds. Of its tune we shall have more to say later. You can easily hear the minstrel recounting the story in the verses, and the people joining in the refrain.

The other obvious example is "The First Nowell" (*Oxford* 27), which is complementary to "God rest you merry" in using the other normal ballad-metre, being written in rather halting verses of triple-time four-stress lines, and in recounting the story of the visit of the Wise Men. This again has a chorus in which everybody can respond to the narrative. It is a crude piece of writing, and as it happens it has, like "God rest you merry", a tune which will have to be examined at a later stage.

Legendary Carols (The Cherry Tree)

But more interesting than these for the reader who has time to move off the well-beaten track are the legendary carols. The first of these which we shall consider is "The Cherry Tree" ("Joseph was an old man"), to be found at *Oxford* 66. This is the subject of an extensive note by Baring-Gould in his preface to *Carols for Use in Church*. He begins—

> "I was teaching carols to a party of mill-girls in the West Riding of Yorkshire some ten years ago, and among them that by Dr. Gauntlett, 'Saint Joseph was a walking', when they burst out with, 'Nay! we know one a deal better nor yond,' and, lifting up their voices they sang, to a curious old strain;

'Saint Joseph was an old man,
And an old man was he;
He married sweet Mary
And a virgin was she.'

The incident says much both for the tenacity of the carol-tradition in
a mid-Victorian industrial society and for the taste of the girls. The
good vicar is referring to the carol "As Joseph was a walking", No. 26
in Chope's book whose preface he is writing, and a nice demure piece
it is:

As Joseph was a walking he heard an angel sing,
His song was of the coming of Christ the Saviour King.
The good man, long-dejected, had knelt to him who hears;
The blest refrain now swelling removed his doubts and fears.

"Be not afraid when hearing the choirs seraphic sing;
This night shall be the Birthtide of Christ the heavenly KING.
He neither shall in housen be born, nor yet in hall;
Nor bed, nor downy pillow, but in an oxen-stall."

Both words and tune are ascribed to H. J. Gauntlett in Chope, but in
fact the tune is an arrangement of a traditional melody (found also at
Oxford 66, ii), and the words are a revision, with a few original lines
retained, of that "Cherry Tree Carol" which the mill-girls preferred,
and which now stands in *Oxford*. Beginning at verse 2, and going on
to verse 7, this is how the traditional version runs:

Joseph and Mary walked
  Through an orchard good,
Where was cherries and berries
  As red as any blood.

Joseph and Mary walked
  Through an orchard green,
Where was berries and cherries
  As thick as might be seen.

O then bespoke Mary
  With words so meek and mild,
"Pluck me one cherry, Joseph,
  For I am with child".

O then bespoke Joseph
  With answer most unkind,
"Let him pluck thee a cherry
  That brought thee now with child".

O then bespoke the baby
  Within his Mother's womb—
"Bow down then the tallest tree,
  For my Mother to have some".

Then bowed down the highest tree
  Unto his mother's hand.
Then she cried, "See, Joseph,
  I have cherries at command".

This is the kind of legend the minstrels loved to use in their carols.
It is a delicate rustic disguise for the doubt in Joseph's mind whether

he should "put her away privily" when he learns that Mary is with child, but more than one strain of folk-lore can be found in it. One is certainly that which Baring-Gould mentions, the widespread use in folk-lore of the gift of a cherry (or some fruit carrying its own seed) as a divine authentication of human fertility. Baring-Gould quotes a Finnish epic, *Kalewala*, with a parallel story, and gives references from the Latin poet Ovid and from Arabia. But another strain seems to come from a story in the apocryphal Gospel of Pseudo-Matthew, chapter 20, which has the story that Mary, on the way home with the family after the flight into Egypt, sat down under a palm-tree and expressed a wish that she could have some of the dates to eat. Joseph could find no way to scale the tree, but at the bidding of Jesus the tree bent its branches, and Mary gathered the fruit. This has nothing to do with fertility, of course; it is one of the many infancy-miracles that are to be found in that wonderful farrago of rumour, gossip and fantasy, the Apocryphal New Testament. The reason for the currency of these stories in late medieval England was their use by the preaching friars as illustrations or even as texts for their homilies.

But the Christian instinct in putting the two legends together would take the singer and the hearer on to firmer ground than these speculations and unauthenticated tall stories. He would see in it what the early Fathers of the church called a "recapitulation"—that is, the spiritual truth that the sin of Eve is reversed and redeemed by the obedience of Mary. Transposing it into a story, the singer says that Eve took a fruit and sinned, and Mary took a fruit and knew that the Lord was with her.

The Cherry Tree carol runs on to eighteen verses, and after this opening episode tells the story of our Redemption, all the way to Easter, through a dialogue between Mary and her Son:

Then Mary took her young son   "O I shall be as dead, mother,
    And set him on her knee,   As stones are in the wall,
Saying, "My dear son, tell me,   O the stones in the streets, mother,
    Tell how this world shall be".   Shall sorrow for me all.

    "On Easter day, dear Mother,
      My rising up shall be;
    O the sun and the moon, mother,
      Shall both arise with me."

Throughout the carol, whether in legendary reference or in such an echo of biblical phrases as "the stones in the streets shall sorrow", we have reminiscences of the reading and preaching of popular religion with which the hearers would have been familiar.

The carol was actually in print well before Baring-Gould met the mill-girls, for it is to be found in Sandys, who also prints the tune. Sandys (as we shall later see) was incapable of writing a tune down in an intelligible fashion, and his version of this makes no sense. *Oxford* (66, i) prints it in duple time, Terry (in *Gilbert and Sandys' Christmas Carols*) in triple. There is no means of telling which is authentic. The second tune in *Oxford* we have already mentioned as having been collected by Gauntlett. The third looks suspiciously like a cousin of the first.

The Holy Well

Another classic of this kind, which draws on legend and imagination and yet never deviates from Christian dogmatic teaching, is "The Holy Well" ("As it fell out one May morning"), *Oxford* 56:

> As it fell out one May morning
>   And upon a bright holiday,
> Sweet Jesus asked of his dear Mother
>   If he might go out to play.
> "To play, to play sweet Jesus shall go,
>   And to play now get you gone;
> And let me hear of no complaint
>   At night when you come home."
>
> Sweet Jesus went down to yonder town
>   As far as the Holy Well,
> And there did see as fine children
>   As any tongue could tell;
> He said, "God bless you every one,
>   And your bodies Christ save and see!
> And now, little children, I'll play with you,
>   And you shall play with me".
>
> But they made answer to him, "No!
>   Thou art meaner than us all;
> Thou art but a simple fair maid's child
>   Born in an ox's stall!"
> Sweet Jesus turned him round about,
>   Neither laughed, nor smiled, nor spoke;
> But the tears came trickling from his eyes
>   Like water from the rock.

Sandys writes this quatrain thus:

> But they made answer to him, "No".
>> They were lords' and ladies' sons;
> And he the meanest of them all,
>> Was but a maiden's child, born in an ox's stall.

How the last line fitted the music he wisely does not attempt to say.

Two verses follow, in which Jesus reports to his Mother how the children have taunted him for his humble birth, and then his Mother says (verse 6):

> "Though you are but a maiden's child
>> Born in an ox's stall,
> Thou art the Christ, the King of heaven,
>> And the Saviour of them all!
> Sweet Jesus, go down to yonder town,
>> As far as the Holy Well,
> And take away those guilty souls
>> And dip them deep in hell."

> "Nay, nay," sweet Jesus smiled and said,
>> "Nay, nay, that may not be,
> For there are many sinful souls
>> Crying out for the help of me."
> Then up spoke the angel Gabriel
>> Upon a good set *steven*,   (*voice*)
> "Although you are but a maiden's child,
>> You are the King of Heaven!"

What can this be, but a versification of a homely sermon, or children's address, of the late medieval kind? That is how the friars would have preached to simple people (see G. R. Owst, *Preaching in Medieval England* (1926)), and it is the kind of story that would have remained in the popular mind. There is nothing exactly to correspond with it in the apocryphal Infancy Gospels, although there is a dreary and disedifying story there of how Jesus struck dead a child who jostled him in the street (*Gospel of Thomas*, iv). But the carol is better than that. It is a simple homily on the subject of the royalty of Christ's forgiveness, delivered with that earthy touch which removes the ballad carol so far from modern religious culture. The Mother of Jesus is portrayed as a sharp-tongued peasant housewife, busy, hasty and affectionate. But there is a deeper note as well. Both her invincible belief in the messiahship of Jesus and her making judgments which he contradicts have Gospel precedent, as in St. John 2.1-4 and St. Mark

3.32 ff.). None of this is bolder than our Lord's own technique in the parables which compares God to a lazy friend (St. Luke 11.5 ff.) and commends a dishonest steward (St. Luke 16.1 ff.). For the tune, see below pp. 100.

The Carnal and the Crane

Another long ballad carol that deals in legendary material is "The Carnal and the Crane" ("As I passed by a river-side"), *Oxford* 53, 54 and 55. *Oxford* gives it in twenty-three verses and Sandys in thirty. It is cast in the form of a dialogue between a carnal (which is probably a crow) and a crane, and the dialogue narrates the redemption-story. It includes at one point a reference to a miraculous harvest:

> Then Jesus, aye and Joseph
>   And Mary that was *unknown*,   (*virgin*)
> They travelled by an husbandman
>   Just while his seed was sown.

> "God speed thee, man!" said Jesus,
>   "Go fetch thy ox and wain,
> Any carry home they corn again,
>   Which thou this day hast sown."

The notion of a harvest springing straight out of new-sown seed may be compared with the story in the *Acts of Thomas* 10, where Jesus scatters a handful of seed which at once produces a hundred measures of wheat. Once again, an idea from the Apocryphal New Testament has been translated by a better Christian consciousness into a beneficent act on our Lord's part. A little later in the same carol we have this, in the context of the Flight into Egypt:

> And when they came to Egypt's land,
>   Amongst those fierce wild beasts,
> Mary, she being weary,
>   Must needs sit down to rest.

> "Come, sit thee down," says Jesus,
>   "Come, sit thee down by me,
> And thou shalt see how these wild beasts
>   Do come and worship me."

> First came the lovely lion,
>   Which Jesus's grace did spring,
> And of the wild beasts in the field,
>   The lion shall be king.   (Sandys, p. 154)

This comes straight from *Pseudo-Matthew* 35.

Dives and Lazarus

Another legend of a different kind, and universally known, is that of "Dives and Lazarus", which is made into a carol beginning "As it fell out upon one day", *Oxford* 57:

> As it fell out upon one day,
>   Rich Dives made a feast,
> And he invited all his friends,
>   And gentry of the best.

The story is well known because it forms part of a famous discourse of our Lord's recorded in St. Luke 16. That parable is the most extended example we have of our Lord's use of a folk-tale. It is generally agreed that "Dives and Lazarus", the story of the rich man ill-treating the poor man and of their being respectively sent to hell and to heaven in the end, is in the Gospel simply a re-telling of a story familiar to everybody who was listening—a story of compensation in another world for the injustices of this one. The tailpiece of the parable is, of course, what matters from the point of view of our Lord's teaching— the solemn warning about the impenitence of human nature, no matter what signs are given to authenticate the divine Word; that is no part of the folk-tale. By itself, "Dives and Lazarus" is the kind of legend that grows up in any society when men become conscious of, and rebellious against, the inequalities of social life.

The same story comes into a verse of the carol "Job" ("Come all you worthy Christian men"), *Oxford* 60, which shares a tune with "Dives and Lazarus". Here we have a carol which uses two stories, that of Job and Dives, to illustrate a simple homily on the dangers of inordinately valuing the things of this world:

> Come, all you worthy Christian men,
>   That dwell upon this land,
> Don't spend your time in rioting;
>   Remember you're but man.
> Be watchful for your latter end;
>   Be ready for your call.
> There are many changes in this world;
>   Some rise while others fall.

The Angel Gabriel

We may mention here the finest of the English carols based on the Lucan story of the Annunciation, "The Angel Gabriel from God was sent to Galilee" (*Oxford* 37), not because of the legendary quality of its main theme, but because of its very characteristic introduction of an assumption based on legend that we find in other carols as well— namely, that Joseph was an old man:

> Mary anon looked him upon
>   And said, "Sir, what are ye?
> I marvel much at these tidings
>   Which thou hast brought to me.
> Married I am unto an old man,
>   As the lot fell unto me;
> Therefore, I pray, depart away,
>   For I stand in doubt of thee."

This recalls a passage in the *Protevangelium of James*, another Apocryphal Gospel, which runs as follows:

And when she was twelve years old, there was a council of the priests, saying: Behold, Mary is become twelve years old in the temple of the Lord. What then shall we do with her? . . . And the high priest . . . prayed concerning her. And lo, an angel of the Lord appeared saying unto him: Zacharias, Zacharias, go forth and assemble them that are widowers of the people, and let them bring every man a rod, and to whom- soever the Lord shall show a sign, his wife shall she be. And the heralds went forth over all the country round about Judaea, and the trumpet of the Lord sounded, and all men ran thereto.

And Joseph cast down his adze and ran to meet them, and when they were gathered together they went to the high priest and took their rods with them. And he took the rods of them all and went into the temple and prayed. And when he had finished the prayer he took the rods and went forth and gave them back to them: and there was no sign upon them. But Joseph received the last rod: and lo, a dove came forth of the rod and flew upon the head of Joseph. And the priest said unto Joseph: Unto thee hath it fallen to take the virgin of the Lord and keep her for thyself. And Joseph refused, saying, I have sons, and I am an old man, but she is a girl: lest I become a laughing-stock to the children of Israel. And the priest said unto Joseph: Fear the Lord thy God, and remember what things God did unto Dathan and Abiram and Korah, how the earth clave and they were swallowed up because of their gainsaying. . . . And Joseph said unto Mary, Lo, I have received thee out of the temple of the Lord: and now do I leave thee in my house, and I go away to build my buildings, and I will come again unto thee. The Lord shall watch over thee.

This is one of the more agreeable apocryphal traditions, and is here built into one of the most beautiful of the ballad carols.

Lullaby

The "lullaby" carol is, of course, a very common form in all the carol-eras. There are several in Greene, and many among the ballads and the Continental *noels*. A very beautiful one is "This endrys nyght" (*Oxford* 39, cf. G. 151), which seems to stand astride the boundary between the manuscript carols and the ballads. Three versions are given in Greene, and four in the transactions of the Early English Text Society. The version from the Bodleian manuscript (G. 151A) begins thus:

> Lullay my child, and weep no more,
>   Sleep and be now still
> The King of bliss thy Father is,
>   As it was his will.

>   This endrys night
>   I saw a sight,
> A maid a cradle keep,

>   And ever she sung
>   And said among,
> "Lullay, my child, and sleep".

>   "I may not sleep,
>   But I may weep;
> I am so woebegone;
>   Sleep I would
>   But I am cold
> And clothys I have none."

The carol in this form includes verses of the Passion, beginning (at the seventh):

>   "Here shall I be
>   Hanged on a tree,
> And die, as it is skill;
>   That I have bought
>   Less will I nought,
> It is my Father's will."

Similarly the other two manuscript versions have stanzas on the Passion; but the version in *Oxford* remains throughout its seventy lines a carol of the Nativity. The tune was first noted down just before or just after 1600 in the following form:

Here we have the ballad-tune (which is, of course, not among the manuscript tunes noted in *Musica Britannica*) incorporated into a very agreeable piece of chamber-polyphony characteristic of the Elizabethan age. "This endrys night", then, has a double tradition both as a manuscript carol and as a ballad, but both its metre and its tune are of the ballad kind, and the *Oxford* recension makes a delightful Nativity carol:

> This endrys night
> I saw a sight,
> A star as bright as day;
> And ever among
> A maiden sung,
> Lullay, by by, lullay.
>
> This lovely lady sat and sung,
>   And to her child did say:
> "My son, my brother, father, dear,
>   Why liest thou thus in hay?
> My sweetest bird, 'tis thus required,
>   Though thou be king veray;
> But nevertheless I will not cease
>   To sing, by by, lullay."

Greene has altogether fourteen lullaby carols in his collection, and we meet some more in the polyphonic carols of the Tudor and early

Stuart period; they are naturally more appropriate to the intimate occasion than to the open-air minstrelsy of the ballads, but they are to be found in great numbers among the foreign *noels* of the fifteenth and sixteenth centuries.

"I saw three ships" and "Down in yon forest"

Before we leave the legendary and go on to the doctrinal and the purely festive, we must attend to two of the most remarkable of the legendary carols, both based on legends of a different kind from those apocryphal stories which gave rise to the carols we were dealing with a few pages back.

The first is "I saw three ships", one of the best known of all carols (*Oxford* 18: compare *Oxford* 3). It was appropriate that this, with its nautical image, should have been collected from Tyneside. Sir Cuthbert Sharpe (1781–1849), who was Collector of Customs at Sunderland and Newcastle-on-Tyne, wrote down in his *Bishoprick Garland* a secular nursery-rhyme which he had heard in that district, beginning:

> I saw three ships come sailing in . . .
> On New Year's Day in the morning.
>
> And what do you think was in them then? . . .
> Three pretty girls were in them then.

This is a parallel version of the carol, and it goes to one of the tunes associated with it. But the legend behind it is connected with the Magi. The Wise Men from the East (first called "Kings" by Tertullian (see the *Oxford Dictionary of the Christian Church* (1957), p. 842, s.v. *Magi*) about A.D. 200) were the first Gentiles to believe in Christ. Origen (early third century) is the first Christian writer to say that they were three in number, no doubt deducing this from the three gifts that they brought. The tradition was that their remains were brought to Byzantium by the Empress Helena (the mother of the Emperor Constantine who renamed the city), and later taken to Milan. From Milan the skulls of the Three Kings were taken to Cologne by Frederick Barbarossa in 1162, and are believed to be still preserved as relics in the cathedral there. The "three ships" are traditionally the ships by which they were brought to Cologne. The carol has simply transferred the ships from the Magi to Christ himself. It is interesting, but not at all surprising, that there is a sailors' song (referred to by Miss Gilchrist in JFSS V, pp. 31 [f]) along the same lines describing the journey from the "port" of Bethlehem to the port of Cologne. So in popular imagination what began as a cortège becomes a triumphal procession by sea. I am not sure but that we may add this, that the carol appeals to a deep-rooted psychological instinct in the imagination which associates the sea with the Great Division between heaven and earth, and a sea-journey successfully completed with a major gesture against the powers of darkness. You have that thought in, for example, the Book of Revelation 21.2, "There was no more sea", and in the Old Testament passages that speak of the sea as the abode of the monstrously evil things (e.g. Psalm 89.9–10); and the legend of the death of King Arthur is only the most familiar of the appearances of the same conceit in Western folklore. This may well be a third strain to be added to the quasi-historical, in the Three Kings of Cologne, and the obviously nautical, in the place of its English origin:

"Down in yon Forest", or "The Fawcon hath borne my love away", or "All bells in Paradise" (to name only three of its titles) is a more remarkable example of multiple mythology. This is the carol of which we said that it exists in a manuscript version, and was independently picked up by collectors in Derbyshire. Greene prints (322) four versions. The manuscript version went as follows:

> Lully, Lullay, lully, lullay
> The fawcon hath born my *mak* away.   (*lover*)
>
> He bare hym vp, he bare hym down;
> He bare hym into an orchard brown.
>
> In that orchard ther was an hall,
> That was hangid with purpill and pall.
>
> And in that hall ther was a bede;
> Hit was hangid with gold so rede.
>
> And yn that bed ther lythe a knyght,
> His wowndes bledyng day and nyght.
>
> By that bedes side ther kneleth a *may*   (*maid*)
> And she wepeth both nyght and day.
>
> And by that beddes side ther stondith a ston,
> *Corpus Christi* wretyn theron.

The second version, collected from North Staffordshire, begins (without a burden):

> Over yonder's a park, which is newly begun,
>   All bells in Paradise I heard them a-ring;
> Which is silver on the outside and gold within,
>   And I love sweet Jesus above all things.

This is preserved at *Oxford* 184. The third version, from Derbyshire, begins:

> Down in yon forest there stands a hall,
>   All bells of Paradise I heard them ring;
> It's covered all over with purple and pall,
>   And I love my Lord Jesus above anything.

This appears, with its traditional tune, at *Oxford* 61. A fourth version collected from Scotland, begins:

> The heron flew east, the heron flew west,
> The heron flew to the fair forest;
> She flew o'er streams and meadows green,
> And a' to see what could be seen.

The Scottish version has neither burden nor refrain, but the English traditional versions repeat their double refrain throughout. We will now quote the North Staffordshire version in full. This was heard in the middle of the nineteenth century, and contributed in 1862 to *Notes and Queries*:

> Over yonder's a park, which is newly begun:
>   *All bells in Paradise I heard them a-ring.*
> Which is silver on the outside and gold within:
>   *And I love sweet Jesus above all thing.*

> And in that park there stands a hall
>   Which is covered all over with purple and pall.

> And in that hall there stands a bed
>   Which is hung all round with silk curtains so red.

> And in that bed there lies a knight
>   Whose wounds they do bleed by day and by night.

> At that bedside there lies a stone
>   Which our blest Virgin Mary knelt upon.

> At that bed's foot there lies a hound
>   Which is licking the blood as it daily runs down.

At that bed's head there grows a thorn
Which was never so blossomed since Christ was born.

The literary history of this astonishing composition is highly con-
jectural. Apart from the burden of the manuscript version, which
mentions the falcon, and which has crept into the Scottish version with
its opening lines about the heron, we have four distinct mythologies
interwoven in the carol. Where that burden came from, it is hard to
say. Greene is content to guess that it was the burden of a medieval
secular love-song. In that case it was attached to the carol by the
medieval scribe, and the only conceivable reason for this is that it
provided a suitable tune for the whole carol. In itself it expresses a
sense of bereavement which is not foreign to the rest of the carol, but
we may well conjecture that the ballad is in this case older than the
manuscript version.

Moving on to the stanzas, we have references to these four mythologies—of the Passion, of the Mass, of the Glastonbury thorn, and of
the Arthurian legends. The "park" is the wooded country of Somerset
in which traditionally Avalon is situated, and the "hall" is the castle
of the Grail. The "bed" is both a deathbed and, symbolically, the altar
on which the Sacrifice is made daily effective for the faithful in the
Mass: hence also "by day and by night" in verse 4, and "daily" in
verse 6, which emphasise the continual efficacy of the Sacrifice once
made. The red curtains are the draperies of the altar, red being the
liturgical colour appropriate to the Passion in the order of those days;
and purple, of course, is the traditional funeral colour. The wounded
knight is the Keeper of the Grail, and, behind him, the crucified Christ,
and the "hound" may be a symbol of the faithfulness of Joseph of
Arimathea who (as the tradition says) brought the Grail, the Cup used
at the Last Supper, to Britain and left it in the "hall" or "abbey" of
Glastonbury. In the folk-version the "stone" means little, but the
manuscript version says that *Corpus Christi* is written on it. The thorn
is, of course, the Glastonbury thorn, traditionally planted there by
Joseph of Arimathea, and still to be seen.

Modern historians have poured plenty of cold water on the Glastonbury legend (for example, Beatrice Hamilton Thompson in her
pamphlet, *Glastonbury, Truth and Fiction*, Mowbray's, 1939), but in less
critical times it was firmly believed not only that Joseph of Arimathea
visited the place and planted the thorn, but that our Lord as a young
child accompanied him on one of his visits, and lived for a while at
Priddy, a village near by. When William Blake wrote his well-known
lines :

> And did those feet in ancient time
>   Walk upon England's mountains green?
> And was the holy Lamb of God
>   In England's pleasant pastures seen?

he had this legend in mind. But to move from Glastonbury through the Arthurian epic to the Mass and the Passion makes a multiple mythology of the kind that the carol-makers loved, and we have here the richest example in English of a conflation of Christian belief, church practice and local legend in a folk-song.

Carols of Redemption and other Doctrines

But the telling of the story of our Redemption without recourse to fanciful or apocryphal stories still provides material for the carol-maker's imagination and sense of the dramatic. We find this at its simplest, with no "frills" and yet with never a dull line, in that admirable carol of the Nativity, "A child this day is born" (*Oxford* 2). Its metre is unusual in the ballads (though familiar in hymns)—ballad metre with a foot missing from the first line of each couplet. It is worth comparing it with one of the best of Christmas hymns, "While shepherds watched" (see below, p. 156): the carol is brilliant where the hymn is innocently obvious:

> Then was there with the angel
>   An host incontinent
> Of heavenly bright soldiers
>   Which from the High'st was sent,

> Lauding the Lord our God
>   And his celestial King:
> "All glory be in Paradise",
>   The heavenly host did sing.

But the minstrels did not believe that the Nativity was the only dramatic story in the Gospels, as we see from the carol, "Awake, awake, ye drowsy souls" (*Oxford* 44). This, collected by Cecil Sharp in Shropshire, looks like a Passiontide variant of "God rest you merry", and it could be sung (though we cannot say that it ever was sung) to the same tune. Its first four verses follow closely the Gospel narrative of the Passion, the next four deal with Easter, and the last two are a conventional salutation, "God bless the master of this house. . . ." From its refrain it seems to have been associated with celebrations of the New Year; in its course it mentions the crown of thorns, the flight of the

A MEDIEVAL MANUSCRIPT CAROL

"Abide, y hope hit be ye beste"

(Bodleian Library Arch. Seld. B 26, folio 29 verso)

G. D. & A. D. Parkes

THE BOAR'S HEAD WINDOW
Horspath Parish Church, near Oxford

disciples, the crucifixion, the darkness over the earth, the rending of the tombs and the centurion's confession; the Easter section gives us the journey of the Marys to the tomb, the appearance to Thomas and the ascension-charge to the disciples. This last is spread over two verses, giving this part of the carol a hortatory tone which is never far from the ballads. The second of these (the eighth of the carol) goes like this:

> Go seek you every wandering sheep
>   That doth on earth remain,
> Till I myself have paid your debts
>   And turned you back again;
> Come, all you heavy-laden,
>   I'll ease you of your pain,
> *So God send you a joyful New Year.*

The carol appears in a collection known as *A Good Christmas Box* (1847), published at Bilston, near Wolverhampton, and it seems to have been popular in the Marches as well as in what we now call the Black Country.

An important new aspect of the manner characteristic of all the ballads begins to appear at this point. It was by no means foreign to the ballad-maker's principles to think of the Passion at Christmas-time, or to attach a cheerful and hospitable refrain of goodwill to verses dealing with the solemnities of the Passion and Resurrection of Christ. Again and again we find evidences of this flexibility in medieval religion. Nothing could be farther from the medieval genius than the doleful temper in which modern religious folk approach the Passion, with hymns like "O come and mourn with me awhile" and cantatas like Stainer's *Crucifixion*. The two familiar Passion-tide hymns from the middle ages begin "Sing, my tongue, the glorious battle" and "The royal banners forward go"—and that is the key in which the medieval minstrels think of the Passion. They never forgot that the whole act of God is a Divine Comedy—a terrible story with a triumphant ending. Their native genius for seeing the shape of a story, a genius entirely extinguished in our own time by any obsessive approach to the Passion, caused them to see clearly that the Nativity involves the Passion, and the Passion the Resurrection, and that it all stands for hope and joy for people who have, and want, no other anchor in the world.

Exhortations to repentance in the light of what Christ has done for our redemption are, of course, numerous. In the May carol, "Awake, awake, good people all" (*Oxford* 47) the solemn and the merry are quaintly juxtaposed:

Awake, awake, good people all,
  Awake, and you shall hear;
Our Lord, our God, died on the Cross
  For us whom he loved so dear . . .

The life of man is but a span,
  And cut down in its flower,
We are here to-day and to-morrow are gone,
  We are all dead in an hour.

To-day you may be alive, dear man,
  Worth many a thousand pound;
To-morrow may be dead, dear man,
  And your body laid under ground.

My song is done, I must be gone,
  I can stay no longer here.
God bless you all, both great and small,
  And send you a happy new year.   (Sandys, pp. 159f.)

Another May carol, which has a close relation to that just quoted, contains the lines:

So dearly, so dearly has Christ loved us
  And for our sins was slain;
Christ bids us leave off our wickedness
  And turn to the Lord again.

A branch of May I bring to you,
  And at your door it stands;
It is but a sprout, but it's well budded out
  By the work of our Lord's hands.

A more discordant juxtaposition is to be found in a familiar verse of the "Seven Joys of Mary" (*Oxford* 70), which bids us sing:

The next good joy that Mary had,
  It was the joy of six,
To see her own Son Jesus Christ
  Upon the crucifix.

But the most poignant example, in one of the most exquisite of all ballad carols, is in "All under the leaves, the leaves of life" (*Oxford* 43). This is the record of a dream or vision, in which the dreamer meets "seven virgins", of whom one is our Lord's Mother, and witnesses the crucifixion through their eyes. I cannot forbear to quote it in full.

Here, in the transition from the tenth to the eleventh verse, is the very essence of that calculated incongruity which is at the heart of medieval popular religion:

All under the leaves, the leaves of life
   I met with virgins seven,
And one of them was Mary mild,
   Our Lord's Mother from heaven.

"O what are you seeking, you fair maids,
   All under the leaves of life?
Come, tell, come tell me what seek you
   All under the leaves of life?"

"We're seeking for no leaves, Thomas,
   But for a friend of thine;
We're seeking for sweet Jesus Christ
   To be our guide and thine."

"Go you down, go you down to yonder town,
   And sit in the gallery;
And there you'll find sweet Jesus Christ
   Nailed to a big yew-tree."

So down they went to yonder town,
   As far as foot could fall,
And many a grievous bitter tear
   From the virgins' eyes did fall.

"O peace, mother, O peace, mother,
   Your weeping doth me grieve;
O I must suffer this," he said,
   "For Adam and for Eve."

"O how can I my weeping leave,
   Or my sorrows undergo,
Whilst I do see my own Son die
   When sons I have no mo?"

"Dear mother, dear mother, you must take John
   All for to be your son,
And he will comfort you sometimes,
   Mother, as I have done."

"O come, thou John Evangelist,
   Thou'rt welcome unto me,
But more welcome my own dear son
   That I nursed upon my knee."

Then he laid his head on his right shoulder,
   Seeing death it struck him nigh:
"The Holy Ghost be with your soul,
   I die, mother dear, I die."

Oh, the rose, the rose, the gentle rose,
   And the fennel that grows so green!
God give us grace in every place
   To pray for our king and queen.

Furthermore for our enemies all
   Our prayers they should be strong.
Amen! good Lord! your charity
   Is the ending of my song.

On that great moment Lord David Cecil comments that its author "sweeps from heaven to earth as boldly and suddenly as a bird from sky to meadow grass" (*Oxford Book of Christian Verse*, p. xv of Introduction)—and this sweeping from heaven to earth, this mingling of the dimensions, this freedom of the exalted and of the homely, was the most gracious trait in that religion which the carols expressed and sought to encourage.

Two carols on the theme "Remember, O thou man" are familiar today. "Remember, O thou man . . . thy time is spent" (*Oxford* 42) is strictly sober and homiletic. Its metre, at first sight unusual, is a form of "Long Metre" expanded to triple time, and its haunting tune was noted first by Thomas Ravenscroft in his *Melismata* of 1611. A version of it appears in Thomas Hardy's *Under the Greenwood Tree*, where in chapter IV the carol-singers are "going the rounds":

"Number seventy-eight," he softly gave out as they formed round in a semicircle, the boys opening the lanterns to get a clearer light, and directing their rays on the books.

Then passed forth into the quiet night an ancient and time-worn hymn, embodying a quaint Christianity in words orally transmitted from father to son through several generations down to the present characters, who sang them out right earnestly:

Remember Adam's fall,
  O thou man:
Remember Adam's fall
  From Heaven to Hell.
Remember Adam's fall;
How he hath condemn'd all
In Hell perpetual
  There for to dwell.

Remember God's goodness,
  O thou Man:
Remember God's goodness,
  His promise made.
Remember God's goodness,
He sent his son sinless
Our ails to redress;
  Be not afraid!

In Bethlehem he was born,
  O thou Man:
In Bethlehem he was born
  For mankind's sake.
In Bethlehem he was born
Christmas-day i' the morn:
Our Saviour thought no scorn
  Our faults to take.

Give thanks to God alway,
  O thou Man:
Give thanks to God alway
  With heart-most joy.
Give thanks to God alway
On this our joyful day:
Let all men sing and say,
  Holy, Holy!

The version in *Oxford* is part of a ten-verse version from Ravenscroft, and is therefore older; to compare it with that in Hardy is to see again, all at a glance, how a long carol would be pruned, and its words slightly altered in oral transmission: the short version is made appropriate to Christmas, but the dark note of repentance is still quite clearly heard.

The "Sussex Mummers' Carol", beginning "O mortal man, remember well" (*Oxford* 45), deals not with the incarnation but directly with the Atonement as the focus of our repentance. This very solemn carol, with another serene and beautiful tune, is written in strict Long Metre: but it adds to its three verses of meditation on the Cross three more of old-fashioned hospitable import. Originally the carol opened with a verse on the Annunciation, but this is now dropped from customary use.

Wassail

It must be supposed, from the carols of festive Yuletide hospitality that have come down to us, that long after the medieval feudal system had passed away, that least disagreeable aspect of it—the relaxation of its disciplines at Christmas—persisted. Under a feudal régime the tenant was the landlord's liege and servant; but at Christmas he was entitled to beg in a good humoured way for the alms and food that he knew would be provided in excellent measure, and even to exhort (in such fashion as we have already seen) the exalted master and mistress of the Great House. Traditionally the men of humble station were invited into the presence of the lords and ladies of the manor, and those among them who were "waits" or "minstrels" would lead in "singing for their supper". In they would come, singing their "Wassail songs".

"Wassail" means "Good health to you"; indeed, its second syllable conceals the root, "hail" which we have in "health", "hale", and "Hallo". The best known of the Wassail Songs is "Here we come a wassailing", a carol of true Yorkshire breeziness:

We have got a little purse,	Bring us out a table
Of stretching leather-skin;	And spread it with a cloth,
We want a little money	And bring us out a mouldy cheese,
To line it well within.	And some of your Christmas broth.

This, with two tunes, will be found at *Oxford* 15 and 16.

The Somerset Wassail, "Wassail and wassail, all over the town" (*Oxford* 32), whose tune is reminiscent of one of the Yorkshire "Wassail" tunes (see below), suggests that the waits are calling at a large farmhouse.

> Wassail and wassail all over the town,
> The cup it is white and the ale it is brown;
> The cup it is made of the good ashen tree,
> And so is the malt of the finest barley.

This verse probably concealed a sly local reference that would raise a good laugh:

> There was an old man who had an old cow,
> And how for to keep her he didn't know how,
> He built up a barn for to keep his cow warm,
> And a drop or two of zider will do us no harm.

Much local satisfaction would be given by the last verse:

> The gurt dog of Langport he burnt his long tail,
> And this is the night we go singing Wassail.

The "dog of Langport" refers to a tradition that Langport, Somerset, was the farthest west that the Danes penetrated in their invasions of the ninth century. Tradition has it that it was forty miles nearer London, at Ethandun (now Edington, Wilts) that the final defeat was inflicted in the year 878 by King Alfred.

Another wassail song of similar pattern comes from the neighbouring county of Gloucester (*Oxford* 31); this is a kind of "Barley-Mow" of the cattle, being largely taken up with toasts to the health of "Cherry and Dobbin" the horses, and "Colly, Fillpail and Broad May", the cows.

Holly and Ivy

Another type of carol based on hospitality, but that takes us back again to the remoter regions of folklore, is the carol of holly and ivy. Of this group most of us know best the Gloucester carol:

> The holly and the ivy
> Now they are full well grown
> Of all the trees that are in the wood
> The holly bears the crown.

Here, in a somewhat lighter mixture than we have in the Glastonbury carol, traditions of secular folklore and of Christendom are blended together. In "The holly and the ivy" (*Oxford* 38), the chief purpose is the recitation of the acts of our Redemption, which are conventionally symbolised in the blossom, the berry, the prickle and the bark of the Holly tree. Ivy is mentioned merely in the chorus. In the "Sans Day" carol (so called from its place of origin, St. Day in Cornwall), "Now the holly bears a berry", the stanzas take a similar line, but the point of reference is always the berry of the holly, which is fancifully described in successive verses as white, black, green and red, and the ivy is not mentioned at all (*Oxford* 35).

To us, holly is a seasonable plant at Christmas time, ivy less so: mistletoe is more in evidence than ivy. But this is only the surface of the matter. We find several "Holly and Ivy" carols in Greene, and the primitive ones among them usually introduce a contention for the mastery between the two plants. Greene quotes an old folk-song, which in modern English would look like this:

> Holly and Ivy made a great party
> Who should have the mastery
> In lands where they go.
>
> Then spoke Holly: I am free and jolly,
> I will have the mastery
> In lands where we go.
>
> Then spoke Ivy, "I am loud and proud,
> I will have the mastery
> In lands where we go".
>
> Then spoke Holly, and set him on his knee,
> "I pray thee, gentle Ivy, call me no villein,
> In lands where we go".

(Greene, p. xcix)

In this, which looks like a game-song, the holly-ivy strife is a friendly rivalry between man and woman, each of whom bears authority in the household. The earliest holly-ivy carol is less courtly:

> Holly stands in the hall, fair to behold;
> Ivy stands without the door; she is full sore a-cold.
>
> Holly and his merry men, they dance and they sing,
> Ivy and her maidens, they weep and they wring.
>
> Ivy hath a kybe; she caught it with the cold;
> So may they all have aye that with Ivy hold.
>
> Holly hath berries as red as any rose;
> The foster, the hunters keep him from the doors.
>
> Ivy hath berries as black as any sloe;
> There came the owl, and ate her as she go.
>
> Holly hath birds, a full fair flock,
> The nightingale, the woodpecker, the gentle laverock.
>
> Good Ivy, what birds hast thou?
> None but the owlet, that cries "How, How!"

G 136 A, spelling modernised, and "woodpecker" written, according to Greene's note, for "poppinguy". *Kybe* = "chilblain".

All this is very much to Ivy's disadvantage, but the balance is redressed in another carol:

> Here comes Holly, that is so gent:
> To please all men is his intent. Alleluia!
> Whosoever against Holly do cry
> In a *lepe* shall he hang full high.   (basket)
>
> Ivy, chief of trees it is,
> *Veni, coronaberis.*   (come and be crowned)
>
> The most worthy she is in town,
> He that saith other doth amiss,
> And worthy to bear the crown,
> *Veni coronaberis.*   (G. 137)

The only overtly Christian carol in this group (if we discount the magnificently irrelevant "Alleluia" above) is one addressed solely to Ivy, which has this verse:

> I shall tell you a reason why
>   Ye shall love Ivy and think no shame;
>   The first letter beginneth with I,
>   And right even so—Jesus' name.   (G. 139)

All this has its roots, of course, in the elemental struggle of the sexes. In medieval society the notion would be conventionalised and sometimes coarsened into the kind of humour we now associate with jokes about mothers-in-law and henpecked husbands. A passage from G. M. Trevelyan offers comment on this:

> To the educated medieval man and woman, marriage was one thing, love another. Love might, indeed, chance to grow out of marriage, as doubtless it often did. If it did not, the wife tried to assert her rights by her tongue, sometimes with success. But the "lordship" was held to be vested in the husband, and when he asserted it by fist and stick, he was seldom blamed by public opinion.

A large medieval manor was a counterpoint of authorities between the husband, whose authority was over the tenants, and the wife, whose authority was over the domestic staff. It might work eminently well, but if it did not it could lead to a complexity of vexations whose only relief for the underlings would be found in folklore of this kind. Thus a naturalistic mythology, running close to the region of fertility-cult (mistletoe, by the way, is the other side of that frontier), and absorbed into civilised custom, produces the carol of "The Holly and the Ivy" that we know. The irrelevance of the "holly-ivy" convention to the religious content of these carols is some indication of the haziness of the church's thinking on some of these fundamental matters.

And so Christmas domesticity, with a roaring fire, a Yule log, a cold night and a good supper, is reflected in the carols. It is not surprising, with all this evidence of communal roistering good humour, to learn what substantial trenchermen the medievals could be. One of the boar's head carols (G. 135) enumerates the rest of the Christmas dinner—crane, bittern, heron, partridge, plover, lark, woodcock, snipe, crushed almonds, venison, capon and fruit. But then the medievals worked hard in the open air, and the church taught them how to fast as well as how to feast; Advent was then the season not of Christmas shopping but of protracted preparatory fast, and this fact played no small part in the high spirits that prevailed at Christmas. It was quite natural that the puritan, who hated the ecclesiastical fast as much as the feast, should see in Christmas, without the fast, little beyond an occasion for vulgar gluttony.

Number Carols

A curious but not unnaturally attractive form of folk-song is the numerical mnemonic, of which the best example in carols is "The Seven Joys of Mary" (*Oxford* 70). This is a conventionalisation of the catalogue-carol in which the seasons of Christmas are enumerated. "Welcome Yule" (*Oxford* 174) is such a carol of the non-numerical kind: it runs simply through the days of the Christmas season:

> Welcome Yule, thou merry man,
> In worship of this holy day.
>
> Welcome be thou heaven-King,
> Welcóme born in one morning,
> Welcome, for whom we shall sing
>   Welcome Yule.   (*Dec.* 25)
>
> Welcome be ye, Stephen and John (*Dec.* 26, 27)
> Welcome Innocents every one, (*Dec.* 28)
> Welcome Thomas, Martyr one . . . (*Dec.* 29)
>
> Welcome be ye good New Year (*Jan.* 1)
> Welcome Twelfth Day, both in fere (*Jan.* 6)
> Welcome Saintes lief and dear . . .
>
> Welcome be ye, Candlemas   (*Feb.* 2)
> Welcome be ye, queen of bliss,
> Welcome both to more and less.

  For two manuscript versions, see G. 7; one of these, which varies from the above version chiefly in excluding Candlemas, is attributed to John Awdelay (*fl.* 1559-1577), stationer and printer.

But with "The Seven Joys of Mary" we come almost into the realm of nursery-rhyme. The primitive versions of this in the medieval manuscripts limit the joys to five:

> The Nativity
> The Crucifixion
> The Resurrection
> The Ascension
> The Assumption

The sevenfold pattern in the familiar carol drops the Assumption and the Ascension and adds four non-credal Gospel categories:

The Nativity
Making the lame to walk
Making the blind to see
Preaching
Raising the dead to life
Crucifixion
Resurrection.

Other versions take the number as far as twelve (see *G.* 230–3). The reader may refer to the note at *Oxford* 70 for references to the categories used in the twelve-fold versions, some of which are quaint to the point of unintelligibility, like the tenth clause in one of them, which reads

> To see her own Son, Jesus Christ
> Bring up ten gentlemen.

Folk-song of this kind has, of course, persisted in popularity from very early times. One can recall many, ranging from "The animals went in two by two" and "This old man" to "One man went to mow" and "Ten green bottles". A modern folk-song much in vogue at Christmas time, written on the accumulating numerical principle, is "The Twelve Days of Christmas", to which we shall refer again later (p. 237). But the most fascinating of all, which leads us into a devious byway, is "A New Dial" ("In those Twelve Days let us be glad"), *Oxford* 64.

There is a venerable and familiar folk-song, "Green grow the rushes-O", written in antiphonal style:

> A. I'll sing you one-O
> *Green grow the rushes-O:*
> B. What is your one-O?
> A. One is one and all alone
> And evermore shall be so.

This is hardly a carol in its own right, but it is a song of extremely antique associations, coming from an original in Hebrew; and it stands somewhere in the background of "A New Dial". The Christian carol is thus called because it is cast in the form of a meditation on the twelve hours of the day. "A New Dial" means, as it were, "A new use for the clock-face". It appears in Sandys in three versions:

(1) *A New Dyall* (p. 59), in rhyming octosyllabic couplets (i.e. Long Metre).

(2) *Man's Duty*, or *Meditation for Twelve Hours of the Day* (p. 133) in couplet-rhymed four-line decasyllabic verses.

(3) *In those Twelve Days* (p. 135), in couplet-rhymes four-line stanzas of octosyllables with a burden—i.e. like *Oxford* 64, but with four long lines instead of three in each stanza.

In *Oxford* the items are taken from all three sources. The accompanying table (p. 77) indicates how the items are arranged in the four versions of the carol, and in "Green grow the rushes-O".

Most of the references are self-explanatory. *Six ages* is a shade obscure, but it is perhaps a reminiscence of the kind of chiliasm which, as preached by the thirteenth-century Abbot Joachim of Fiore, announced the beginning of a new age and the end of "this world" in the year 1260; 1260 is six times 210, and 210 years, "an age" is made up of seven generations of thirty years. The same number (1260) appears as the length of an ultimate period in Revelation 11.3 and 12.6. The biblical and patristic affection for the numbers 3, 7 and 12 was at the bottom of these arithmetical fantasies, and we may hazard that this is behind the "six ages". The *nine degrees of angels* refers back to a Gnostic belief that the Most High is insulated from the contamination of the created world by a system of orders of being, which in some Gnostic sources were called angels. (The astrological temper of "Green grow the rushes-O" strongly suggests Gnosticism.)

The *eleven thousand virgins* recall a famous *mumpsimus* in Christian folklore. In an inscription there was a reference to two virgin martyrs, Ursula and Undecimilla. These are both given names, Undecimilla being a natural development of the convention that produces names like Tertius and Septimus, and meaning "the eleventh child, and she a girl". A scribe misreading the inscription interpreted it as "Ursula et undecim mille", that is "Ursula and eleven thousand others". His credulity was quite equal to the spectacular vision of eleven thousand young women storming heaven at once—a vision such as hardly occurred even to the makers of the film, "A Matter of Life and Death" —and Christian popular imagination swallowed it whole.

Epilogue

The ballad carol is a creature of contrasts, of high colours and of lyric tenderness. But although we have encountered already the profound and the haunting, we have not yet met the most audacious of them all. For sheer passionate humanity, nothing comes near "To-morrow shall be my dancing day" (*Oxford* 71). From two directions at once this carol affronts the now-accepted principles of religious

	Green grow the rushes-O	A New Dyall (c. 15) Sandys, p. 59	Man's Duty Sandys, p. 133	In those Twelve Days Sandys, p. 135	Oxford
ONE	All alone (i.e. One God)	One God, one Faith, one Baptism	God, Faith, Baptism	One God alone	God, Faith, Baptism
TWO	Lillywhite boys (i.e. Jesus and John the Baptist)	Testaments	Testaments	Testaments	Testaments
THREE	"The Rivals" (obscure: possibly the Trinity or the Wise Men)	Trinity	Trinity	Trinity	Trinity
FOUR	Gospel-makers	Evangelists	Evangelists	Evangelists	Evangelists
FIVE	"Symbol at your door" (i.e. the Pentagram)	Senses	Senses	Senses	Senses
SIX	"Proud walkers" (corrupted from the six water-pots at Cana)	Days to labour	Days to labour	Ages this world shall last	Days to labour
SEVEN	"Stars in the sky" (Ursa major group)	Liberal arts	Liberal arts	Days in the week	Liberal arts
EIGHT	"Bold rainers" or "April rainers" (corruption from "angels"?)	Souls saved in the Ark	Souls saved in the Ark	Beatitudes	Beatitudes
NINE	Bright shiners (stars?)	Muses	Muses	Degrees of angels	Muses
TEN	Commandments	Commandments	Commandments	Commandments	Commandments
ELEVEN	"Eleven went up to heaven" (i.e. faithful apostles)	Faithful apostles	Faithful apostles	11,000 virgins	11,000 virgins
TWELVE	Apostles	Apostles	Gates in heaven / Tribes in Jerusalem / Articles of the Creed	Apostles	Apostles / Articles of the Creed

decorum. Each verse ends with the word "dance", the dance is its
very context and framework: it is more of a dance than anything that
was ever written in the dance-form in those religious manuscripts;
it recapitulates for us the ancient origin of all carols. That is bad
enough, but it is nothing to the daring with which it celebrates the
whole story of our redemption in terms of the human love of man and
woman. The love here evoked is not that spiritual love of which
the Apostle writes in I Corinthians 13; it is strictly *eros*, as when
Ignatius wrote, "My *eros* is crucified". Nowhere are the staggering
incongruities of the religion of the middle ages so shamelessly revealed
as they are in this product of their genius. Nowhere is human love so
boldly used as a type of the divine love.

Nowhere—save in the Scriptures. Daring though this is, it does not
go beyond the Bible. David could dance before the Lord, and could
call his people to praise him in the cymbals and dances. And the prophets
could liken the love of God to the love of a human betrothed:

> You shall be called, "My delight is in her" (Hephzibah), "and your
> land", "Married" (Beulah), for the Lord delights in you, and you shall be
> married. For as a bridegroom rejoices over the bride, so shall your God
> rejoice over you (Isaiah 62. 7-8).

Our Lord, at some of the most solemn moments of his ministry, loved
to refer to himself as the Bridegroom. It is only another of these
disconcerting incongruities with which the middle ages are always
confronting us, that a song like this should exist side by side with those
demure patristic and medieval interpretations of the *Song of Solomon*
which persist in the headlines of our Authorised Version to this day.
Few modern scholars (except G. A. F. Knight) have dared to expound
the Song of Solomon otherwise than typologically, and as for the
deeper issues of theological *eros*, nobody since Dante has faced them
and explored them, save only Charles Williams. "The words of My
dancing-day" expose the last positive quality, perhaps the single
fundamental quality, of the old ballad-carols, which is that they are
world-affirming, not world-denying. They are the very essence of what
the Dean of King's, Cambridge, has recently called "Holy Worldliness". They are innocent of that anxiety which cannot enjoy the best
things because it dare not face the worst. It is not because they are
written in gay or prosperous days, by men who knew neither insecurity
nor suffering. The Middle Ages were full of terror, and we are told
that in the days of Queen Elizabeth a man's expectation of life at birth
was less than thirty years. There were witches in the middle ages,

there were plagues, there were famines and there were tortures. But the ballad carols were, amid all that, world-affirming, and none more so than this, in whose vision even Judas is whirled into the dance of love.

> To-morrow shall be my dancing-day,
> I would my true love did so chance
> To see the legend of my play,
> To call my true love to the dance.
>   Sing, O my love, O my love, my love, my love;
>   This have I done for my true love.
>
> Then was I born of a virgin pure,
> Of her I took fleshly substance;
> Thus was I knit to man's nature,
> To call my true love to my dance:
>
> In a manger laid and wrapped I was,
> So very poor, this was my chance,
> Betwixt an ox and a silly poor ass,
> To call my true love to my dance:
>
> Then afterwards baptised I was;
> The Holy Ghost on me did glance,
> My Father's voice heard from above,
> To call my true love to my dance:
>
> Into the desert I was led,
> Where I fasted without substance;
> The devil bade me make stones my bread,
> To have me break my true love's dance:
>
> The Jews on me they made great suit,
> And with me made great variance;
> Because they loved darkness rather than light,
> To call my true love to my dance:
>
> For thirty pence Judas me sold,
> His covetousness for to advance;
> "Mark whom I kiss, the same do hold:
> The same is he shall lead the dance":
>
> Before Pilate the Jews me brought,
> Where Barabbas had deliverance;
> They scourged me and set me at nought,
> Judged me to die to lead the dance:

Then on the cross I hanged was
   Where a spear to my heart did glance;
There issued forth both water and blood,
   To call my true love to my dance:

Then down to hell I took my way
   For my true love's deliverance,
And rose again on the third day
   Up to my true love and the dance:

Then up to heaven I did ascend,
   Where now I dwell in sure substance,
On the right hand of God, that man
   May come unto the general dance:
      Sing, O my love, O my love, my love, my love:
      This have I done for my true love.

(Photo by courtesy of the Vicar of Addington)

THE HOME OF THE FESTIVAL OF NINE LESSONS:
ADDINGTON PARISH CHURCH
and
TRURO CATHEDRAL, FROM THE NORTH-EAST

(Photo: Norman Dash, Truro)

CAROL SINGING IN THE SEVENTEENTH CENTURY
"The Waits" by Robert Buss (1804–75)

The Music of the Ballad Carols

Sources of Folk-music

THE music of five of every seven manuscript carols has perished; that of the other two-sevenths is preserved in a definitive form which modern scholars have interpreted. By contrast, every ballad-carol has its tune, even if in some cases several carols share a tune, and in a few more than one tune share a carol. Oral tradition determines this; for when you are collecting a ballad from an aged villager, as the folk-song collectors did at the beginning of this century, you do not expect the villager to recite the words without a tune. Indeed, it is very probable that he will be unable to.

Written sources for the music of the ballad-carols are, with a very few exceptions (like "Remember, O thou man", "This endrys night" and the carols that come from pageant-plays), of recent date. We have manuscript collections, or early printed collections, which form the first written sources of certain ballad-carols. There is the famous and amusing collection of Richard Hill, a London grocer, who kept a commonplace book during the first third of the sixteenth century in which he made notes of anything he thought memorable, whether it was a table of weights and measures, a recipe for brewing beer, the date of one of his children's birth—or a carol. There was a rather gloomy little book edited about 1550 by one Richard Kele, to which we shall refer in a later chapter; and there was during the following generations a fairly continuous stream of small books. But for the tunes we have in almost every case to rely on the latter-day collectors.

Gilbert and Sandys

The earliest of these was Davies Gilbert, whose collection of carols appeared in 1822 under the title *Some Ancient Christmas Carols with the tunes to which they were formerly sung in the West of England*. Appended to this modest collection is some music, including some traditional dance music and eight carol tunes. Among these are THE LORD AT FIRST DID ADAM MAKE (*Oxford* 1, 1st tune), which appears twice, once in duple and once in triple time, A VIRGIN MOST PURE (*Oxford* 4, 1st tune), the tune THE ANGEL GABRIEL (*Oxford* 37) set to other words, and GOD'S DEAR SON WITHOUT BEGINNING (*Oxford* 13). With the words "While shepherds watched" we find the tune CROWLE (*E.H.* 463), from J. and J. Green's *Psalmody* (1715)—a straight hymn tune. Yet another tune, HARK, HARK WHAT NEWS THE ANGELS BRING, is a "repeating" hymn tune of the Methodist kind. So we see that Gilbert is not a rich or fertile source: but at least he makes a start.

Sandys published his *Christmas Carols New and Old* in 1833. This is a more extensive work, having an erudite introduction of 144 pages, 178 pages of texts, and eighteen tunes. The bulk of his material comes from the West of England, but he adds a few carols from northern France, with three relevant tunes.

In view of what I wrote in my first paragraph of this chapter, it will seem odd that these collectors wrote down so few tunes, especially Sandys, whose carol-texts (which he did not number and which I have not counted) must number about 150. It is odd. Nobody has explained it. I am still sure that they cannot have heard these carols without their tunes; even if they collected many of them from the broadsheets which were in circulation, and on which tunes were not printed, they could have found the tunes had they wanted to. It is probable that their reason for not noting the music was that their interest in music was much less eager than their interest in texts. We shall see in a moment that Sandys at least had little notion how to write down the music he did collect.

However, he is an important tune-source, as will be seen from the fact that he gives us the first written versions of A CHILD THIS DAY IS BORN (*Oxford* 2), THE FIRST NOWELL (27), THIS NEW CHRISTMAS CAROL (29), A VIRGIN MOST PURE (the version at *Bramley and Stainer* 3), GOD REST YOU MERRY (*Oxford* 11: not the more familiar tune), TOMORROW SHALL BE MY DANCING DAY (71), I SAW THREE SHIPS (18), THE CHERRY TREE (66, 1st tune), WHEN JESUS CHRIST WAS TWELVE YEARS OLD (72), A NEW DIAL (64) and SAINT STEPHEN (26). Apart from these, Sandys takes over Gilbert's rather tedious tune to HARK, HARK, WHAT NEWS; then follows a version of the well known hymn tune, MILES LANE, which we sing to "All hail the power of Jesus' name" but which is here set to other words. Then come two foreign tunes for the French carols, both of which were hardy travellers in Europe: one is the tune that has come into English hymn books under the name JESU DULCIS MEMORIA (*E.H.* 238, 2nd tune), but which is also associated with several French carols and with at least one Basque carol (*University Carol Books*, II, 11); the other is what we know as the Welsh hymn tune

ARFON (*E.H.* 116), which seems to have had wide currency in Northern France as well as in Wales. Finally, Sandys appends a dance-tune which he calls LORD THOMAS, with no words prescribed. This appears with modern words at *Oxford* 163.

Sandys is no musician. He provides basses for all the carol melodies, and attempts harmonies for one or two. As the following example will show, his efforts in this direction resemble the brave improvisations of Auntie on the parlour piano.

It was Sandys who gave us our first sight of THE FIRST NOWELL; but although Terry has lovingly transcribed the melody as Sandys gives it, and harmonised it with great piety (p. 22), it is a gawky affair, and there is no reason to believe that he wrote down very faithfully what he heard. Probably what we now sing is a serviceable reproduction of what they sang in Sandys' day and before: but for history's sake, here is what Sandys put down:

He has no notion of how to bar a tune: his version of A VIRGIN MOST PURE is barred throughout as if in two-time:

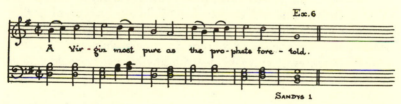

What the Cornish squire and the London lawyer began, others carried on. Large musical collections begin to appear under expert editorship in the mid-nineteenth century. Outside our own country we hear of the collection of Irish melodies edited by George Petrie (1789–1866) in 1855, and of the Abbé Migne's *Dictionnaire de Noels et de Cantiques* (Paris, 1867). William Chappell in 1859 produced his famous *Popular Melodies of Olden Time*, but this turns out to be a collection chiefly of urban rather than of rustic songs, and of country dances, mostly collected from written sources. William Husk's *Songs of the Nativity* (1868) is a fine collection, with some excellent music (including THE HOLY WELL as at *Oxford* '56). Among smaller collections there is E. F. Rimbault's *A Little Book of Christmas Carols* (1846) which gives us the well known GOD REST YOU MERRY tune, and the Percy Society's reprint of some of the fifteenth century manuscript carols, edited by Thomas Wright (1847).

The Later Folk-song Movement

But it was after 1880 that the folk-song movement expanded to what would be journalistically called a "nation-wide coverage". The pioneers of this movement were Miss Lucy Broadwood, Cecil Sharp, J. A. Fuller-Maitland and R. Vaughan Williams. The record of their developing researches in the *Journal of the Folk-song Society* reads like a detective story. They were concerned not only with carols, but with songs and dances of every kind—with anything they could find in the length and breadth of England.

Folk-song and Geography

Length and breadth it was. For the reader's interest, I here furnish a sketch-map of England, indicating the places at which the traditional carols which appear in *Oxford* were picked up. The map is not of high scientific importance. The thing to do with it is to hold the page at arm's length and see how the pattern forms itself. You will see at once that the "folk-song belt", as it were, runs north-north-west from Cornwall to Yorkshire, with its thick end in the south-west, a bulge on the Marches, and some not negligible entries in the dales of Derbyshire and the West Riding. In the East the entries are much more scattered.

Nothing could put the picture more clearly. For the survival of folk song in its purest form you seem to require two things—a settled agricultural society, and a remoteness from progressive civilisation. Cornwall is ideal. (Devonshire is full of entries on our map, because it is a convenient interpretation of "West Country"; actually Somerset and Cornwall, of named localities, are more productive than Devon— and they are more agricultural.) Cumberland is no use at all; it is

N
↑
0

(130)

10, 15ᴬ, 15ᴮ,
(66)

17, 18,
51, 61 = 184

67

(7), 43
44

(9),(50),(34)
(59),(155)

(60)

69

53·5
56, 57   22   48
68 (115)   7   47
(131)

Oxford
° 19

4ᴮ, 31, 38

LONDON
12

8, 32
60, 70   3   (138)

WEST
COUNTRY
1, 2, 4ᴬ, 11, 13, 26, 27
37, (56), 64, 66   20, 25   24, 45
71, 72, (114)
(142), (163)
35 49 41

KEY TO THE MAP

1. The Lord at first did Adam make
2. A child this day is born
3. As I sat on a sunny bank
4. A virgin most pure
7. Come all you faithful Christians
8. Come all you worthy gentlemen
9. Dark the night
10. Come, love we God!
11. God rest you merry (Cornwall)
12. God rest you merry (London)
13. God's dear Son without beginning
15. Here we come a Wassailing
17. It was on Christmas Day
18. I saw three ships
19. The Boar's Head
20. Let Christians all with joyful mirth
22. The Coventry Carol
24. On Christmas night all Christians sing
25. Rejoice and be merry!
26. Saint Stephen was a holy man
27. The First Nowell
31. Gloucestershire Wassail
32. Wassail and wassail all over the town (Somerset)
34. All poor men and humble ("O Deued Pob Cristion")
35. Sans Day Carol

37. The Angel Gabriel from God
38. The Holly and the Ivy
41. When righteous Joseph wedded was
43. All under the leaves
44. Awake, awake, ye drowsy souls
45. Sussex Mummers' Carol
47. May Carol
48. May-Day Garland
49. Helston Furry
50. Now the joyful bells (Nos Galan)
51. All you that are to mirth inclined
53-5. The Carnal and the Crane
56. The Holy Well
57. Dives and Lazarus
59. Awake were they only ("Roedd yn y wiad honno")
60. Job
61. Down in yon forest
64. A New Dial
66. Cherry Tree Carol
67. Song of the Nuns of Chester
68. This is the Truth sent from above
69. The babe in Bethlem's manger laid
71. To-morrow shall be my dancing day
72. When Jesus Christ was twelve years old.

The numbers correspond with those in the *Oxford Book of Carols*
Numbers in brackets refer to *tunes* only

remote in all conscience, but not agricultural, and, because of its geographical quality, without any high community sense. The Home Counties are less prolific, because though agricultural, they are not remote. (But note that this is about *carols*, not folk songs and dances generally. If I included folk-song *tunes* that have come into use for hymns, or that are associated with dances, there would be a good cluster in Surrey—which fact is not unconnected with the fact that Dr. Vaughan Williams lived many years at Dorking. But we have had few carols—words plus tunes—from that area.)

Progressive civilisation in the seventeenth century was much allied with the puritan ethos; for it was from the merchant class that Puritanism gathered its most powerful adherents. When this progressive civilisation manifests itself through social legislation, it is near the Capital that that legislation finds both more sympathy and greater ease of enforcement. George Sampson, in that fine essay, *The Century of Divine Songs*, wrote eloquently of the West-Country journeys of John Wesley:

> This man, who went wherever horse could carry him, who faced bestial mobs of drink-sodden men and furious half-naked women in remote regions where the laws of God and man were scarcely known—this man re-christianised half of England, and brought into the darkest and foulest dens the light of divine love and hope of salvation.

Exactly. The dens were not necessarily in London. They were also in Penzance. They were most certainly in Wednesbury and Burslem. As for Cornwall, which eighteenth-century writers called "the land of West Barbary", we read in the *Gentleman's Magazine* for 1754 the splenetic opinions of a progressive metropolitan character who says that Cornwall has "the worst roads in all England", and expresses his earnest wish to see "one good road running from the metropolis of the kingdom to the Land's End, and, consequently, travelling in wheeled vehicles will be rendered easy and commodious which, at present, is a bold undertaking, and not to be attempted without manifest danger". I am indebted for this quotation to G. C. B. Davies, *The Early Cornish Evangelicals, 1735–60* (S.P.C.K., 1951), where it appears on pp. 1–12. One could wish that that writer had lived to see A 30 on an August week-end in the nineteen-fifties.

What is here said of Cornwall could have been said equally well of most parts of England more than six score miles from London in the eighteenth century. Now compare our map with a study of the church history of the puritan and Wesleyan periods, and you will be led to the interesting conclusion that the richest carol-country is the part of England where Wesley made his most spectacular impact, and where, to a large extent, Methodism still flourishes with very little challenge from the other non-anglican churches. Cornwall, the Marches, the Black Country (which was country in those days), Yorkshire. Discounting what happened after the Industrial Revolution by way of shifting the population to the great new cities, you have there the areas where the darkness encountered and enlightened by Wesley was at its deepest. The historic puritan foundations of Congregationalism and the Baptists are thicker on the ground in East Anglia and in the Home Counties both in those days and, with important but not decisive exceptions, in our own.

Wesley will appear again, of course, when we have to deal with Christmas hymns. He had nothing to do with the carol-revival as such, although one may guess that he would have been more sympathetic to it than were the puritans. But the places where he found the greatest necessity for evangelism were the places in which Gilbert and Sandys, and later Cecil Sharp and Lucy Broadwood, found much of what they were looking for. The ballad carol, in a very real sense, comes up from the mud of agricultural life, and if we are right to say that it is essentially world-affirming, then it was a gracious product of a society that had much sin and sourness in it, and that might have engulfed it in squalor and despair had not puritanism's denial come, in a paradoxical way, to rescue it from its environment. George Sampson and other writers about Wesley say with perfect truth that medieval society had disintegrated. There was a disastrous rustic slump in the eighteenth century, and it is better history to say that the collectors—themselves a product of puritan efficiency—rescued the carol just in time than to say that had the remote, lawless, godless areas of England been left to themselves we should now have better carols.

Community of Tunes

It is worth our while, then, to attend to a few of the tunes that go with our folk-song carols. In the ordinary way one carol has one tune; but there are exceptions. On the one hand, you find one carol with different tunes in different localities, and on the other, you find a single tune appearing here and there in different forms for different words. Or again, you find a phrase cropping up in different tunes which after the common phrase take different courses.

The folk-song is essentially anonymous, and there would naturally be a tendency for singers, where memory failed, to improvise by drawing on the common coin of current music. Plagiarism, a cardinal sin in an age of individualism where everybody is property-conscious, is a notion unknown to the community of folk-song (see *M.C.H.*, pp. 57, ff.).

GOD REST YOU MERRY

An excellent example of "community" both in tune and words is provided by the carol, "God rest you merry". *Oxford* prints it in two slightly different versions with its Cornish tune at No. 11 and its London tune at No. 12. The tune of No. 12 is the one everybody knows, beginning thus:

God rest you mer-ry, gen-tle-man, let no-thing you dis-may   OXFORD 12

That was collected in the London area by E. F. Rimbault, and first printed in 1846. The other tune was noted earlier, by Sandys, and begins thus:

God rest you mer-ry, gen-tle - men; let nothing you dis - may   OXFORD 11

The two tunes make a striking contrast. Ex. 8 is modal, smooth and written in long phrases; Ex. 9 is of conventional tonality, but constructed in primitive, short, repetitive phrases with a piquant change of rhythm at the refrain, but no pretensions to polish. From inspection it is possible to guess that Ex. 8 is in fact the older tune, and its wide circulation (as we shall see) supports that judgment. If indeed it was native to the Home Counties, of course, it would get a better "start" than a tune native to Cornwall. Ex. 9 seems to be more primitive in culture but of later date. What happened? Surely some West Country singer, knowing the words but having forgotten the tune (or possibly disliking it or thinking it impracticable in his own circle), invented another tune in the idiom of his own culture. That kind of tune is not uncommon in Cornish songs—up the scale and down again, with no nonsense about it, like the Helston Furry Dance.

But nobody else agreed with the Cornish singer. Ex. 8 is a member, if not the progenitor, of a large family. Gilbert was able to hear this in Cornwall (which suggests that even in his own county the hypothetical singer did not find universal agreement):

and this tune to the Wassail song was heard by Dr. Martin Shaw's father in Leeds a hundred years ago:

A form of the tune set to a patriotic song, which seems to date from the period when national anxiety was at its highest because of the threatened invasion from the Continent, about 1745, is preserved in *J.F.S.S.* IV 7:

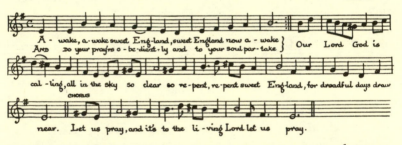

And a far-flung emigrant turns up in Nova Scotia, set to a twelve verse version of "The Joys of Mary":

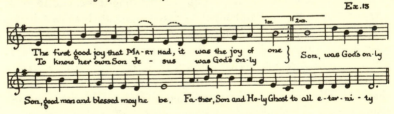

Traditional Songs from Nova Scotia, collected by Helen Creighton and Doreen H. Senior (Ryerson Press, Toronto, 1950), p. 275. The editorial note reads as follows:

"Miss Norma Smith, Halifax, who sent me 'Grandpa Saunders' " version, enclosed the following note: 'My grandfather used to sing this every Christmas Day until he passed on. He came to Canada from Hoddesdon, Herts. He would only sing this on Christmas Day, no matter how much we would coax to have it at other times. When he was a tiny boy the Waits used to sing in in the village, and when he was old enough he would steal away from home and sing it with them. He was born in 1833. Because of the demi-semiquavers at the end, he said only an Englishman could sing it.' "

In the version printed in our source, the demi-semiquavers have been ironed out. The versions of tunes which are preserved to us always do this: but discreet (and sometimes not quite discreet) decorations of the kind often appear in the psalm tune-books published *c.* 1750-1850, and we may well believe that in the days of unaccompanied singing (or where accompaniment was performed on a rudimentary instrument by a downtrodden musical hack) the kind of ornament which we now get from a good organist or pianist by way of varied harmony and contrapuntal descant would have often appeared in the singing as the occasional grace-note.

Here and there the tune appears in the major mode. Three examples appear in *Oxford*, one of which is set to a West Country variant of "God rest you merry" itself:

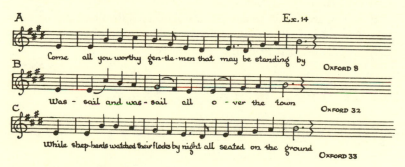

A contributor to *J.F.S.S.* suggests that there is a reminiscence of the carol tune in Giles Farnaby's "Flatt Pavan", which begins

If this is true, we can be quite clear that GOD REST YOU MERRY is at least as old as the sixteenth century; but these coincidences rarely have the strength to carry much weight of inference.

A VIRGIN MOST PURE

Another carol which seems to have enjoyed universal popularity is that which is variously known as "A virgin most pure" or "A virgin unspotted" (*Oxford* 4). It is written in a merry, dancing metre, and seems to have many tunes. It is impossible to say whether what we may call the "well known" one is the original tune, or which of its versions has priority, but at any rate it is recorded by both Gilbert and Sandys, and is the only traditional carol tune of which that can be said. Gilbert's version, the first of the following examples, is the more unusual and attractive; but Sandys's is a rollicking good tune. They begin thus:

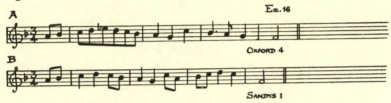

Folk-song enthusiasts will assuredly vote for Gilbert, but nobody can say whether Sandys is Gilbert and water or whether Gilbert is Sandys with rum sauce.

But there are many variants, and it is often difficult to say whether the variants are fresh tunes or not. *Oxford* has two, of which the first may well be derived from the tune above:

This is of much the same shape as Ex. 16 (A), but it gives the impression of being the result of a fault not uncommon among amateur singers—that of beginning a tune too high, so that its higher reaches are inaccessible, and the tune takes a new shape (in this example, in its third phrase). One recalls the anecdote of Sir Hubert Parry, quoted by Sir Walford Davies, of the old sailor who tried to play Mornington's chant in E flat on a bo'sun's pipe which had only one octave compass, and achieved this:

Ex. 18

There is an extraordinary example of this kind of transposition, surely
for a similar reason, in the two forms of a German folk song turned
hymn tune, called WAS LEBET, WAS SCHWEBET. Another West Country
version (falsely attributed to Sandys in *Oxford*) looks much the same,
but this time the top note is safely reached:

Ex. 19

OXFORD 114

Then there is this, from the midlands (*English County Songs*, p. 56):

Ex. 20

In Beth - le - hem ci - ty, in Ju - dae - a it was } All
That Jo - seph and Ma - ry to - ge - ther did pass

for to be ta - xed when thi - ther they came for Cae - sar Au -

gus - tus com - man - ded the same

And finally, there is the tune called ADMIRAL BENBOW in Chappell,
which reappears under the name A VIRGIN UNSPOTTED (but not to
those words) at *E.H.* 29:

Ex. 21

Let me list to the bil - lows as they break at my feet }
For the song of the min - strel near to me was so sweet

as the wild rug - ged mu - sic I can hear in their voice, when my

heart is de - spon - ding they would bid me re - joice

The words to which *E.H.* sets this tune are by Bramley of *Bramley &*
Stainer, but in *Bramley & Stainer* (No. 26) those words are set to our
Ex. 17 above.

All these tunes seem to be at least cousins. On the other hand, there
is this haunting and (to modern ears) outlandish tune collected in
Shropshire by Cecil Sharp, which preserves the musical form, but
moves in that Dorian mode of which Welsh folk music is so fond, and
shows obvious signs (as do many of the other melodies from the
Marches, if our map be collated with *Oxford*) of Celtic influence:

Ex. 22

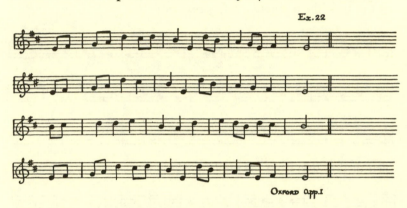

Oxford App.I

KINGSFOLD

But the most impressively pervasive of all the folk-tunes which
come into our field is that which the hymn books call KINGSFOLD. We
will call it that for convenience, because its other name, DIVES AND
LAZARUS, suggests a primary association with the carol of that name,
which *Oxford* denies. *Oxford* sets it to the carol "Job" in the following
form:

Ex. 23

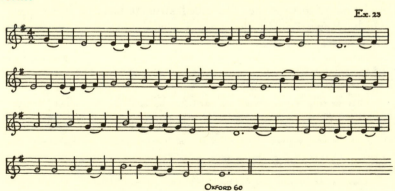

Oxford 60

In that form, says *Oxford*, it was noted in Westminster, and printed in *English County Songs* with "Dives and Lazarus" (p. 102). That is very nearly the form in which it is now used as a hymn-tune, normally as a very felicitous setting of the ballad-like hymn, "I heard the voice of Jesus say". But it is a tune that we find everywhere. *J.F.S.S.* (II, 115) notes that it has been heard in England at Weobley (Herefordshire), Lew Trenchard (Oxfordshire), Kingsfold (Surrey), and in Norfolk and North Devon. It is found in a cognate form associated with the Scots ballad "Gilderoy", and as the tune of the Irish song, "The Star of County Down". Within the single volume of *English County Songs* it appears three times; once as above, and as the following examples with "A bold Thresherman" (p. 68) and "Cold blows the wind" (p. 34)— the last a thoroughly watered-down version:

The internal form of the tune suggests an Irish background, and the thriving woollen trade between Ireland and East Anglia during the later middle ages may have brought it into England from Ireland through the ports; in that case, like that even more evidently Irish tune that we usually call an English folk song, KING'S LYNN (*E.H.* 562), its first English home may well have been East Anglia. But however it was, it found its way everywhere. If, as the rather ambiguous note at *Oxford* 60 implies, the tune there printed opposite KINGSFOLD came from Somerset, we may well conjecture that in it we have yet another form of the same melody; its chief differences from the KINGSFOLD version are at the cadences and in the sixth phrase, but there is not much doubt of their common parentage. Dr. Vaughan Williams has composed an orchestral piece called *Five Variants on Dives and Lazarus*, which introduces five versions of this tune. (Compare also *Cambridge* 5.)

THE FIRST NOWELL

Then there is the very curious business of THE FIRST NOWELL. When one is writing about hymns, one has to pay much attention to music justifiably to be classed as second-rate. With folk-song the question hardly ever arises, because in the nature of the case the weakest goes to the wall in oral tradition. We shall have to deal with bad words and music in carols only when we reach chapter 8. But may we not whisper that THE FIRST NOWELL, beloved though it is, is really a rather terrible tune? If it be sung in full according to *Oxford* 27, the singers sing one two-line phrase twenty-seven times. In the ordinary version they sing it eighteen times. Something has gone amiss, surely, with the transmission of this tune.

As might have been expected, the folk-song authorities have not missed this oddity. The efficient cause of our knowing it at all is Sandys, who (as we saw above) preserved it in what may or may not be an authentic version. But whether in Sandys or in Stainer, it is in two ways a peculiar tune. It is repetitive to the point of hideous boredom, and its melody only touches the keynote at one point in each long phrase, and that at the beginning. Each of these peculiarities may be made the starting point of a chain of conjecture: unhappily, not both at once.

If we say that here we have half a tune, or a third of a tune, the rest of which the singer either forgot or discarded because he was content with the fragment, then we may speculate on how the original tune went. *J.F.S.S.* (V, 26 and 240) gives two clues here. One (Ex. 26) is a "Nowell" carol from Camborne, Cornwall, picked up in 1913 "from Mr. Spargo, 75–80 years of age", the other (Ex. 27) is a wassail-carol

from the same county, heard in Redruth. It will be seen that both
return to their keynote in the normal way.

Ex. 26

No-well and no-well the angels did say while shep-herds then in the fields did lay, laying

in one night and fol-ding their sheep a win-ters night both cold and bleak   No-

well and no-well, no-well and no-well Born is the King of   Is - ra - el.

Ex. 27

The mis-tress and mas-ter our was-sail be - gin, Pray   o-pen your

door and let us come   in with our was - sail, was - sail, was-

sail, was - sail, and joy come to our jol-ly was - sail.

The first of those examples may well be the original of our "The
First Nowell", and if it is so, then the cause of the fragmentariness of
our tune is simply the failure of the memory of the singer whom
Sandys heard, or of some singer somewhere along the line that ended
with Sandys. There is a parallel to this in another tune recorded by
Sandys, THIS NEW CHRISTMAS CAROL, reproduced at *Oxford* 29. Here
we have a single phrase repeated four times to make a complete verse.
An attempt to make the tune less monotonous was made in the
predecessor of *Oxford*, *The English Carol Book* (edited by Martin Shaw
and Percy Dearmer, 1919) at No. 10, where the third of the four
phrases is transposed a tone lower: but this, of course, was quite
artificial. Terry in the end discovered the original in a Breton dance-
song, ME ANVEZ EUR GOULMIK, which he harmonised and set out in
Gilbert and Sandys' Christmas Carols, p. 32.

But if we follow the other clue—that furnished by the peculiar form
of the phrase—it may be guessed that we have in it a descant to some
tune which has since disappeared, and that the descant was what stayed

in the mind of the singer who transmitted it. Miss Anne Gilchrist in *J.F.S.S.* V 240 starts what at first looks like a possible hare by quoting an old hymn tune with its descant. The hymn tune (it was later found) comes from Playford's *Divine Companion* (1801), and may possibly have been, like several other tunes in that book, by Jeremiah Clark (1659–1707). If it was, it was not one of his best. The tune with the descant was written in a manuscript tune book of about 1820, and set to the Christmas hymn, "Hark, hark what news the angels bring"— the hymn to which belongs that quaint repeating tune which we have mentioned as being in both Gilbert and Sandys. The third strain, which is all that matters here, with its descant, is this:

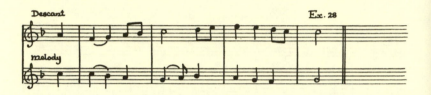

That is all very well, but it involves our believing that the singer made up his FIRST NOWELL tune out of that single phrase—which is not the first of a descant set to an unmemorable tune—a tune, moreover, which was certainly not the tune normally associated with those words in the West of England. Probabilities seem to wear a little thin at this point. Eighteen hundred and twenty, anyhow, is a precariously late date, unless the descant is a good deal older.

Yet the notion of the familiar scrap of melody as a descant to some other tune is not lightly to be set aside. There was plenty of part-singing in the eighteenth century. In those days and circles when Puritan principles forbade it, it was impossible even for Calvinists to eradicate that aspect of sin which makes some members of the congregation sing the tune only approximately. I have suggested elsewhere (*M.C.H.*, p. 52) that it was this kind of process that produced the tune COLESHILL out of the tune WINDSOR (*E.H.* 492, 332). Within familiar knowledge there are two possibilities. There are two carols which begin with a common first line—REJOICE AND BE MERRY, and TO-MORROW SHALL BE MY DANCING-DAY (*Oxford* 25 and 71). Both come from the West Country, and either forms a reasonable *cantus firmus* to THE FIRST NOWELL; *Oxford* 25 fits it throughout, 71 fits it in its first and last lines. The Sussex carol, ON CHRISTMAS NIGHT (*Oxford* 24), can with a little ingenuity be fitted to it.

These are, of course, not even very firm guesses. They merely demon-
strate that THE FIRST NOWELL could have come from a descant to some
tune like those suggested. Their common first line was clearly a stock
phrase in carol tunes, and if this theory is right, it need not be either
of these tunes that provides the true answer. But in any case, if we have
to choose between the two theories, we may be wise to choose the
former, and to suppose that our "First Nowell" tune is a deformation
of the Camborne "Nowell" at Ex. 27.

Other Ballad-tunes

Most of the tunes associated with the ballad-carols are easily accessible, and there is no need to give much space to them here. We may
note, of course, their astonishing variety and individuality. There is
not one of them, preserved in anything like its original form, which
has not some marked character. Perhaps after all it is as well that so
uncritically zealous a collector as Sandys did not live a generation later
than he did, for then we might have been left with a dozen "First
Nowells", truncated, misshapen, and dull. But what genius went to
the making of the carol-tunes!

Since we attended to "The Holy Well" in our last chapter we may
mention three tunes associated with it here. The tune set in *Oxford*
(and wrongly attributed to Sandys) is a broad, spacious melody which
first appeared in Husk's *Songs of the Nativity* (1868), and which may be
suspected of Irish origin from its wide compass and its a-b-b-a form.
It has come into use as a hymn tune in one or two modern books
(*AM* 277). Another tune, simpler and more high-spirited, was picked
up at Camborne, and is recorded as follows in *JFSS* V 1:

Ex.30

Thirdly, it has been heard to the very modest ballad tune now called
BUTLER, to be found at SP 378; and several other tunes, not in general
currency now, are noted at the same place in *JFSS*.

FURRY

This is perhaps the place to refer to the celebrated HELSTON FURRY
SONG; it is a folk-dance rather than a carol, but carol-like words are
associated with it, and it is in *Oxford* (No. 49). This is a May song
associated with one of the few surviving processional dances—a dance
which has become a function of national renown. Its origin is as
obscure and complicated as such things usually are. Terry says that
"Furry" originally means "Foray", and that the dance finds its origin
in an annual raid carried out on the surrounding countryside by the
bellicose inhabitants of Helston which, long before records began to

be kept, became a merely friendly and symbolic occasion (much as the rivalry between towns and regions which in the dark ages might lead to bloodshed is now given expression on the football field). But the dance which is now familiar, leading in and out of the houses on the main streets, suggests a placating (or defying) of the pagan gods of the threshold. Gilbert, who lived on the spot, knew nothing of its modern form, and explained it through the notion of the predatory excursion. Gilbert lived just too early to know that remarkable country parson, the Reverend Robert Stephen Hawker of Morwenstow (1803–75), but Hawker's famous ministry recalls something of that "barbarity" which Wesley and the contributor to the *Gentleman's Magazine* found in Cornwall. Hawker was described by J. A. Noble as "a missionary among wrecking, smuggling and superstitious savages, upon whom his influence was . . . radically transforming". It is known that he was the pioneer of the modern Harvest Festival, in a Festival of ingathering which he held for his sea-going·flock about the year 1850; and who knows but that he may have had one eye on the principle that it is better to rejoice over the ingathering of your own harvest than over the ingathering of your neighbour's. (See also an article in *The Month* (1953) pp. 332–7, by Tudor Edwards, entitled "The Hermit of Morwenstow".) Hawker, at all events, worked in that climate of near-barbarity in which, as we have already seen, the carols were still flourishing, and it was some influence akin to his, no doubt, that tamed the Furry.

However that may be, it is not too far from our purpose to note that the Furry tune has a first cousin in Lancashire, in the Abram circle dance. Those readers who are not Lancastrians will need to be told that this has nothing to do with the patriarch, but is assocated with the village of Abram, three miles south-east of Wigan. Its tune appears in the *Journal of the Folk Song and Dance Society* (see I 55 and III 221 ff) thus:

Ex.31

GREENSLEEVES

But when all is said, there is no ballad tune that has kept so close to the hearts of Englishmen as GREENSLEEVES. It cannot possibly be called a carol-tune by origin; and yet there it is, in *Bramley and Stainer* (14) and in *Oxford* (28). The *Oxford* association is a good one, for the words are a New Year carol from 1642 that was marked on its publication for use with the tune, although, of course, the original association was a love-song. Everybody knows it in something near its authentic version, but it is not surprising that the eighteenth century "improvers" reduced it to this:

Ex.32

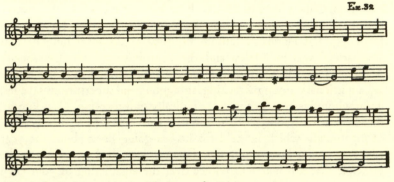

That is how it appears in *The Beggar's Opera*.

There remains little to say—and yet in a sense there remains everything to say. A whole book could be devoted to detailed commentary of the beauty and freshness and variety of the ballad carol tunes. Just as you have in the "48" of J. S. Bach the prefiguration of every kind of music that was written in the next two centuries, so in the ballad carols you have a compendium of all that has ever been said by the English song-writers of later times. There is no better training in the lyric language of music than a close study of the carols. Consider the rugged strength of THE LORD AT FIRST DID ADAM MAKE (*Oxford* 1, first tune), the care-free innocence of A CHILD THIS DAY IS BORN, the serene beauty of the only carol-tune in Part I of *Oxford* to be marked with the musical direction, *Slow*—the SUSSEX MUMMERS' CAROL (45), the deceptive reticence of TO-MORROW SHALL BE MY DANCING DAY (71), the pure, natural gravity without a touch of mournfulness in DOWN IN YON FOREST (61)—and so forth. It is all there, the influence of carol-minstrelsy has gone out through the whole history of music-making. What more striking testimony to the pervasiveness of the carol-technique can be found than the extraordinary similarity between THE FIRST GOOD JOY THAT MARY HAD (70) and that most excellent and innocent of all Ira D. Sankey's tunes, THERE WERE NINETY AND NINE (*E.H.* 584)? Or between REMEMBER, O THOU MAN (42) and the National Anthem (if you think of it in the minor mode)? These are probably the merest coincidences, and yet they show the way towards an argument, which would require another book altogether, that when men have sought to write music for the people—hymns, national songs, songs of faith and courage and even repentance—they have reached out towards the carols, and have been prevented only by convention and over-civilisation from finding what they sought.

PART TWO

THE CONTROVERSY

The Medieval Genius for Play

THE Puritans, it is commonly said, disliked, despised, suspected and did what they could to abolish carol-singing. We have already made one or two references to the "puritan mind" that suggest that it is the enemy of carol-making. In this part of our story we shall have to examine the truth of these generalisations, to see what it was that the Puritans said and did, and to try to discover what it was in carol-making and singing that gave them anxiety. And although we shall find that only part of the generalisation is strictly true, we all know that somewhere in the seventeenth century there comes a "great divide" which separates the medieval from the modern ethos of religious life. We are at this moment, as it were, moving up that slope of the "great divide" which leads up from the medieval plain: we shall in our next chapter reach its summit and see something of what it is made of and what its shape is: and then in the chapter after that we shall consider the new kind of religious song which had to replace the carol—the hymn, and especially, in this context, the Christmas hymn.

But just now we are still in the medieval country, and it is here that we ought to consider some of the late medieval customs and habits which give point to our reading of the great controversy that drove the carol underground. This means mentioning certain customs that antedate the manuscript-carols and the ballad-carols by decades or even centuries; but all of them have to do with the carol-making mind, and some of them actually gave us carols. While I do not reckon here to present an exhaustive study of medieval religious customs—for that is chiefly the business of folklore specialists, liturgists and musicologists—I choose here simply those customs of which you can already hear the puritan mind saying, "That is the sort of thing I mean".

THE PROCESSION

Let us begin with the religious procession. I mean now not the processional dance—to which the religious procession is indeed at some points related—but the church-procession. We can begin with the kind of procession most familiar to Anglican churchgoers nowadays: the procession that is used on saints' days and their vigils at evensong. This nowadays usually consists of a movement by the choir out of their stalls, round the church, and back to the place where they started. The Dean of Lincoln (Bishop Dunlop) reminded us some years ago that this is but a pale reflection of the real use of procession; but none the less this movement of the choir, with banners, during the singing of some cheerful if not very literary hymn like "For all the saints" or "Spouse of Christ", marks the day as a day of festive thanksgiving, and everybody enjoys it greatly. Not infrequently the Litany is sung in procession: and when that is done, we can discern a clear reminiscence of "burden and stanza" when at certain points a halt is made. A similar form is certainly to be detected in the Procession of the Stations of the Cross, where the Stations are, precisely, *stanzas*.

But, as Bishop Dunlop points out, there is much more to be said, aesthetically and historically, for a procession whose movement is significant as well as symbolic. It is well that the act of procession should symbolise the movement of the church through history, with a touch of the "church militant" in its gay colours and flying banners. But if the procession goes somewhere, and is not simply a movement from here to there and back again, it has more significance, and comes nearer to the medieval spirit. Of such kind is the Rogation procession now observed in many parishes; of the same kind is the procession at an Anglican Induction to the Font, the Pulpit, the Lectern, the Reading-desk and the Altar, with "stations" at each (a practice which is also to be seen in churches of the Dissenting tradition), or the processions at the consecrating of a churchyard.

But the medieval procession went further than this, in being not infrequently something like a carnival. Processions in the open air are more medieval than those inside church, processions that move from here to there are more medieval than those which move in a circle, and processions that involve the whole worshipping company are more medieval than those which involve only the choir in movement. True—but we must add the irrepressible popular humour that went with processions in the Middle Ages. The most familiar of these is the Procession of the Ass at Sens, where in the thirteenth century a young woman rode through the village on a donkey, carrying a baby in her arms, to symbolise the Flight of the Holy Family into Egypt, while everybody joined in a carol:

Orientis partibus
Adventavit asinus
Pulcher et fortissimus
Sarcinis aptissimus;
    Hez, sire Asnes, hez!

"Out of the eastern lands comes the Ass, beautiful and brave Ass, Ass most patient of burdens. Hail, sir Ass!" But perhaps "Hail" is too demure a word; probably the original was onomatopoeic, and meant "hee-haw".

The tune associated with this carol in a manuscript dated 1222 has survived as ORIENTIS PARTIBUS (*E.H.* 129), and the "Alleluya" with which it finishes is the original "Hee-haw" of the chorus. Here is a capital example of a traditional procession which was perhaps half-Christian, but hardly more. No doubt such occasions were a friendly rebuke of the church against "unedifying entertainment"; but they were great days for the populace. You catch a breath of the same atmosphere in some of the pilgrimage-hymns of Roman Catholic piety, and in their tunes: for after all, a procession extended to the grand scale becomes a pilgrimage.

But the symbolism of a procession remains with us both in sacred and in secular life. There are, on the one hand, the Sunday School processions of the north country, and it was no accident that it was Baring-Gould, that devoted medievalist, who wrote the archetypal modern processional hymn, "Onward, Christian soldiers", for just such an occasion, in his Yorkshire parish. If, however, you want the gaiety and entertainment of the medieval procession, you must nowadays go to the seaside-town carnival; a conspicuous figure will be Father Neptune, a gesture of patronage towards a paganism that has for us passed into history, but the real medieval part is in the clowns who wear enormous artificial heads and improvise horse-play as they go. These carnivals are for amusement only: but I suppose that the medieval procession is nowhere more thoroughly integrated into the commercial ethos of modern life than in Toronto, where on the day preceding that which Christians call the Sunday before Advent a procession, focused on Father Christmas, and containing twelve different bands, that takes about forty minutes to pass any given point, is organised by the authorities of the largest store in the town by way of inaugurating the Christmas shopping season.

DRAMA

Processions are symbolic and dramatic, but a more organised form of the symbolic is to be found in the charades, pageants and plays that

make up the medieval *corpus* of religious drama. "Mysteries"—
re-enacting the Christmas scenes, "Miracle plays", dealing with the life
of Christ, and "Moralities", like *Evèryman*, which handle some of the
great issues of life, seem to have abounded at all levels of formality in
the later middle ages. We have the "Mystery" cycles of Wakefield,
Chester, Coventry and York preserved to us, and as may be expected
these form the sources of certain familiar carols. The incompleteness
of their preservation has often robbed us of the music: but we have the
famous "Coventry Carol", perhaps the simplest and most beautiful
of all the "Lullaby" carols (*Oxford* 22) from the pageant of the Shear-
men and Tailors' Company at Coventry. The earliest historic record
we have of this play is its being witnessed by Queen Margaret in 1456;
the earliest written text (G. 112) is that of Robert Croo (1534), and the
earliest written form of the tune (the first in *Oxford*) is dated 1591.
Another carol from the same pageant has survived in words alone,
"Tyrley, Tyrlow" (G. 79), and is set to a modern tune at *Oxford* 169.
From the Chester Mysteries comes the "Song of the Nuns of Chester",
"*Qui creavit coelum*", with its lovely tune (*Oxford* 67).

It was all a very natural development. Religious drama is more
ancient than Christianity; indeed, there was more of what modern
man calls "worship" about the audience at a play of Euripides in
400 B.C. than in the attitude of the witnesses to an Olympian sacrifice
or of the initiates at the mysteries of Eleusis. The Greeks had a mythological religion, of course, not an historical one, and all their serious
plays were Moralities. The historic content of the Christian story is
what makes it a natural gift to the playwrights. It is all there in the
Nativity story—the anxiety of Mary and Joseph, the crowded village,
the blind bureaucracy that was responsible for it all (the old carols love
to bring in Caesar Augustus—see *Oxford* 114), the birth in its incongruous setting, the shepherds, the angels and the wise men, all ushered
in by the Annunciation and brooded over by the senile frenzy of
Herod—if ever there was some story to appeal to "something young in
the spirit" of a people, this is it. Nativity plays remain the most popular
and simplest to produce of all plays, and there is, of course, a great re-
surgence of interest in them, as also in plays of the "Morality" kind, in our
own time. "Mysteries" have been almost abandoned, until the whole
country was startled by the impact of *The Man Born to be King*. (And it
may be noted, apropos of our reference to the "youthful" in a civilisation
that accepts this kind of presentation of religious truth, that Miss Dorothy
Sayers's play-cycle was originally designed to be broadcast in the children's programmes, and was only later appropriated by the grown-ups.)

THE LORD OF MISRULE

Processions and religious drama are familiar to us in our own age, both through revival of medieval customs: but what can we say of that attractive figure, "The Lord of Misrule", or, in Scotland, "The Abbot of Unreason"? Here is something quintessentially medieval. This officer was traditionally appointed on All Hallows Eve to be in charge of the charades and revelries that took place in royal and noble houses. There are accounts of a royal Christmas at Guildford in 1348, where instructions are given *ad faciendum ludos domini regis ad festum natalis domini celebratos apud Guldeford.* Charades are indicated in the order for "Twenty-one linen coifs for counterfeiting men of the law in the King's Play" at Christmas, 1391. There is a most suggestive record, more than two centuries younger, of some sort of burlesque pantomime held in Gray's Inn in 1594, entitled *Gesta Grayorum*—a take-off of certain solemn and strictly edifying entertainment of the day (no doubt inspired by that puritan opinion which was already well formed by that date) called *Gesta Romanorum.* The "Lord of Misrule" for this performance was one Mr. Helmes, who in the concluding Masque of the whole pantomime (which was presented before the Queen) is thus styled:

> The High and Mighty Prince, Henry Prince of Purpoole, Arch-duke of Stapulia and Bernardia, Duke of High and Nether Holborn, Marquis of St. Giles and Tottenham, Count Palatine of Bloomsbury and Clerkenwell, Great Lord of the Cantons of Islington, Kentish-Town, Paddington and Knightsbridge, Knight of the most Heroical Order of the Helmet, and Sovereign of the Same.

Though all this comes from a late date, it furnishes a useful clue to the real nature of the Lord of Misrule. Behind him stood that mighty principle of laughter which the middle ages understood so well. Medieval humour is of the primitive sort that rests firmly on the juxtaposition of incongruous things. The most incongruous things of all are, of course, the devil and laughter, and the medievals were at their best when they were laughing at the devil. But they knew—all society, "both more and less", knew—how healthy it is in a social order based on a strict scale of authorities for what is taken seriously for 364 days in the year to be laughed at on the other one and great day. What the Lord of Misrule reminds me of most, I confess, is the kind of rag-pantomime at a boarding-school in which, once a year, the masters are burlesqued and the academic solemnities for a season dethroned.

And Christmas, when "the mighty are put down from their seat" is the season for this laughter, this turning upside-down of solemn things, this "Misrule" and "Unreason". Of course it can only happen where there is an underlying sense of reason and rule, where society is of the kind that makes men of "progressive" mind mourn for its oppressiveness. And indeed, though the elephantine humour of Gray's Inn may suggest something of sober wit, we need not suppose that the puritan mind had no ground for being anxious at the state of things in those places where the centre of gravity had shifted, and "misrule" was indeed toppling over into anarchy. Here is your Lord of Misrule, dressed in cap and bells, leading a wild dance, organising competitions and forfeits and party-games, bringing in a pillory, stocks and gibbet as emblems of his authority, and all the while perhaps they are singing

> Let no man come into this hall
> Nor groom nor page nor yet marshall,
> But that some sport he bring withall . . .
>
> If he say he naught can do,
> Then for my love ask him no mo',
> But to the stocks then let him go! (G.11, *Oxford* 172)

and it is all very fine, until that dreadful moment when somebody suddenly sees that it is not funny at all. How delicately balanced such things must always be! How doubtful some people must have become about the wisdom of the "devil's dance" that finished this medieval "floor-show", when the Lord of Misrule came in, dancing wildly and extravagantly, with a trail of teddy-boys behind him—and not merely because this raised thoughts in their minds like those which some people now think of jive and "rock 'n' roll" (which are much the same as these revelries), but because of the very real possibility that the devil's dance might become a dance led by the devil. Nothing is worse than the sudden evaporating of humour from an essentially humorous situation. It is like a funeral at a house with a comic name. But something like that seems to have happened to the Lord of Misrule and what he stood for.

THE BOY BISHOP

Even more obviously a refined joke, and even more "un-funny", I suppose, to those who were not fully "in the picture" was the custom by which once a year in certain places a child was solemnly appointed bishop on the 6th of December (St. Nicholas's day), dressed up in episcopal garments, paraded through his "diocese", and invited to preach a sermon. The connection between this and Christmas is hardly more than in that the name of St. Nicholas, patron saint of children, is perpetuated in our "Santa Claus"; but this kind of elaborate fun was of the essence of the carol-making ages. Seen from one angle, it is a good moment when the prelates and curates listen to the words of a child and pay him homage; seen from another, as it will be if anything in the delicate picture is a shade out of drawing, it will look pointless and undignified. And it is not quite enough to insist that the puritan mind said that everything must be dignified and have point. Human nature is too unstable to leave such delicacies unspoilt. We may add that although nothing remotely approaching the "boy bishop" happens today, that is partly because in these days, in which a medieval would feel that children are near-canonised compared with the way they were treated in his time, there is hardly need for any further pointing of our inflated and sentimental respect for youth.

This is all a difficult and hazardous subject to deal with. I am reminded—irreverently, but then these were irreverent times of which I am writing—of a good line in one of Mr. Nicholas Blake's detective stories:

> "He's a physical coward. And he has no sense of humour. Mark me words, he has no sense of humour. Now it's only when you're in dead earnest that you can afford to joke about it. We cartholicks are the only people that jokes about our religion. Y' see the implication?"

There was a sense in which the medieval church "joked about its religion", especially in this country; and there was a sense in which this betokened a certain kind of courage and a certain kind of "dead earnest" behind the impudent exterior. At all events, the humour that the medievals allowed into their religion was all part of the pervasiveness of their religion. Religion was, in a sense which modern protestantism has lost, "mixed up" with life to a high degree, and the inevitable consequence was, precisely, incongruity.

THE CHURCH'S YEAR

I believe that this can be easily seen in the way in which the medieval man went about his church-going. Aside from all the liturgical differences of practice between medieval catholicism and modern protestantism, consider simply the distribution of feasts and commemorations in the church's year. The Reformed ideal, which is still often expressed, was that every Lord's Day is Easter Day, and that upon it the whole

Gospel should be presented. It is no business of mine to controvert that exalted ideal, but simply to say that that was not how the medieval churchgoer saw it. For the Protestant (and I here exclude many anglicans) the rhythm of worship is almost uniformly regular: he goes to church for worship on Sundays and on Sundays only, so that at every seventh day worship punctuates his life. There are very few occasions indeed when he goes to church to worship on any other day of the week: and except where the observance of Christmas Day has returned in Protestantism, he will never go to church in the morning on any day but a Sunday and Good Friday.

But in the medieval church—whose practice is retained in the Roman Catholic church and in parts of the Anglican church—the rhythm was much more complex. Across the regular rhythm of the Sundays there cuts the irregular rhythm of the saints' days and days of commemoration, so that if a man attended church daily (and few outside the monasteries did), the flashes of colour, as it were, lit up the regular routine of the Mass at irregular intervals and not only on Sundays, while if he attended only on feasts of obligation, then he would still be attending in a rhythm more complicated than the mere Sunday rhythm.

Take for example the period between 1st November and 2nd February, 1957–8. In strict Reformed observance, this period is ecclesiastically punctuated by twelve Sundays; religion is injected into life on twelve equally spaced occasions. In the medieval calendar you have these high days—days on which normal daily offices are replaced by special observances: 1st November (All Saints), 30th November (St. Andrew), 26th December (St. Stephen), 27th December (St. John the Evangelist), 28th December (the Holy Innocents), 29th December (St. Thomas), 1st January (The Circumcision), 6th January (The Epiphany), 25th January (The Conversion of St. Paul) and 2nd February (The Purification, or Candlemas)—three Saturdays, two Fridays, two Wednesdays, a Thursday and a Monday apart from one Sunday. Days of commemoration, requiring no special liturgical acts and marked only by special collects, are added in considerable number, for example (in January alone), St. Antony on the 17th, St. Wulfstan on the 19th, St. Fabian on the 20th, St. Agnes on the 21st, and St. Vincent on the 22nd.

It is not necessary to the point I am here making to believe that everybody went to church every day. All I am saying is that you have here a system that *presupposes* daily worship—that cannot be worked without it—and which, if daily worship be practised, lends a dramatic and irregular rhythm to the impact of worship on life. Daily worship very naturally is more "mixed up with life", less allied with "Sunday best" than weekly worship on a day socially set aside for such activities. And a worship of irregular impact is more "mixed up with life" than a worship whose impact will fall predictably every seventh day.

Here then you have a line that leads directly back to the genius of medieval piety. Whatever were the corruptions of the church in the year 1500, whatever means it found to spoil its inheritance, we can be quite clear that in intention its worship was earthy and its influence pervasive. Consider what a difference it makes to a whole universe of piety that worship for so many of us now is a leisure-time activity, while for others it is still something that fits into the day's routine, in which a routine of its own is punctuated by festive days and Sundays.

It was natural, surely, that a worship thus designed to get "mixed up with life" should to some extent get "mixed up with" the worshipper's own personal nature: that its appeal to all his senses should be closely connected with its appeal to all his life. The medieval church welcomed images of every kind, and the protestants welcomed only concepts: and there is one simple way of stating the whole difference between them. To the medieval, if a carol went home partly on the strength of its tune, he was content not to express too much anxiety as to whether the words themselves made sense or spoke the whole truth. The spoken word was not to him the only means by which the truth could be communicated, and the written word was hardly a means of communication at all. What could not enter by "ear gate" might enter equally by "eye gate", and the liturgical pageantry of the Mass together with its music supplied him with an image which the foreign tongue in which the words were spoken would, left to itself, have denied him. Nor was the sense of smell overlooked, for they had their incense. Good medieval doctrine still gave primacy to the Word: "Love proceeds from the Word", wrote St. Thomas Aquinas, and the same Angelic Doctor wrote in his eucharistic hymn (as Gerald Manley Hopkins translated it):

> Seeing, touching, tasting are in thee deceived;
> How says trusty hearing? That shall be believed;
> What God's Son hath told me, take for truth I do;
> Truth himself speaks truly, or there's nothing true.

And Romano Guardini, writing of the splendour of the Mass, says:

Pride of place, though not of rank or worth, belongs not to beauty but to truth. The connection between beauty and truth established in that noble phrase *spendor veritatis* splendour of truth . . . is the anchor against the relativity of beauty. . . . Truth does not mean a mere lifeless accuracy of comprehension, but the right and appropriate regulation of life, a vital, spiritual essence. . . . And beauty is the triumphant splendour which breaks forth when the hidden truth is revealed.

"Seeing, touching, tasting are in thee deceived": quite so, and an acquiescence in the deception of images is the puritan's main contention against the middle ages. But consider what happens in religious behaviour when the critical faculty is turned only towards that which is communicated from mind to mind. In such a case, the only thing which can be right or wrong is a statement, a sentence, a proposition: all that matters in a service of worship is that the preaching be true and the prayers relevant. Whether the music be good or trivial, whether the building be beautiful or hideous, whether the eye and the affections be assaulted by aesthetic horrors or calmed by aesthetic beauties—these questions must take care of themselves. They must be turned over for judgment to the secular arm: and we know what confusion that has caused throughout protestantism, in all matters of taste and aesthetic.

The Wrath of the Puritans

THE puritan ethic, then, found everything to suspect in the medieval ethic. Where the medievals took their worship out of doors, the puritans kept it securely under cover of the meeting-house roof. Where the medievals used processions and liturgical movement within the church, the puritans preferred a form of worship which could be conducted by the minister without moving his feet. Where the medievals permitted and enjoyed the representation of sacred subjects on the stage, in church or from the back of a cart in the market square, the puritans condemned the stage and everything pertaining to it. Where the medievals spiced their religion with humour, the puritans turned a severe eye on all levity. Where the medievals spread their religious observances all over the week, the puritans kept it for the Lord's Day.

That we have seen: but there was more in the controversy than this. In the first place, the puritan and Calvinistic theology insisted with a new and devastating force on the "otherness" of God, and therefore on the "otherness" of religion. This has two immediate consequences. First, the relics of superstition or of paganism in the carols are abhorrent to the puritan mind. The puritan cannot bear all this about holly and ivy. His attitude to the scriptures, excluding the Old Testament Apocrypha from the church and, *a fortiori*, the New Testament Apocrypha from all religious consideration whatever, disposes at a stroke of "The Carnal and the Crane" and all the other legendary carols. Nothing but what is written in Scripture will be fit to sing about in church or to be associated with any religious observance. What is heathen is no worse than what is doubtful: both must go. Second, that insistence of Calvin upon the transcendent sovereignty of God which coloured so much of English religious thinking in the puritan period discouraged men from singing the kind of narrative ballad about the historic Jesus which had become so popular. To treat Jesus as the ballad-makers treated him seemed to the puritan mind irreverent and tending away from edification. The otherness of God and of the religious life in which they so firmly believed formed in their minds a presumption which collided head-on with the "mixed-up" character of medieval piety. Even the addiction of the carols to nature and naturalistic imagery would be repellent to the Calvinistic mind.

We must then add that, partly in consequence of the rise of the puritan attitude to things in general, but partly causing it, the shape of English society was radically altering, and the new shape was not one into which the carol could very easily be fitted. The rise of the merchant-class in England was the bridge between the middle ages and the industrial revolution. There was still an aristocratic class, whose activities will in a moment concern us. But the class which was so vitally affecting the texture of society was a new merchant-class, whose most noticeable characteristic was the very serious attention—the new kind of attention—they paid to the difference between work and play. If you read the Puritan divines of the seventeenth century you are often struck, I think, with a sense of surprise and even of incongruity by the abrupt way in which such a spiritual consellor will, after painting a terrifying picture of hell, and an equally glowing picture of the rewards of the faithful, say, "But anyway, the dissolute life is very expensive." Examples are, from Thomas Goodwin's *The Work of the Holy Ghost in our Regeneration*: "Are not godly men's thoughts to be taken up with their worldly business?" . . . (Answer): "A good man must do diligently that business to which he may be called" (Eccles. 9.10): (ed. of 1863, page 483): and from Philip Doddridge's *Rise and Progress of Religion in the Soul* (1740): "What the world calls a life of pleasure, is necessarily a life of expense too, and may, perhaps, lead you, as it has led many others . . . beyond the limits which providence has assigned." (XXI, 3–4). There is a shameless honesty about this which is by no means to be lightly dismissed. It was not a mere Forsytean philistinism that caused one of the major offences for which men were excluded from Dissenting churches in the eighteenth century to be the crime of debt. It was the way English society was going. Life was beginning to take a commercial shape which was more conveniently served by a religious observance that confined itself to the Day of Rest.

Moreover, the new commercial ethic was better served by the puritan ethos of personal life than by the medieval. The medievals were always delighting in a community-life which was neither church nor home but, as likely as not, tavern or village green. The puritans are entirely uninterested in any community except the home and the gathered church. They are neither clubbable, nor in the sense of the medieval peasant or the modern working man, sociable. Of course they frown on the tavern, and still frown on the pub. And equally they found no use for the kind of song, religious or otherwise, that suggested this kind of midway community. At their worst, they can fairly be held to have been saying, "While you're not at home, you're supposed to be working in the firm's time". At their best, of course, they expected the honourable man to be devoting his spare time to Bible-reading and the education of his children.

There were, then, theological reasons (the "otherness" of God), philosophical reasons (the suspicion of images and the elevation of concepts and written words), and social reasons (the requirements of the new commercial texture of life) that led the puritans either to dislike or to neglect the carol-making way of life. And since this is a book about carols, we are bound to give the puritans a somewhat unfavourable showing. That cannot be helped. I cannot be expected to praise them for trying to abolish my subject. But before continuing the story there is one thing that must be said on the other side.

Status pupillaris

The whole of Reformed theology was designed, from Luther on-wards, to permit an access to God on the part of man which the Reformers held had been denied by medieval society and medieval religious habit. In a word, the Reformers on the continent and the puritans in England were persuaded that medieval religion kept the laity in a condition of *status pupillaris* beyond what was just. If the puritans can be accused of denying that "youthful" quality which is the essence of the carol-maker's art, it must be admitted that they knew exactly what they were doing. It was, they said, for the church to educate men and then leave them to some extent free to make their own grown-up responsible approach to God. Certain customs in the medieval church were particularly mentioned by the Reformers as being tainted with what we now call paternalism. Parallel to this agitation on the part of the religious was a social agitation that to some extent allied itself with the puritan movement; this was designed to secure grown-up responsible freedom in the secular sense for the ordinary man, and was expressed by partly in the agitations of the Levellers and Diggers, partly in the insistence of the Brownists on the freedom of the local congregation from episcopal or national direction, and partly in Cromwell's dramatic democratic gesture, and in his whole hatred of tyranny. Now, unbalanced though one must judge the more extreme manifestations of this passion for freedom, we are bound to say that the puritan movement did leave the country with a sense of the responsibility of the individual for large as well as for small concerns which he retained almost until the present day. If therefore the puritans drove yet another nail in the coffin of the traditional carol by telling men to be their age (for there was more in my remark that Christmas revels were like a school rag-pantomime than mere epigram), we must at least admit that there are things which we now value in our national life for which the puritan movement made the world safe, and which under the medieval dispensation were in danger of being suffocated. History does not write itself clearly or unambiguously enough for us to say that carols can thrive only in a corrupt civilisation or that a strong evangelical piety is necessarily poison to the carol. But we can say that at this particular stage, where carol-making was overlapping actually into the beginning of the puritan period, the main controversy ran along these lines, and that it was a controversy of enormous historic importance. The puritans came to power in 1640: but we remember the good Arthur Bedford's conviction (written in a later part of the puritan period) that carols were so-called because they were sung in Charles the First's time. They were indeed. They were not killed by the advent of Martin Luther or John Calvin or Bishop Cartwright or Robert Browne or Oliver Cromwell. It was just that the nation's public opinion came in the end to turn its back on carol-making of the ballad kind, having other things to think about.

The Puritan Enactments

With respect to the observance of Christmas, it will be as well to quote two passages from Daniel Neal's *History of the Puritans*, that we may set the facts in order. It appears that in the year 1643 the ministers of London (Presbyterian) met together to decide whether they should hold services on Christmas day in their churches. Although it looked at one stage as if the sense of the meeting would go against it, John Lightfoot (1602–75, later Master of Catherine Hall, Cambridge, and Prebendary of Ely) persuaded them of the legitimacy of holding such services. But in the next year, 1644, Christmas Day coincided with the monthly fast-day ordained by Presbyterian opinion, and in consequence the following order was published on 19th December:

> Whereas some doubts have been raised, whether the next fast shall be celebrated, because it falls on the day which heretofore was usually called the feast of the nativity of our Saviour; the lords and commons in parliament assembled do order and ordain, that public notice be given, that the fast appointed to be kept the last Wednesday in every month ought to be

observed, till it be otherwise ordered by both houses; and that this day
in particular is to be kept with the more solemn humiliation, because it may
call to remembrance our sins, and the sins of our forefathers, who have
turned this feast, pretending to the memory of Christ, into an extreme
forgetfulness of him, by giving liberty to carnal and sensual delights,
being contrary to the life which Christ led here on earth, and to the
spiritual life of Christ in our souls, for the sanctifying and saving whereof,
Christ was pleased both to take a human life, and to lay it down
again.

The general tenor of this order is amplified and expounded in the
sermon preached by Edmund Calamy (Rector of St. Mary, Alder-
manbury) before the House of Lords on Christmas Day in which
he said:

This day is commonly called Christmas-day, a day that has heretofore
been much abused in superstitition and profaneness. It is not easy to say,
whether the superstitution has been greater, or the profaneness . . . and
truly, I think the superstition and Profaneness of this day are so rooted in it,
that there is no way to reform it, but by dealing with it as Hezekiah did
with the brazen serpent. This year God, by his providence, has buried it in
a fast, and I hope it will never rise again.

Superstition and profaneness—there we have in a couple of words
the main heads of the puritan indignation: against superstition, as men
of the New Covenant who wanted men to grow up as free, responsible
members of the Church who have grown out of bedtime stories; and
against profaneness, as men whose moral conscience matched their
theological zeal, and who were jealous for the "Crown rights of the
Redeemer". Their enactment, made through the Long Parliament,
is described by Neal as having "occasioned the greatest disturbance
over the nation".

Under the year 1645 Neal once again comments on an order of
8th June, abolishing the observance of Saints' days, and also Christmas,
Easter and Whitsuntide; of this order he says that "none occasioned
so much noise and disturbance". This was an extension of the prohibition on Christmas, to show that it was not merely the accidental
coincidence of the fast that moved them to act as they had done the
year before. It shows, too, that it was not only Christmas that was
odious in their eyes. To provide some compensation for the social
deprivations that this enactment brought with it, Parliament gave
instructions that the second Tuesday in every month should be observed,
without religious connotations, as a day of relaxation from labour on

which employers must provide for their servants to have the day free.

It is recorded that the King was highly displeased with this, and that he protested, in a letter dated 23rd April, 1647, when the matter was yet again under debate, that surely, in the matter of Easter, we were not departing from the intention of our Lord expressed in Scripture by celebrating the Resurrection. But the puritans had him there. The Sabbath, said they, was without doubt a scriptural ordinance, and the Christian Sabbath a Christian ordinance. But where does Scripture enjoin the *observance* of Easter? Once they took this literally biblical line, there was no arguing with them.

Then Neal puts the other side of the picture:

> The changing of the festival of Christmas into a fast last winter (sc. 1644), was not so much taken notice of, because all parties were employed in acts of devotion; but when it returned this year, there appeared a strong propensity in the people to observe it; the shops were generally shut, many Presbyterian ministers preached; in some places the common-prayer was read, and one or two of the sequestered clergy getting into pulpits prayed publicly for the bishops; several of the citizens of London, who opened their shops, were abused; in some places there were riots and insurrections, especially in Canterbury, where the mayor, endeavouring to keep the peace, had his head broke by the populace and was dragged about the streets; the mob broke into divers houses of the most religious in the town, broke their windows, abused their persons, and threw their goods into the streets, because they exposed them to sale on Christmas Day.

Neal's judgment on this is that behind the open rioting there was political force, occasion being taken for demonstrations by the supporters of the hard-pressed King. In consequence of the demonstrations arrests were made and certain prominent Papists were punished "as a terror to the rest", but

> during the space of the following twelve years, wherein the festivals were laid aside, there was not the least tumult on account of the holidays, the observation of Christmas being left as a matter of indifference.

We may reasonably gather from this that the social aspects of Christmas (and other festivals) were not, after the institution of the Commonwealth, regarded as an important issue by the puritans. The forces behind the prohibition of Christmas were religious and political, and the punishments for breach of the orders were entirely political.

It is also well known that the puritans frowned on the maypole. The ordinance of 6th April, 1644, which is almost entirely concerned with what may or may not be done on the Sabbath, includes a sentence to this effect: "That all May-poles be pulled down, and no others erected." That is the only general prohibition in the whole order, the rest of which deals with sports on the Lord's Day, and ends with the truculent and revealing injunction, "That the king's declaration concerning lawful sports on the Lord's Day bé called in, suppressed, and burnt". The inference is that the maypoles formed occasions for political demonstration and for breaches of the peace.

Carols of the Puritan Period

The carol, of course, did not die overnight, nor did it die completely. The puritan disapproval was neither a hundred per cent efficient nor a hundred per cent intended. It was possible for Thomas Warmestry (1610–65, a royalist clergyman of puritan leanings, later Dean of Worcester) to write in 1648 that "Christmasse Kariles . . . of holy and sober composures, and used with Christian sobriety and piety . . . are not unlawfull, and may be profitable, if sung with grace in the heart." The appearance of such collections as *Good and True, Fresh and New Christmas Carols* (1642), *New Carols for this Merry Time of Christmas* (1661), and *New Christmas Carols* (*c.* 1662), not to mention the celebrated *Dancing Master* of Henry Playford, which appeared when Cromwell was at the height of his power (1651), sufficiently indicate that the puritans were far from eradicating song and dance from the national life. There is plenty of evidence, much of which was collected by Dr. Scholes in *The Puritans and Music*, from which we can deduce a real love of music and culture among the puritans. No, it was, in the end, like the sailors who could not sing shanties without having their hands on the rope, and the Irish woman who could not keen without a body. The carol that goes with the medieval social context dies when that context is removed. Once the notion had really "sunk in" that there was something disreputable about the whole context of the ballad-carol, the spirit of the carol-maker died.

Therefore from about 1550 onwards we see something else taking the place of what was called "carol" up to then. The ballads survive, but alongside them we find new material that shows quite clearly what is happening.

For example, there is Richard Kele's *Christmas Carols Newly Imprinted* (dated about 1550): how different, this, from Richard Hill's commonplace book, which may not be much earlier (see above, p. 81)! Kele's modern editor, Edward Bliss Reed, comments, "(The carols) have little

THE ENGLISH CAROL

beauty of diction or metre. There is more of pathos than of joy in them; there is more of the puritan than of the wassailer in their spirit. Apparently the good people of that day found a satisfaction in lugubrious song." The contents of this depressing little book bear out this judgment. There is more than a suspicion of Sternhold-like zeal for improving people, a tendency to suggest that people's religious taste errs in being frivolous and light-hearted. The mournful motif in the carols is miles away from the poignancy of "All under the leaves" or "Tomorrow is my dancing day"; it is more like *The Crucifixion* crossed with Mrs. Hemans. Here is some typically didactic stuff, in the manner of a children's sermon in the name "John":

> If thou be Johan I tell it the
>   Hyght with a good advyce,
> Thou may be glad Johan to be
>   It is a name of price;
> The name of Johan well praise I may,
>   It is full good y-wys,
> The grace of God it is to say,
>   It soundeth none amys;
> If thou be a king in royalte,
>   And of wyt full wyse,
> Thou mayst be glad Johan to be,
>   It is a name of price.
>   (repeat first quatrain as chorus) (Reed, p. 24)

If there is a puritan flavour about this book, that is not an epithet that can be applied to all its contents. Some of the carols in it are love-songs of a dreary, witless kind, without the humour that could carry off a doubtful line in a melancholy thing like "The Friar and the Nun". And of course it is early yet to be talking of puritanism except in a very general sense. But in one sense it is here in Kele—in its opposition of a world-denying mind to the carol-makers' world-affirming mind. The world-denying mind, without a complete ascetic system, leads a man to make a virtue of sadness, and in the end leads him to write, and approve, this kind of thing that follows. Remember—the title of the book is "*Christmas* Carols Newly Imprinted":

> Be thou poore or be thou ryche
> I *rede* lyfte up thyn eye   (advise)
> And see in this we be all *lyche*   (like)
> Forsothe all we shall dye.

Sethe began bycause of syn,
  We syn both poore and riche,
Therefore dethe will never *blyn*   (cease)
  To take us all *in lyche.*   (alike)
For our syn I rede we *seche*   (seek)
  To heven that we may hye
For be we never so fresh nor ryche
  Forsothe we all shall dye.
    Be thou poore &c.

Christ that was bothe god and man,
  He dyed for our gylt;
    Nedes must we dye than
    With syn if we be *spylt.*   (corrupted)
    We shall *rote* both heart and *mylt* (rot/spleen)
Mercye lorde we crye,
It shall be, lorde, ryght us thou wilt
  Forsothe all we shall dye.
    Be thou poore &c.

Now Chryst dyed for all our mys,
  I red have in thy thought
To set thy mynde on worldly blys,
  Forsothe I holde it nought;
For worldes blys Christ he *ne rought*   (reckoned not)
  I rede the it defy
Unto thy grave thou shalt be brought,
  Forsothe we all shall dye.
    Be thou poore &c.

(Reed, *op. cit.*, p. 25. The old spelling is retained for the sake of the rhyme-scheme, which is not without interest.) Quite so; and four more verses of the same. If this be a Christmas carol, what would be Kele's notion of a penitential hymn?

This is the new age at its stuffiest. The medievals could approve the notion of our rejoicing in the Cross—awful paradox though it be. Kele just makes us uncomfortable about it all. Kele is of the new age— logical, sensitive to any suspicion of paradox, nonsense, or playfulness. Kele would have appealed in places to Amos Starkadder, but he is cold comfort after the ballads.

Motet Carols
"Out of the orient crystal skies", or "Falan-tiding" (Oxford 121), when you look at its words, is a very good late imitation of the ballads.

Perhaps its first line gives it away (the ballad-makers did not care to heap up adjectives like that), but its last verse has the authentic ring:

> The shepherds dwelling there about
> When they this news did know,
> Came singing all even in a rout,
> *Falan-tiding-dido.*

Falan-tiding is simply a madrigal-like ejaculation, and an indication to the musician that he can go as he pleases. This indicates not only that this is not a real ballad (for the ballads did not care for that kind of dalliance either) but that it comes from the new domestic-polyphonic school of composition. It first appeared with a five-part setting in 1610.

There are several examples of the motet-carol in modern editions of Tudor and Stewart music. The social background of this development is what we should expect. Alongside the popular music a taste for music-making was beginning to develop among cultured people, who no longer thought of music as something beneath their dignity, something which they hired a man of low degree to make for them. In this country and on the Continent there arose in the mid-sixteenth century a madrigal style in which some of the most perfect music in existence is written. No musician of any consequence in those days thought himself above composing this kind of music, and so we have the abundant treasure of Palestrina, and Lassus from overseas, and, within our own borders, of Byrd, Tallis, Weelkes, Wilbye and Gibbons, to name only a few of the many about whom you can read fully in the music histories. Behind the "great names" come a long procession of lesser composers, who were quite capable of making an agreeable setting of a love-song or of a metrical psalm to be sung either in four or five or six parts by people sitting round a table at home, or as a solo accompanied by a lute.

The texture of this music is, of course, light and feathery, and its climate is always cool. But behind this reticence of demeanour there often lies a wealth of contrapuntal skill. It makes no matter to Byrd (for example) whether he is writing for the church choir or for amateurs at home; it is all at the same level of genius. He gives us a *Carowle for Christmas Day* in his *Psalms, Sonnets and Songs* of 1589, and another in his later collection, similarly named, of 1611. These are church anthems, designed for a trained choir, and they stand alongside other pieces obviously designed for use at home. Less demanding, and more in the domestic atmosphere, are two settings of a lullaby-song (this kind being clearly suitable for the refined atmosphere of the places where it would be sung)—"Sweet was the song the Virgin sang". One of these appears at *Oxford* 30, being taken from William Ballet's manuscript *Lute Book* of 1594, and another, by John Attey, can be found in E. H. Fellowes' edition of the English School of Lutenist song-writers (Series II, Vol. 9, No. 14).

Late Ballads

This is almost a swing-back to the manuscript-carol style of the fifteenth century; but we have here of course carols that are popular neither by origin nor by destination. During the period when these were being written (and we must refer the reader to the sources for them because they are too extensive to be quoted here) the ballad carols were still in full swing. The Waits' Carol for the New Year, "The old year now away is fled", marked for use with GREENSLEEVES, which we have already encountered, dates from 1642, well after the polyphonic "Golden Age" was past.

But after 1660 new anonymous carols come in a much thinner stream. The reason for this is, quite apart from the prevalence of a puritan opinion among the middle classes even after the puritans had lost political power, that the Restoration brought with it musical styles that were as far removed as any could be from English folk-song. All the best people were singing Purcell by 1700, and all the likeliest musicians were dining out on the fact that they had had lessons from Lully. Society was taking a new shape; there was a stronger tendency now for the lower orders to imitate the habits of their betters, and an increasing conviction that what the people in London do matters to the rest of the country. The sudden superimposition on English music of foreign styles through the court of Charles II was, broadly speaking, responsible for that "divided mind" in English music which made it impossible for our country to make significant contributions to the progress of music between Purcell and Vaughan Williams. This was another force that drove the folk-musicians to the regions that were "ignorant alike of the law of God and of man". The movement was beginning which, in the end, turned the whole music-making picture upside down: in the fifteenth century the nobility listened to music made by the poor; by the middle of the nineteenth the ordinary man was beginning to listen to music made by the virtuoso. Where did the stream of music made by people for themselves, without primary thought of listeners, run during this period of transition?

We have a few carols that look as if they must have come from this "dead" period.

There is an excellent carol, "All ye who are to mirth inclined" (*Oxford*, 51), which is a selection of 28 verses originally published in 1631. As we have it, it is a carol of the ministry of Christ, mentioning various incidents recorded in the Gospels, and placing them all in a carol-framework formed by the word "mirth" in the first line, and in the last verse by the couplet:

> And how he shed his precious blood
> Only to do his sinners good.

Its metre is Long Metre, not ballad-metre, and it has a faintly hortatory note; indeed in its original twenty-eight verses it reads like a versified sermon, just where a ballad of comparable length reads like a versified story. Its kinship with the ballads, at least in outward style, is probably due to the fact that the book where it is first found, *The Garland of Good-will*, is an enlarged edition of a book originally published in 1593 by that pioneer among story-tellers, Thomas Deloney (about 1543–1600), who himself was a ballad-writer. He did not write these lines, but they would only have been thought fit to stand in an enlarged and posthumous edition of Deloney's collection had they been written in something like his style. It appears to have no "proper" tune, but Gilbert heard it in the West Country, and printed it with a tune that adds a refrain. The tune printed in *Oxford* is said to be a different one from that in Gilbert. As a matter of fact, if Gilbert's refrain be detached, the two tunes are almost certainly versions of a common original. (See Terry, *op. cit.*, p. 20. For the words, cf. *Oxford* 14.)

Of a similar cast, but more ponderous in diction, is the carol called "The Decree", beginning "Let Christians all with one accord rejoice" (*Oxford* 65). This was printed in *Bramley and Stainer* in its original twenty-three verses. Its metre—our first encounter with heroic couplets in a carol—gives it away as almost certainly eighteenth century in origin, and so does its very homiletic manner. Here are two verses on Herod—verses 11 and 12 of the original:

> The Black Decree went all the country round
> To kill and murder children sick and sound:
> They tore young children from their mothers' breast,
> Thinking to murder Christ among the rest.
>
> But God above, who knew what should be done,
> Had sent to Egypt his beloved Son;
> Where with his earthly parents he was fed,
> Until the bloody tyrant he was dead.

We have indeed now come to the age of prose commentary on scripture, when a man can set down a line like "Until the bloody tyrant he was dead". But such commentary does at least give us carols on the life and work of our Lord, and both "The Decree" and "All ye who are to mirth inclined" fill a gap that the ballad-carols usually leave. The extra verses in "The Seven Joys of Mary", bringing the number up to twelve, probably date from this period, bringing in "Making the lame to go", "making the blind to see", "reading the Bible o'er", "bringing the dead alive", and "Turning water to wine" (for all of which except the last, see *Oxford* 70).

We move a stage further when we come to "Jacob's Ladder" (*Oxford* 58). Here is a carol genuinely of the Evangelical Revival. Here is the voice (though not the diction) of Charles Wesley—the personal appeal, the didactic style, the evangelical invitation at the end. It is worth quoting in full, for it is the only thing of its kind that we have:

> As Jacob with travel was weary one day,
> At night on a stone for a pillow he lay;
> He saw in a vision a ladder so high,
> That its foot was on earth and its top in the sky.
> > Alleluya to Jesus who died on the tree,
> > And hath raised up a ladder of salvation for me.
>
> This ladder is long, it is strong and well-made,
> Has stood hundreds of years and is not yet decayed,
> Many millions have climbed it and reached Sion's hill,
> And thousands by faith are climbing it still.
> > Alleluya to Jesus &c.
>
> Come, let us ascend! all may climb it who will
> For the angels of Jacob are guarding it still:
> And remember, each step that by faith we pass o'er,
> Some prophet or martyr hath trod it before.
> > Alleluya to Jesus &c.
>
> And when we arrive at the haven of rest
> We shall hear the glad words, "Come up hither, ye blest,
> Here are regions of light, here are mansions of bliss."
> O, who would not climb such a ladder as this.
> > Alleluya to Jesus &c.

That goes to a rollicking tune which makes one feel that it was a pity Sankey did not know it, and a few more like it, and so spare us some of his worse efforts in a more modern style. Its metre is our old friend, the "Virgin Unspotted" metre, and it may have been written to carry a tune of that family: but the traditional tune seems to have been associated with it from near the beginning. *Oxford* conjectures that the tune already existed with other secular words, and the new marriage may well have been arranged under Evangelical influence.

Nearer the older carol tradition is a splendid tub-thumping song in the Pepysian collection, preserved in *Oxford* (5) as "All hail to the days". Its first two verses are by Tom D'Urfey (1653–1723), a dramatist and poet who wrote them in a book he published in 1681 under the delightful title, *An Antidote to Melancholy: Made up in Pills*. Melancholy certainly stands little chance against this:

> 'Tis ill for a mind to anger inclined
>   To think of small injuries now;
> If wrath be to seek, do not lend her thy cheek,
>   Nor let her inhabit thy brow.
> Cross out of thy books malevolent looks,
>   Both beauty and youth's decay,
> And wholly consort with mirth and with sport,
>   To drive the cold winter away.

The metre and manner suggest W. S. Gilbert at his best, and the tune is one of the best things that ever came out of the Restoration period.

A few other carols may perhaps come from this period, though of these we cannot be certain. "Rejoice and be merry" (*Oxford* 25), from a Dorset Church gallery-book, may well come from somewhere near 1700; its refrain suggests the influence of hymns of a date even later than that—

> Who brought us salvation—his praises we'll sing.

"This is the truth sent from above" (*Oxford* 68), another Long Metre carol, laying emphasis on the Atonement, probably belongs to the same period, and the same may be said of "The babe in Bethlehem's manger laid" (*Oxford* 69), whose tune is very much of the eighteenth century, and whose words tell of the preaching as well as the incarnation of Christ. This latter carol comes from the Black Country collection, *A Good Christmas Box* (1847), in which we may expect to find a trace of Evangelical influence. "When Jesus Christ was twelve years old" takes the same biographical subject matter again (*Oxford* 72), and may come from the same period. But these are merely speculations. By the year 1750 religious folk-song is all but submerged, and when the folk-songs were resurrected in about 1900 they all sounded like a barbarous tongue to our jaded cosmopolitan ears.

The Poets: William Dunbar

Wherever we presented those poets whose verses have become carols, they would be a digression from our main theme; but it seems best to attend to them here, which is at least their historical place. There are many poets of the period before 1700 whose work comes near to the carol-maker's art, even though they moved in a different sphere from that in which the minstrels were at work. Most of the carols we shall mention here are "synthetic" carols—as, indeed, will be a large proportion of all the carols we mention from here to the end of the book. A "synthetic" carol is a carol whose words and music did not appear in original association, the collocation of words and tune being the result of editorial work at some stage. The carol we have encountered that goes with GREENSLEEVES (*Oxford* 28) is a synthetic carol, and so, of course, may be some that we believe to be traditional but whose words and tune further research might show to be not of original association. (In the same way we might speak of a "synthetic" hymn: we do not usually do so, because almost all hymns in modern use are synthetic in that their collocations of words and tune are editorial. "O God, our help in ages past" to the familiar tune is synthetic, because the association was only made 142 years after the hymn was written and 153 years after the tune was written. "O come, all ye faithful", whose words and tune come from the same hand, is one of the few that are purely homogeneous, but we should hardly call "synthetic" a hymn whose tune, although composed by a hand not the author's, is a contemporary setting, and has been the only setting of the words in use: of these there are few, but "Christians, awake" would be one.)

The first and greatest of all the carol-poets is William Dunbar, who comes into our story for his lines beginning *Rorate caeli desuper* (*Oxford* 125). Dunbar was born about 1460 and died some time before 1522, a Scotsman who served his country chiefly as a politician. He wrote a number of poems, religious, amorous, satirical, comic and courtly. We may pause for a moment on Professor C. S. Lewis's comment on him that he is a master in the juxtaposition of the comic and the terrible. Professor Lewis notes the parallel between this and the jokes men made about the gallows under the old penal code, or that boys made about flogging at Eton under Keate, or that Englishmen made about Hitler during the Second World War. "There is nothing funny", he says, "about Hitler *now*". That is to say, Dunbar's ferocious grotesqueries are to be linked with the very real terrors that formed part of popular religion at the time: and this is all part of the great controversy with which we are still engaged. For in the far north the colours are darker than in the south country where the carols flourished. We have little of Scots minstrelsy in the carol world. Where Dunbar was brought up, the horrors were at their deepest, and I suppose that in him we have the farthest reach of that medieval sense of humour, of fearlessly juxtaposing the terrible and the gay as well as the sacred and the secular, which we have already noted in the ballads. Nothing in literature is more packed with the primitive sense of encounter with death, "that strong unmerciful tyrand", than his "Lament for the Makers" (*Oxford Book of English Verse*, 42), or with the bizarre and religiously horrible than "The Dance of the Seven Deadly Sins" (*English Verse, Early Lyrics to Shakespeare*, World's Classics, p. 84). But not so *Rorate caeli*. Of it Professor Lewis writes (p. 95), "(It) might almost claim to be . . . the most lyrical of all English poems—that is, the hardest of all English poems to *read*, the hardest not to *sing*. We read it alone and at night, and are almost shocked, in laying the book down, to find that the choir and organ existed only in our imagination. It has none of the modern— the German or Dickensian—attributes of Christmas. It breathes rather the intoxication of universal spring and summons all Nature to salute 'the clear Sun whom no cloud devours'."

It could not, of course, be put better. The literature of carols, like that of hymns, does not abound in the exalted poetic virtues; it is not its business to do so. That makes this noble poem the more precious.

Dr. Lewis's musical suggestion contains the only unabusive remark that (so far as my knowledge goes) he has written about the organ. But no music has survived as traditionally associated with these words, no doubt because, as he suggests, they "sing themselves". Moderns, however, understandably greedy for so distinguished an enrichment of the repertory, have suggested tunes. That in *Oxford* is a Scottish ballad, which some may feel runs a trifle skittishly for the words. But a surprisingly good setting, shamelessly anachronistic, is the eighteenth-century tune, LONDON (*E.H.* 297), which is set to the words in the *Westminster Hymnal* (1940).

> *Rorate caeli desuper*,
>   Heavens, distil your balmy showers,
> For now is risen the bright day-star
>   From the rose Mary, flower of flowers:
>   The clear Sun, whom no night devours,
> Surmounting Phoebus in the East
>   Is comen of his heavenly towers,
> *Pro nobis Puer natus est.*

Archangels, angels and dominations,
   Thrones, potestates and martyrs *seir*   (various)
And all ye heavenly operations,
   Star, planet, formament and sphere,
   Fire, earth, air and water clear,
To Him give loving, most and least,
   That comes in to so meek manner,
Et nobis Puer natus est.

Sinners, be glad and penance do,
   And thank your Maker heartfully;
For he that ye might not come to,
   To you is comen full humbly
   Your soulis with his blood to buy
And loose you of the fiend's arrest—
   And only of his own mercy,
Pro nobis Puer natus est.

The spelling is here modernised for the reader's convenience. In v. 1, *Rorate caeli desuper* is the opening of the Vulgate version of Isaiah 45. 8, translated in R.S.V.: "Shower, O heavens, from above, and let the skies rain down righteousness." In verse 2, "dominations" is in the original "dompnationis", three syllables, and "Fire" is pronounced in two syllables.

We shall not rise to these heights again, but there are some delightful verses in the lesser poets of the period which the editors have at various times annexed.

Southwell, Jonson and Contemporaries

Robert Southwell (*c.* 1561–94), gives us two carols which we must mention. One is "Behold a silly tender Babe" (*Oxford* 170), in which, of course, "silly" means "simple", and the other is "The Burning babe". The former of these is a charming ballad, written in a consciously contrived and polished style, full of image, alliteration and antithesis:

This stable is a Prince's court,
   This crib his chair of state;
The beasts are parcel of his pomp,
   The wooden dish his plate.

The persons in that poor attire
   His royal liveries wear;
The Prince himself is come from heaven,
   This pomp is praised there.

The other, also written in ballad metre, works out another and more striking image:

As I in hoary winter's night stood shivering in the snow,
Surprised I was with sudden heat which made my heart to glow;

And lifting up a fearful eye to view what fire was near,
A pretty Babe all burning bright did in the air appear,

Who scorched with excessive heat such floods of tears did shed,
As though his floods should quench his flames with which his tears were fed.

Alas! quoth he, but newly born in fiery heats I fry,
Yet none approach to warm their hearts or feel my fire but I!

My faultless heart the furnace is, the fuel wounding thorns;
Love is the fire and sighs the smoke, the ashes shame and scorns;

The fuel Justice layeth on, and Mercy blows the coals;
The metal in this furnace wrought are men's defiled souls;

For which, as now on fire I am, to work them to their good,
So will I melt into a bath to wash them in my blood!

With that he vanished out of sight and swiftly shrunk away,
And straightway I called into mind that it was Christmas Day.

Both these poems provide good examples of the judgment that Professor Lewis makes on Southwell: "He was not in the least 'contemporary'; his work sometimes recalls the past, sometimes anticipates the immediate future which he was unconsciously helping to create, and often seems to belong to no period at all." There is the real ballad-ring about the rhythm and style, and yet something in the imagery that looks forward to the metaphysicals. Southwell, a Catholic priest who was chaplain to the Countess of Arundel from 1589 to 1592, was arrested and ultimately put to death under the same penal laws that brought the puritan martyrs to their death.

Southwell's "Burning Babe" was praised by a distinguished contemporary, Ben Jonson (1573–1637), who has left us a famous carol, "I sing the birth was born tonight" (*Oxford* 168). Like all these poems, it has no traditional tune, but its very unusual metre irresistibly suggests that he had in mind the Genevan tune to Psalm 36 (for which see *E.H.* 544), which had come over to England in 1558 as the tune for the 113th metrical psalm in the Old Version. It is therefore probably good history to set that tune to these words, as has been done by the *Oxford Hymn Book* and *Congregational Praise*. This delightful poem is too well known to need quotation.

The Roman Catholic martyr, Southwell, also brings to mind the Hymn of the New Jerusalem, of which two versions are familiar, a selection from one of which is in *Oxford* at No. 132. The better known version begins "Jerusalem, my happy home", and is dated about 1600. But an earlier version (that in *Oxford*) is dated 1585 and ascribed to W. Prid.

We know nothing of Prid, but that he published in 1585 a treatise entitled *The Glasse of Vain-glorie: Faithfully translated out of St. Augustine his booke, intituled Speculum peccatoris, into English by W. P., Doctor of the Lawes*. His version of this hymn begins, "O mother dear, Jerusalem"; *Oxford* alters its first line to "City of peace, our mother dear". It is originally in 176 lines. The other poem, "Jerusalem, my happy home", is shorter—104 lines (see *E.H.* 638)—and contains many reminiscences and some actual borrowings from Prid. It cannot be positively said which is the older, but "Jerusalem, my happy home", whose author is known to us only as "F.B.P.", was first printed in 1601. There is a tradition that "F.B.P." was a Catholic priest imprisoned and under sentence of death; it is at least a plausible theory that he used his hours of meditation writing what he could remember of Prid, and where his memory failed, writing in lines of his own.

Although it has nothing to do with Christmas, and is not usually thought of as a carol, "Jerusalem, my happy home" has nearer affinities with the carols than have the works of most contemporary poets. Where the ballad-carols tell the story of the Nativity or of the Passion in homely English verse, using often English images, so this anonymous poet takes over the familiar imagery of the Book of Revelation and translates it in terms of the English scene:

> Thy gardens and thy gallant walks
> Continually are green.

The imagery of the Book of Revelation is a kind of folk-song in itself; but Revelation comes to the poet through Augustine's *Meditations* Book I, chapter 25, and both poems are ordered in their thought by the pattern of Augustine's chapter. "F.B.P." at one point includes a delightful gloss on Augustine (whom he, of course, calls "Austin"). Augustine writes at one point:

> There are the melodious choirs of angels . . . there the goodly fellowship

of prophets, whose eyes God opened to take a prospect of far distant mysteries, there the Twelve leaders of the Christian armies. . . . There the noble army of martyrs. . . . There the convention of Confessors, there the holy men and women . . . there the virgins and youths. . . .

recalling the words of the *Te Deum*; and "F.B.P." particularises:

> *Te Deum* doth Saint Ambrose sing,
> Saint Austin doth the like—

an agreeable hidden compliment to his author.

These lines achieved very wide popularity. When the hymn-editors came to use them for a hymn, they found it necessary to make large omissions and to dress up the words in conventional garb before the nineteenth-century congregation would swallow it. A version which is very likely by James Montgomery (1819) will be found in *Hymns A. & M.*; but who could want to sing it, knowing the originals, one can hardly imagine. Indeed, a comparison of *E.H.* 638 ("F.B.P.'s" version) with the hymn at *A. & M.* 282 provides an excellent introduction to what we shall shortly have to say about the difference between a carol and a hymn. (The whole story about these two ancient carols is told in Julian's *Dictionary of Hymnology*, p. 583.)

Herrick and Contemporaries

Three pieces from Herrick's *Noble Numbers* (1647) have come into currency through the devotion of editors. "In numbers, but these few" (*Oxford* 176) is especially attractive, with its delicate choice of words and sweet rhythm:

> The Jews, they did disdain thee,
> But we will entertain thee
> With glories to await here
> Upon thy princely state here,
> And more from love than pity
> We'll make thee here
> From year to year
> A free-born of our city.

Oxford has also "What sweeter music" (122), set to a delightful tune from a German nativity play, and "Down with the rosemary" (126), a carol for Candlemas, traditionally the end of the Christmas season. His "The Wassail" does not seem to have found a popular tune, but it is more carol-like than any of the others—a real country song of good cheer:

Then may your plants be pressed with fruit,
　　Nor bee nor hive you have be mute,
But sweetly sounding like a lute.

Next may your ducks and teeming hen
　　Both to the cock's tread say Amen,
And for their two eggs render ten.

Last may your harrows, shares and ploughs
　　Your stacks, your stocks, your sweetest mows,
All prosper by your virgin vows.

Alas! we bless, but see none here
　　That brings us either ale or beer:
In a dry house all things are *near*.   (mean)

Perhaps it is the rather surprisingly minatory last verses, that express
the sentiments of waits attending on a teetotal family, that have kept
the lines out of the books.

　　With great regret we must judge George Herbert's "Christmas" too
far outside the carol-country to be included here, although it is in
Rickert. Herbert's genius ran at too high a voltage to produce carols,
although some of his verses have been made into acceptable hymns.
William Austin (1587–1633) of Lincoln's Inn, spares us one engaging
lyric in "All this night shrill chanticleer" (*Oxford* 123) which has found
a happy traditional tune, and Bishop Joseph Hall of Exeter (1574–1656)
left lines which have found their way into several books, beginning
"Immortal babe" (*Oxford* 117), and have a gravity that almost pre-
figures Charles Wesley. Both these carols are in *Bramley and Stainer*,
Austin's to a gushing tune by Sullivan, and Hall's to the same deplorable
recension of a great German tune that (surprisingly) appears in *Oxford*.
　　But if we have no Herbert, we have a snatch of Richard Crashaw
(1613–49) in "Gloomy night" (*Oxford* 124). Of the metaphysical poets,
of whom Crashaw was one of the chief, Professor Lewis writes yet
another comment that illuminates our own story. He says that they
are distinguished by their defiance of a convention which he calls
"decorum". "Decorum" is itself the negation of the kind of incongruity
which we noted in the ballads. It is characteristic of the Metaphysicals
to produce "poetic shocks by coupling what was sacred, august, remote
or inhuman with what was profane, hum-drum, familiar and social",
and this, rather than the learning or wide reading that makes it possible,

is what "gives Metaphysical poetry its essential flavour". It is, of course, the medieval love of the incongruous, bred into the late medievals by the inevitable and often harsh incongruities of ordinary life as they lived it, carried up to the plane of high culture. George Herbert is a perfect master of it. (How would the author of "Love bade me welcome" have rejoiced in "My Dancing Day" if he knew it!) Crashaw alone brings the Metaphysical style into our story, and of course the poem that brings him in is a very mild example of it: none the less, it has one line of unexpected significance. His first verse works out the implications of the simple antithesis—Day and Night:

> Gloomy night embraced the place
>   Where the noble infant lay;
> The babe looked up and showed his face,
>   In spite of darkness it was day!
> It was thy day, Sweet, and did rise
> Not from the East, but from thine eyes.

But in his last verse the colours are deeper and the contrasts bolder:

> Welcome, all wonder in one night,
>   Eternity shut in a span,
> Summer in winter, day in night,
>   Heaven in earth and God in man!
> Great little one! whose all-embracing birth
> Lifts earth to heaven, stoops heaven to earth.

It is impossible not to be reminded there of Charles Wesley's lines,

> Our God contracted to a span,
> Incomprehensibly made man.

George Wither (1588–1667), whom we know for "Sleep, Baby, sleep", sometimes called "Wither's Rocking Hymn" (*Oxford* 185), is a very different kind of person. Brought up in the society from which lyric poetry came, he began his grown-up life as a lawyer in Lincoln's Inn; but lyric soon gave way to satire, and his royalist sympathies had fully gone during the twenties, leaving him an enthusiastic parliamentarian, who raised a troop of horse for Cromwell when the call came in 1642. Wither wrote a great deal, much of it in verse, but he never became a stylist. One or two of his pieces have become hymns in modern books, and very good hymns they make, chiefly because of his unpolished, workaday style of diction, which is the style that makes one kind of good hymn. His religious lyrics are to be found in his *Hymns and Songs of the Church* (1623) and in *The Hallelujah, Britain's*

Second Remembrancer (1641). Both books have prefaces of great length and truculence, chiefly explaining his puritan sympathies and denouncing the wickedness of society in general:

> For so innumerable are the foolish and profane songs now delighted in, to the dishonour of our language and religion, that hallelujahs and pious meditations are almost out of use and fashion; yea, not in private only, but at public feasts and civil meetings also, scurrilous and obscene songs are impudently sung without respecting the reverend presence of matrons, virgins, magistrates or divines.

This sounds an unpromising background for a carol; but then Wither was not the first writer of religious lyrics to have the improvement of public taste as one of his major concerns. Indeed, "Sleep, Baby, Sleep" has a brief rubric that restates the principles of his Preface:

> Nurses usually sing their children to sleep, and through want of pertinent matter they often make use of unprofitable, if not worse, songs; this was therefore prepared that it might help acquaint them and their nurse-children with the loving care and kindness of their heavenly Father.

This is perhaps the nearest thing we have to a genuine Puritan carol— designed with didactic and almost censorious purpose, but remaining as a gentle and graceful Christmas lullaby.

Not unlike Wither is Thomas Pestel (*c.* 1584–*c.* 1659), Vicar of Packington, near Ashby-de-la-Zouch, Leicestershire. He is a minor poet who rates a short entry in the *Dictionary of National Biography*, but none in the *Oxford Companion to English Literature*. One can see why. He is absurdly unreliable. But his "Psalm for Christmas Day" contains verses that rise dramatically out of doggerel to inspiration. It opens thus:

> Fairest of morning lights, appear,
>   Thou blest and gaudy day,
> On which was born our Saviour dear;
>   Arise, and come away!
>
> This day prevents his day of doom,
>   His mercy now is nigh;
> The mighty God of Love is come,
>   The Dayspring from on high.

Had it all been on that level I hardly think that Lord David Cecil would have admitted it to the *Oxford Book of Christian Verse*. That is good average Sternhold; ballad metre tamed to the precision of psalmody.

There are the stock expressions, the crude syntax, the line-filling epithets. And then all at once it takes fire.

> Behold, the great Creator makes
> Himself a house of clay,
> A robe of virgin flesh he takes
> Which he will wear for ay . . .

> This wonder struck the world amazed,
> It shook the starry frame;
> Squadrons of spirits stood and gazed,
> Then down in troops they came.

Beginning there, the verses now form a Christmas hymn of unusual and vivid beauty (*E.H.* 20). But see how imagination has taken over at that third verse. The hand that could do no better than "blest and gaudy day" can now write of "squadrons of spirits", and at the end form a verse that is pure carol:

> Join then, all hearts that are not stone,
> And all our voices prove,
> To celebrate this Holy one,
> The God of peace and love.

Here is this faithful Anglican parson, arraigned before a puritan court in 1646 with his son (who by then had succeeded him as Vicar) for using illegal ceremonies in church: when he would write a Christmas psalm, he begins in the manner of puritan Sternhold, and moves by the end into the pure medieval carol-climate, taking in on the way at least two theological statements of extreme dubiety. "Which he will weare for aye" suggests the Apollinarian heresy to certain sensitive souls, and "God in cradle lies" the patripassian heresy to others. He is, as it were, undecided whether he is writing a psalm-like paraphrase of conventional piety, or whether he is writing an imaginative lyric. And that is just where a minor poet in seventeenth century anglicanism would be likely to find himself. With all its vitality and splendour, "Behold, the great Creator" exposes with pathetic clarity the perplexity into which the religiously imaginative had fallen in the seventeenth century when it came to turning the most gracious of Christian mythologies into popular song.

Christmas Hymns

A FESTIVE Christmas at the present time demands, alongside Christmas carols, compositions of a characteristically post-puritan kind known as Christmas hymns. Although they are not carols, they do duty for carols in a sense in which hymns for other seasons do not do duty for carols even of those seasons, and since we have now arrived at that period which marks the extinction of the traditional carol, this is the place to consider them.

Hymns and Carols

It must be noted that the habit of disregarding the distinction between Christmas hymns and Christmas carols is a habit of fairly recent formation. To take the hymn books as a rough guide, the first hymn book to include carols alongside the hymns was probably the *Oxford Hymn Book* (1908), which in a Christmas section of twenty-three hymns (out of 300) includes "A virgin unspotted", "In dulci jubilo" and "The first Nowell" from the early tradition, and "Good Christian men, rejoice", "Like silver lamps in a distant shrine" and "See amid the winter's snow" from the modern period. Designed primarily for college chapels, in which at the date of its publication much of the medieval ethos still survived, that book has now largely passed out of use. Of standard hymn books (by which expression I mean hymn books with a wide circulation in the Church of England (which has no official hymn book) or hymn books authorised by the major non-anglican denominations) the earliest to print carols was the *Congregational Hymnary* (*c.* 1916), which prints eleven carols, including "God rest you merry" and "The first Nowell" at the end of the book, separate from the Christmas hymns: no doubt this was partly due to the fact that its Editor-in-chief, Sir John Maclure, was at the time headmaster of a large public school (Mill Hill), in which a carol-singing tradition persisted much as it would in the colleges. The anglican books have never yet printed carols: there are none (except possibly No. 29, "The great God of heaven") in the *English Hymnal*, and none in any edition of *Hymns Ancient and Modern*. *Songs of Praise* prints "The First Nowell" in its children's section, with a few other carols from various sources, but for the rest relies on *Oxford*, which was edited by the same hands. On the other hand, carols are admitted in the *Church Hymnary* (1927), the *Methodist Hymn Book* (1933) and the *Baptist Church Hymnal*. Of recent hymn books, *Christian Praise* (1957) has a generous section of nineteen Christmas carols in addition to Christmas hymns, and *Congregational Praise* (1951) and the *BBC Hymn Book* (1951) go farther and admit Easter as well as Christmas carols.

That is where we stand today, and the reason for the almost exclusive emphasis on Christmas will be obvious. It is at that season that people who use hymn books in church now want to add carols to the hymns. But it was not always so, and two hundred years ago, or thereabouts, the Christmas hymn came into being to fill the gap left by the decline of the carol-habit among singers who none the less wanted to sing.

It is unnecessary here to go again over the history of post-Reformation hymnody, on which much has already been written. The important point here is that it was the eighteenth century that witnessed the invention of the English hymn as a vehicle of public praise. If some of the compositions of which we now think as hymns are of earlier date, that is because the hymn-singing habit that developed in the eighteenth century encouraged later editors to look in the works of earlier poets for verses that could be used as hymns. In respect of the rise of hymnody to popular favour in the eighteenth century I offer here three observations.

Hymns and Liturgy

The first is that hymns supplied a deeply felt liturgical need. The first hymn books of wide circulation (even though they were not positively the first books to contain hymns) were those of Isaac Watts; and the most important of these (*Hymns and Spiritual Songs*) was published in 1707. At the time, Watts, aged 33, was minister of a fashionable Independent church at Mark Lane, London. Watts's greatest disciple in the next generation was Philip Doddridge (1702–51), who was for twenty-two years minister at an Independent Chapel at Northampton, and Principal of a Dissenting Academy associated with it. This, of which much can be read in other places, is enough to show that hymns come into the worship of the English church from the Dissenting side. It was a puritan mind that ordained that nothing should be sung in our churches, anglican or Dissenting, but metrical psalms, and it was a minister of the puritan tradition, Isaac Watts, who first defied that ordinance on a large scale. When you look at Dissenting worship in 1700, you see why.

At that date Dissenting worship was conditioned by a near-fanatical hatred of the Book of Common Prayer. That Book symbolised the principles on which Dissenters had been persecuted between 1662 and 1689, and the kind of ecclesiastical authority over which immediately before 1662 they had been in controversy with the anglicans. Unedifying though the 1662 controversy is to any but liturgists and church historians, it has some importance just here for our story. In 1661 representatives of the Presbyterians and Independents met at the Savoy Palace with representatives of the anglican church, to submit proposals for a revised Prayer Book. The liturgy which they presented as their constructive contribution to the discussion was (it is usually thought) substantially written by Richard Baxter, the Presbyterian minister at Kidderminster. It is a form of worship of great rhetorical power and of classic Calvinist completeness, but it is entirely destitute of congregational sense: there are no responses, no public recitals of the Creed, the Confession, or the Lord's Prayer. All these (Creeds included) are prescribed to be read by the minister. A psalm (84, 95 or 100) is appointed to be sung at one point, and at the end of the liturgy is a long "hymn", which turns out to be a prose *catena* of lyrical phrases from Scripture, and which no doubt was designed to be read.

The puritan genius, even before the dispersion and persecution that followed the breakdown to which the Savoy Conference was foredoomed, was all against congregational participation in worship. But during and after the dispersion it was, effectively, against liturgy of any kind; and in Isaac Watts's time, which is some fifteen years after the Act of Toleration, we find that worship in an Independent chapel is likely to consist of an opening psalm, a short invocatory prayer, a reading and exposition of Scripture, another psalm, a long prayer, the Sermon, another prayer, and the blessing. The psalms apart, the congregation's duty was to be silent and attentive. It is not surprising, then, that the young Watts, as the story goes, complained to his father of the aridity of public worship at Southampton, where they lived, and in particular of the metrical psalms, and, when challenged by his father to do better, wrote his first hymn at the age of sixteen.

That story about Watts is an epitome of the whole situation in Dissenting worship; and anglican worship, though it never lost the priceless boon of the Book of Common Prayer, was in other ways not much better. Watts's gesture was to place the New Testament, as well as the Old, in the mouths of the people. There was all the difference in the world between singing "When I survey the wondrous Cross" (even though you sang it, as you probably did at first, to the OLD

HUNDREDTH) and singing some petrified version of Psalm 58. It meant that the congregation could make some kind of New Testament response to the New Testament preaching of the puritan pulpit; and indeed, when one recalls that the whole burden of puritan anti-liturgical feeling was based on the proposition that liturgies and ceremonies are of the "Old Covenant" and that men of the "New Covenant" should have grown out of such necessities, a demand for New Testament hymns, and for psalms translated in a New Testament fashion, in the manner of Watts's "Jesus shall reign", is just what one expects to hear.

Hymns as the Folk-song of Evangelism

But all this was happening in church. As we have before observed, puritan opinion, impatient of all associations of men but the family and the gathered church, took little notice of the kind of casual associations, neither sacred nor domestic, that produced carol-singing. And in this sense, the prevailing opinion all through the country (apart from the highest circles of aristocracy) was puritan. This fact explains that remarkable reaction to the evangelism of the Wesleys which gathered round the proposition that it was wrong, or ungodly, or vulgar, to worship God out of doors, especially at five in the morning (which hour was a favourite with John Wesley for field-preaching). Watts and Doddridge form the first chapter of English hymn-singing; but the second is the Evangelical Revival, which brought a new stream into the tradition. Charles Wesley was, as everybody knows, the most prolific of all English hymn-writers, and his brother John, as a translator from the German, was little behind him in literary accomplishment. But the immediate context of the Wesleyan hymnody was open-air evangelism, and it was open-air evangelism that of all Wesley's techniques (except perhaps his ordination of presbyters), most greatly offended his contemporaries. The fact was, in short, that the Wesleys brought back into English religion a touch of that medieval informality, even medieval gaiety, which of all things would most offend a conventional eighteenth-century mind. More—they brought it to places where there was virtually no religion, where the contrast between the promises of the Gospel and the realities of life was at its starkest, where medieval squalor had long outlived medieval cheerfulness. This open-air religion, this religion of "assurance" was medieval in a sense in which conventional English bourgeois religious observance was not.

The Wesleys owed much of their singing techniques to the Moravians, who look straight back to John Hus, and in whom there was more than a trace of late medieval religious enthusiasm. True, in the Hussite compositions, both of the fifteenth and of the eighteenth centuries, religious ecstasy tends to overlay the earthy vulgarity of the carol; but the Hussites, like all religious groups from that part of Europe, were singers in a way in which eighteenth-century Englishmen were not singers. The Wesleyan revival was, in part at least, an injection into English religion of a religious technique that would have been recognisable to an eighteenth-century German enthusiast, or to a fourteenth-century Italian enthusiast, but which to the educated Englishman seemed as foreign as Handel's music: and yet it was as easily assimilated, once you had got over the repulsion that made you hurl the word "enthusiast" at Wesley as an epithet of abuse, and within his own lifetime Wesley's Gospel (as Handel's music within his) became an inalienable part of English culture.

It was this that made hymns into the kind of sacred folk-song that they have become. It was this that brought about the now familiar fact that the hymns of his church are the last thing that a renegade Christian forgets. It was only after the Wesleyans and the anglican Evangelicals had taken over the technique of hymnody that the Church of England found itself obliged to accord technical recognition to hymns as a vehicle of worship no longer to be withheld from its members. Isaac Watts's hymns would never have become the heritage of universal English-speaking protestantism had not the Wesleys shown the world how to sing them; it is this overflowing of hymns from a narrowly "church" setting into life in general that matters to our present study of the carol. Apart from open-air evangelical enterprises, it is still only Christmas hymns that are at all commonly sung out of doors by the majority of Christians; but we have the Wesleys to thank for that.

The Hymn as an eighteenth-century literary development

But thirdly we must say that the hymn is what it is—and is importantly different from the carol—because it was the eighteenth century that gave it birth. It is primarily the eighteenth-century love of formality, its readiness (which we see in its architecture) to build from the outside inwards, its cult of the urbane, that makes it what George Sampson memorably called "The Century of Divine Songs". The seventeenth century was the age of metaphysical poetry and epic, but it could not have been the age of hymnody. For hymnody you need the neat, the formal, the epigrammatic, the verbal play, the chiasmus, the elegant rhyme, and that is what the eighteenth century provides. While Bernard Manning rightly draws our attention to Watts's debt

to Milton for his imagery and large vision, he equally stresses the force
of classical form and elegant wit in the impact which the hymns of
that age made on all subsequent ages. Inspired with Christian zest a
hymn must, of course, always be, but it must also, in the general
opinion of singing congregations, be written strictly to form. It must
not use those subtle rhythmic devices which make poetry what it is.
It may not use the tripping syllables and tied syllables that diversify
the true ballad metre. It is hardly too much to say that a well-made
hymn ought to sound artificially metrical, and, if read aloud without
its music, almost intolerably monotonous. Wesley is himself without
doubt the most rhythmically daring of English hymnodists, permitting
himself lines like "With inextinguishable blaze" and "Those amaryn-
thine bowers, inalienably ours", and "And prove thine acceptable
will". Moreover, he more than any other hymnodist allows himself
to write far beyond the accepted *length* to which others write. "O for
a thousand tongues" was originally in eighteen verses, and others were
even longer. This, of course, he learnt from the Germans, who also gave
him most of his unusual metres. But writing a hymn is a discipline
from which every English poet of any stature, save only the eighteenth-
century Cowper and the classically-minded Bridges, has shrunk. These
opinions, and these evident facts about our familiar religious behaviour, all derive from the eighteenth-century birth of hymnody.

So most of the best hymns are formal and epigrammatic, and their
virtues are quite different from the proper virtues of the ballad carol.
Where a ballad is narrative, a hymn is dogmatic. Where a ballad is
picturesque, a hymn is ecstatic. Where in a ballad the dialogue may be
between Mary and Joseph, or between a carnal and a crane, in a hymn
it is between Christ and the human soul.

The hymn, then, was invented to fill a liturgical need among people
whom it was impossible to interest in a severely conceptual view of
worship; it was made into folk-song by the evangelical revival; and it
owes its special form and virtues to Dryden, Pope and Addison. That
said, we can turn to some of the hymns without which no Christmas
season is complete to a present-day Christian. There are three archetypal
Christmas hymns, all indispensable to Christmas worship and festivity,
and all written within the same decade of the eighteenth century.
They are, "O come, all ye faithful" (about 1742), "Hark, the herald
angels sing" (about 1739), and "Christians, awake" (1749).

"O come, all ye Faithful"

"O come, all ye faithful" used habitually to be described as a carol in the King's College Festival; and though this was an inaccuracy, it is easy to see what caused it. It is, among all Christmas hymns, the one which most nearly approaches the anonymity and (in its music) the minstrel-quality of the carols. Now that we do know its origin, we are not in the least surprised to find that its tune and its Latin words were almost certainly the work of the same man: and this confirms the judgment that it stands on the very border of the carol-country.

The story of its composition is complicated, and fascinating as well if one follows the detective steps that led to the discovery of its true origin. In 1900 it was still widely believed that the original Latin was the work of St. Bonaventura, and that the tune was written either by a Portuguese monk of uncertain date and identity, or by an English musician called John Reading. All three conjectures have been set aside by Dom John Stéphan of Buckfast Abbey in a pamphlet which remains the classic source of information about the hymn. The author of this learned and delightful little work proves beyond reasonable doubt, on manuscript evidence, that both words and tune are the composition of a young Englishman named J. F. Wade (c. 1711–86), who worked all his life as a copyist and music teacher at Douay, the renowned Roman Catholic centre in France. Dom John reckons that the date of composition is between 1740 and 1744, and that the hymn became well enough known at Douay and in the surrounding region to become the ground of a vulgar burlesque in a long-forgotten comic opera produced in 1744 under the title *Acajou.*

Dom John's pamphlet reveals that the tune, as first written down, went in triple rhythm as follows:

Ex.33

In the manuscript (dated 1751) it is written in that diamond-shaped notation which persisted in Catholic music-notation to the end of the eighteenth century: this is modernised in the example. The first appearance of the tune in the rhythm with which we are familiar is in one of the manuscripts (dated 1760) preserved at St. Edmund's College, Old Hall, Ware, Herts. There the tune is almost exactly as we know it, except that the last line runs (in duple time) as in the above example. We owe our present form of the last phrase to Helmore's *Hymnal Noted* of 1852—a book of which we shall have more to say later.

Nothing else is known to be Wade's composition, unless Dom John is right in his conjecture that he wrote the excellent hymn tune called ST. THOMAS (*E.H.* 623). The early alteration in the rhythm of ADESTE FIDELES suggests a parallel case in the very well known tune EWING which we sing to "Jerusalem, the golden", written by a soldier who is not known to have written any other music at all, which originally appeared in triple time, but has always been known to English congregations in common time as we now sing it (see *Companion to Congregational Praise*, at Hymn 352). ADESTE, then, is the work of an English Catholic amateur musician, and this we may accept. It found its way to England, as *Julian* credibly states, through the bringing in of manuscript copies, and through its performance at the Portuguese Embassy, which was (with other similar Embassies) one of the very few outposts of Catholic culture in England during the eighteenth century, and to which English hymnody owes a good deal of its popular treasures (see *M.C.H.*, p. 158). Its first English Protestant associations were not, of course, with the Christmas hymn (which was not translated into English until well into the next century), but with hymns in what was then called "104th metre", that is, the metre of the 104th psalm in the metrical versions and of "O worship the King" in modern hymn-books. In Rippon's *Selection of Psalm and Hymn Tunes* (about 1796) at No. 263, it is thus set to "Begone, unbelief":

Ex. 34

RIPPON 263

As late as 1837, Novello's *The Psalmist* continues to print the tune as suitable for that metre (see No. 199), and Sankey's *Sacred Songs and Solos* (see No. 526 in the edition of 1200 pieces) sets the tune to the hymn "How firm a foundation". This collocation persists in the United States, where the *Hymnbook* (1955) of the Presbyterian Church of the USA continues to print those words to ADESTE (No. 369).

The Latin words in the earliest manuscript of Wade run as follows from verse 2 onwards (verse 1 is given with Ex. 33):

> Deum de Deo
> Lumen de lumine
> Gestant puellae viscera;
> Deum verum,
> Genitum non factum,
> Venite &c.

> Cantet nunc "Io"
> Chorus angelorum
> Cantet nunc aula caelestium,
> Gloria
> In excelsis Deo,
> Venite &c.

> Ergo qui natus
> Die hodierna,
> Jesu, tibi sit gloria
> Patris aeterni
> Verbum caro factum,
> Venite &c.

These are the four verses corresponding to the four printed in *Hymns A. & M.* (59), and in the shorter version in *E.H.* (28). The words of the refrain were altered from *Venite adorate* ("Come and worship") to *Venite adoremus* ("O come, let us worship") as early as 1751 (though not in the 1751 manuscript quoted above), and Dom John Stéphan comments on the liturgical propriety of the alteration which enables the singer to identify himself with, and not to address, the rest of the congregation. (That is well said, but it is a nicety which was very often overlooked by the didactic Wesleys and their imitators.)

In the course of time the text became corrupted and extended. In the *Thesaurus Animae Musicae* (Mechlin, probably about 1850) it appears in eight verses. The subjects of the extra verses, which appear after verse 2 of the original, are (3) the shepherds, (4) the Magi, (5) the Godhead veiled in flesh, (6) the poverty and helplessness of the holy

Child. In the seven-verse translation at *E.H.* 614 verses 3, 4 and 6 are translated, but the beautiful fifth verse has never, to my knowledge, found its way into English use:

> Aeterni parentis
> Splendorem aeternum
> Velatum sùb carne videbimus,
> Deum infantem
> Pannis involutum
> Venite adoremus &c.

"We shall see the Eternal Splendour of the Eternal Father veiled in flesh. God as a child wrapped in swaddling-clothes."

The extra verses are a dignified reconstruction of the Gospel record, and although they make the hymn longer than Wade's original purpose required, they add a carol-like atmosphere to the whole. But at one point in the source which gives us the extra verses the ecclesiastical writer found Wade too informal and carol-like, and so for Wade's *Cantet nunc io* (which means something very like, "let the angelic choir shout Hooray") he substituted the more demure *Cantet nunc hymnos*.

The translation most of us know best was made by the Reverend Francis Oakeley (1802–80) in 1841, while he was incumbent of what is now known as All Saints', Margaret Street, London. Oakeley was received into the Roman Catholic Church in 1845, and became a Canon of Westminster Cathedral. His translation originally began:

> Ye faithful, approach ye,
> Joyfully triumphant,

and covered only the original four verses. The words we know first appeared in a revised text in 1852. Other translations have appeared, which often attempt to fit the tune more exactly syllable for syllable, and the *Church Hymnary* (1927) actually prints the translation of William Mercer alongside that of Oakeley: this only gives us the opportunity of judging how abysmally prosaic an author who tried to be poetically consistent could become. Dissenters, for some reason, always sing in verse 2 the clumsy expression "True God of true God, Light of light eternal", which spoils the effect of "Very God" at a later point in that verse. There is little sense in doing this, except if you refuse on principle to learn to sing Oakeley correctly.

The reader may well be feeling at this moment that to pass from the story of the carol into the story of hymnology is rather like an abrupt transition from rustic paths to urban streets, or like what happens when you approach Wolverhampton by train from the north. But that is how it is with hymns. They are written by identifiable people, patched up by others, set to music (usually) by others again, and set to different music by different people who did not care for what the first person wrote. (There is even an alternative tune to "O come, all ye faithful", one of R. L, da Pearsall's more preposterous gestures: see Ex. 185 (p. 282) in *M.C.H.*). But for all that, and with all apologies for leading the reader round the back-streets, we can conclude that "Adeste" is the nearest thing we have to a medieval manuscript-carol, written by a devoted son of the Catholic Church, popular by destination and not by origin, severely credal yet full of sacred rhetoric.

"Hark, the herald angels sing"

"Hark, the herald angels sing" is, of course, largely by Charles Wesley. Although it is as intimately associated with the Christmas season, it differs from "Adeste" in being a hymn of the Incarnation rather than a hymn for the festival of Christmas. Originally it was written in ten verses of four lines each, beginning:

> Hark, how all the welkin rings
> Glory to the King of kings.

Eight of those original verses are preserved at *E.H.* 23. Already, reading it thus, we miss the specifically Christmas emphasis of "the new-born King". It was George Whitefield, Wesley's friend and collaborator, who gave us the first couplet as we know it. To get back to Wesley's original intention, however, we must forget that first couplet, and forget also the well-known tune. Here are the last four of Wesley's original verses:

> Come, Desire of Nations, come,
> Fix in us thy humble home;
> Rise, the woman's conquering seed,
> Bruise in us the serpent's head.

> Now display thy saving power,
> Ruined nature now restore;
> Now in mystic union join
> Thine to ours, and ours to thine.

Adam's likeness, Lord, efface,
Stamp thy image in its place,
Second Adam from above,
Reinstate us in thy love.

Let us then, though lost, regain
Then the Life, the inner Man;
O, to all thyself impart,
Formed in each believing heart.

No doubt Charles Wesley had in mind that it should be sung to some simple four-line tune, perhaps to that tune SAVANNAH (*E.H.* 135), which his brother had recently brought over from the Moravians at Herrnhut, but Bishop Frere conjectures from an examination of Butts's *Harmonia Sacra* (*c.* 1756) that in early Methodist days the hymn was sung to the EASTER HYMN (*E.H.* 133), with Alleluias. To sing it so today would indeed be a surprising historical exercise.

The ten-line verses which we always sing now date only from 1856, more than a century after the hymn was originally written; in that year W. H. Cummings, organist of Waltham Abbey, adapted a chorus from Mendelssohn's secular cantata, *Festgesang* (composed in 1840 to celebrate the invention of printing), as a setting for the hymn. This was first published separately, but it appeared in Chope's *Congregational Hymn and Tune Book* (1857), and in the first edition (1861) of *Hymns A. & M.* A line of the original Mendelssohn in reduced score will show the spirit of the music that Cummings arranged.

Ex.36

It is of interest to notice that in Mercer's *Church Psalter and Hymn Book*, published just before "our" tune was printed, the hymn is set to the German chorale called SALZBURG (*E.H.* 128); and what is of even more interest is to observe that when the first edition of *Hymns A. & M.* appeared, its editors (who were very sensitive indeed to anything that might appear secular) backed up Cummings's tune with another. Of their 273 hymns only six are set to more than one tune (aside from those hymns one of whose tunes is plainsong); but MENDELSSOHN was clearly regarded as unsafe. The horror that follows, their second choice, was composed by one C. Batchelor, of whose music I am thankful to say I know no more:

A.M.(1961) 43

"Christians, awake"

When we come to "Christians, awake", we are in easier country. Although even here what we sing is not precisely what its author wrote, we have at least in "Christians, awake" an authentic piece of eighteenth-century architecture, both in words and music. Look at the tune: what perfect poise and proportion! How admirably the long phrases balance each other, and how excellently the high notes are placed! It would be easy to show that this is the most successful of all the magnificent hymn tunes written in the eighteenth century—and a glance through the composers' index of a well-edited hymn book will at once show what competition there is. Balance and proportion, poise and studied rhetoric, of course, we expect in any good eighteenth-century tune. Where this scores over them all is in what it attempts and successfully achieves; for only somebody who has tried to write a really congregational tune in this broad metre knows how difficult that is to do. YORKSHIRE (for that is the inappropriate name of the tune of "Christians, awake") is the only tune in the whole literature in "six tens" that brings it off successfully. I do not even except Orlando Gibbons's SONG I (*E.H.* 384), the tune of "Eternal Ruler of the ceaseless round", for, beautiful though it is, exquisitely proportioned, it yet remains a "musician's tune", and I would rather teach "Christians awake" than Gibbons to a congregation who knew neither.

A romantic story, perfectly well attested, is told of the words. Their author is John Byrom (1691–1763), one of the more remarkable of the gallery of distinguished characters that the century provides. A trained and respected classical scholar, a qualified physician who never practised, a Jacobite who for the sake of his conscience threw up a Fellowship at Trinity, Cambridge, because it depended on a Hanoverian oath, his enduring contribution to English culture was (of all things) a system of shorthand. For most of his life he made his living by teaching this system to literary people, and among the many who had cause to thank him for what was in those days a near-miraculous time-saver as well as an intriguing social accomplishment were the two brothers Wesley. It appears that the Pitman system itself is based on Byrom's.

As to the hymn, it seems that it was a Christmas present to his daughter given in the year 1749. His daughter, Dolly, had said that of all things she would like a poem for Christmas: she was eleven, her father, fifty-eight: and on her plate on Christmas morning she found this:

> Christians, awake, salute the happy Morn
> Whereon the Saviour of the World was born.
> Rise to adore the Mystery of Love
> Which Hosts of Angels chanted from above;
> With them the joyful tidings first begun
> Of God incarnate and the Virgin's Son.
> Then to the watchfull Shepherds it was told,
> Who heard th'Angelic Herald's Voice—behold!
> I bring good Tidings of a Saviour's Birth
> To you and all the Nations on the Earth.
> This day hath God fulfilled his promised Word,
> This day is born a Saviour, Xt the Lord.
> In David city, shepherds, ye shall find
> The long foretold redeemer of Mankind
> Wrapt up in swadling Cloaths, be this the Sign,
> A Cratch contains the holy Babe divine.

He spake, & straightway the celestial Quire
In Hymns of Joy unknown before conspire
The Praises of redeeming Love they sung
And Heav'n's whole Orb with Hallelujahs rung.
God highest Glory was their Anthem still,
Peace upon Earth, & mutual Good Will.
To Bethlehem straight th'enlightened Shepherds ran
To see the Wonder God had wrought for Man.
They saw their Saviour as the Angel said,
The swaddled Infant in the Manger laid.
Joseph and Mary a distressed pair
Guard the sole Object of th'Almighty's Care;
To human eyes none present but they two
Where Heaven was pointing its concentred View.
Amaz'd the wondrous Story they proclaim,
The first Apostles of his Infant Fame.
But Mary kept and pondered in her Heart
The heav'nly Vision wch the Swains impart.
They to their flocks & praising God return
With hearts no doubt that did within them burn.

Let us like these good Shepherds then employ
Our grateful Voices to proclaim the Joy.
Like Mary let us ponder in our mind
God's wondrous Love in saving lost Mankind,
Artless and watchful as these favour'd Swains,
While Virgin Meekness in the Heart remains.
Trace we the Babe who has retrieved our Loss
From his poor Manger to his bitter Cross.
Follow we him who has our Cause maintain'd,
And Mans first heav'nly State shall be regain'd.
Then, may we hope, th'Angelic Thrones among,
To sing, redeem'd, a glad Triumphal Song.
He that was born upon this joyful Day
Around us all his Glory shall display;
Sav'd by his Love, incessant we shall sing
Of Angels and of Angel-men the King.

The story goes on that, when the next Christmas came round, a group of singers led by John Wainwright, of Manchester, visited Stockport, where the Byroms lived, and as Christmas Day began, a minute after midnight, sang "Christians, awake" to Wainwright's tune under their windows. From this most agreeable beginning probably comes the custom still observed in certain parts of the north country of singing "Christians, awake" as the midnight of Christmas Eve turns.

What details lie within and behind this story we cannot hope to tell. From the hymn-singing point of view, we note that none of the three paragraphs of the poem (16, 20 and 16 lines respectively) divides exactly into six-line groups. Perhaps in performance the poem was abridged to six-line verses, yet the visitors, intending a compliment to Byrom might well have scrupled to do that. Since the tune often appears in old tune-books with directions for repeating the last line, it is just possible that they repeated the last two lines of the tune whenever that became necessary. It is a wonderfully adaptable tune and can be thus treated without positive mutilation.

The hymn in the form we know, with the alterations that are now accepted, first appeared, edited by James Montgomery, in the eighth edition (1819) of Cotterill's *Selection*, used at St. George's Church, Sheffield. But Wainwright's tune was printed as early as 1760, so the hymn was probably in some kind of common use from the beginning.

In these three hymns, then, we have a triptych that portrays the whole field of Christmas hymnody. In "O come, all ye faithful":

> God of God
> Light of light,
> Lo, he abhors not the virgin's womb.

In "Hark, the herald":

> Peace on earth, and mercy mild
> God and sinners reconciled.

In "Christians, awake":

> Artless and watchful as those favour'd Swains,
> While Virgin Meekness in the Heart remains.

Dogma, Evangelical religion and daily piety are their respective contexts, and in all three they are drawn from the historic event of the Nativity. None of the Christmas hymns we shall be considering goes far beyond the terms of reference laid down by these three greatest. Those written by later authors take these as their model; those selected from earlier authors are selected on the ground of their conformity with these.

"While Shepherds watched"
"While shepherds watched their flocks by night" is the hymn in

respect of which my reader will have been saying, "Not three, but four." "While shepherds watched" is neither inferior in merit nor less in popularity than those other three: but historically it is of a different kind. It is older than they, being first published in 1696 as one of a handful of New Testament hymns appended to Tate and Brady's metrical translation of the Psalms (commonly called the *New Version*). "While shepherds watched", though not itself a psalm, is in the style of the metrical psalms, being a literal versification of St. Luke 2, 8–15. It is not a free composition in the sense that Watts's hymns were free compositions, and was only admitted to the book because it was a version of a New Testament lyrical passage.

The authorship of this attractive paraphrase—which is easily the best thing in the whole of the *New Version*—is usually ascribed to Nahum Tate, the senior partner in "Tate and Brady". Tate was appointed Poet Laureate in 1690, and until you have fully realised to what extent mediocrity prospered in the arts in those days it is almost unbelievable that this Laureate's most considerable creation during his period of office was called *Panacea—a Poem on Tea*. We have it on the authority of the *Dictionary of National Biography* (or we should not believe it for a moment) that his alteration of *King Lear*, in which Cordelia survives and marries Edgar and lives happily ever after, was considered a practicable and even popular play until about 1840. As for the pane-gyric on tea—the late James Moffatt (whose contribution to hymnology was hardly less, in proportion, than his contribution to biblical studies) writes at the end of his short biography, with a deep Presbyterian frown, that Tate "later fell into dissolute habits and died in debt". From that gaudy and confused age, with the mad Earl of Rochester recently dead and a man called Staggins in charge of the King's Musick, comes the most innocent of all Christmas hymns.

There is no evidence to what tune it was originally sung. In those days it mattered not which tune you used to which psalm, and many congregations knew no more than half a dozen tunes. The hymn is now almost always sung to WINCHESTER OLD, a psalm-tune dating from 1592, which therefore could have been sung in Tate's time, but which was only clearly associated with the words by the editors of the 1861 edition of *Hymns Ancient and Modern* (who set the same tune also to "Jesus, the very thought of thee"). But the carol-like, narrative texture of the paraphrase caused it to be taken over as a welcome addition to the almost empty carol repertory of the period, and in consequence we find many different musical associations for it in differ-ent books and in different parts of the country. There is a most excellent tune which, though of unambiguously eighteenth-century cast, impudently defies the frontier-posts between sacred and secular; it is called CRANBROOK in the 1904 *Methodist Hymn Book*) but the reader will know it by another name. With cheerful adaptability it goes equally well to Common Metre or Short Metre, and it has certainly been sung in Yorkshire to "While shepherds watched":

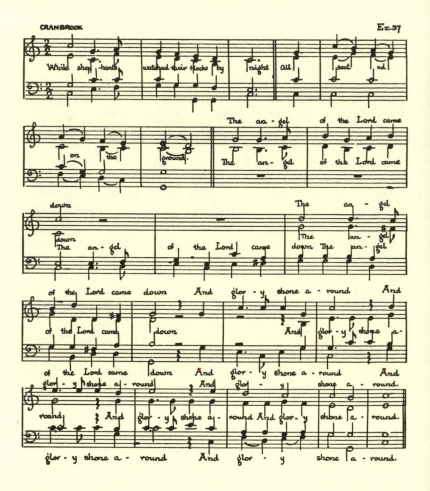

This kind of "repeating" tune has been especially associated with these words. In the Appendix to *E.H.* (No. 8) there is a tune attributed to a Cornish traditional origin called NORTHROP, and the words have often been sung to a tune called LYNGHAM or (because of this association)

NATIVITY (No. 8 in the Appendix to the *Methodist Hymn Book*, 1933). Yet another, again of an eighteenth-century cast, appeared in a small collection edited by the Rev. C. H. Mayo called *Traditional Carols for Christmas-tide, Sung for Many Years at Long Burton, Dorset*, whose melody runs as follows:

Ex. 38

While shepherds watched their flocks by night All - seated on the ground, all sea - ted on the ground An angel of the Lord came down and glory shone a- round, and glo-ry shone a-round, and glo - - - ry shone a - round.

LONG BURTON 10

This kind of hymn-tune became so popular towards the end of the eighteenth century that it became almost a folk-song form in its own right. It was natural that—especially in Cornwall and in Yorkshire, where Methodism had taken so strong a hold—these tunes should become associated with this very well known Christmas hymn. But there are many others that have been sung to it. *Oxford* sets it to an ordinary ballad-tune which it describes as "proper to the words" at No. 33 (see above, Ex. 14). Other books have set it to the BELLMAN'S CAROL (*Oxford* 46), and so on. The multiplicity of settings is the natural result of the carol-famine in that age, and the eagerness with which folk would welcome anything that looked like a carol that had the authentic touch about it. That, of course, is precisely what "While shepherds watched" amounts to, far though any such intention was from the mind of its court-buffoon of an author.

Christmas Hymns of the Nineteenth Century

Of the later Christmas hymns we need say little in detail, for they are well known, and are copiously annotated in the books on hymnology. James Montgomery's "Angels from the realms of glory" is a classic, but of the Epiphany rather than of the Nativity. It has become the custom to sing it to the French carol tune which we now call IRIS (because that was the name of a radical journal which Montgomery edited in Sheffield); that setting is at *Oxford* 119, and in some hymn books. The French carol tune (for which see below, p. 206) provides for a florid *Gloria*, and English congregations always have some difficulty in fitting the words "Come and worship" of Montgomery's refrain to the music written for the *Gloria*. This collocation is agreeable enough, but since G. R. Woodward's admirable carol, "Shepherds in the field abiding" (*Cowley* 68), which begins with a line borrowed from Montgomery, is available for that tune, and accommodates its *Gloria* without change, an ordinary hymn tune is probably better for "Angels from the realms of glory"; but having said as much, I am at a loss where to find a hymn tune carol-like enough to do justice to Montgomery, and hymn-book editors have certainly not come to a common mind on this point.

The best thing that the anglican movement in hymn-writing gave us, of course, is Mrs. Alexander's "Once in royal David's city". Mrs. Alexander, whose husband became Primate of all Ireland, wrote it in 1848 as one of a series of hymns designed to explain the Catechism to children, but, like "There is a green hill", another of the same series, it has become the property of the whole congregation. It found its ideal partner at once in Gauntlett's tune, IRBY, which has the extra-ordinary quality of sounding as effective in the homely piano-accom-panied gathering for which it was originally composed as it does amid all the splendour of King's College chapel. That is as much as to say that Dr. Gauntlett, who wrote ten thousand hymn tunes of which a few are magnificent and the rest as dull as old rope, here caught the popular note and wrote something like a genuine carol.

America has given us (besides one very popular carol, to which we shall come in its place) two Christmas hymns. The older is "It came upon the midnight clear", written by E. H. Sears, a Unitarian minister, in 1850, and the younger, "O little town of Bethlehem", written by Bishop Phillips Brooks of Massachusetts when he was an episcopal rector at Philadelphia, in 1868. They make a strange pair, and repre-sent two very different schools of American hymn writing.

"It came upon the midnight clear" is a controversial piece of writing. It was first printed in this country in 1870, and in the second English hymn book that printed it, the *Hymnal Companion* of 1871, it appears not as a Christmas hymn but in the section "The church Triumphant", next to "Hark, hark, my soul". It is, indeed, not a Nativity hymn in any sense, but a hymn exhorting men to follow the way of peace, based on the Song of the Angels in Luke 2.14. It is interesting to see that its last verse in the *Hymnal Companion* was altered to read like this (the expression-marks are too good to be left out):

mf For lo, the days are hastening on,
    By prophets seen of old,
cr When with the ever-circling years
    Shall come the time foretold,
f When the new heaven and earth shall own
    The Prince of peace their King,
ff And the whole world send back the song
pp Which now the angels sing.

The words in the original last verse are difficult for modern Christians to sing, with their reference to the return of an "age of gold", but no other editor has taken up the alteration of the *Hymnal Companion*, and as we sing it, in its original form, the hymn is little more than an ethical song extolling the worth and splendour of peace among men. Even though the business of war has become a thousand times more horrific than it was when the words were written, more than a century ago, there are many who feel that it still will not do to limit the Christmas message to the satisfaction of a human need, even when it is as desperate as we now know this need to be.

A small piece of detective work waits to be done on its tune. Sullivan's NOEL, a very graceful tune, unlike his usual flamboyant church style, is founded on a folk-song which turns out to be the tune now called EARDISLEY:

Ex. 39

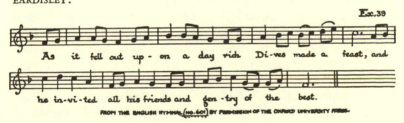

As it fell out up-on a day rich Di-ves made a feast, and
he in-vi-ted all his friends and gen-try of the best.

FROM THE ENGLISH HYMNAL (NO. 601) BY PERMISSION OF THE OXFORD UNIVERSITY PRESS.

This tune was first printed in the Journal of the Folk Song Society, II, 125, as a tune to "Dives and Lazarus" (see above, p. 56), and soon afterwards at No. 601 in *E.H.* But Sullivan wrote NOEL more than thirty years before, and one wonders where he had heard it. He has, of course, tamed the tune fairly drastically, and treated it much as Sandys treated A VIRGIN MOST PURE.

Sullivan's is now the tune universally used in England, but it was not the first. The first was a succulent adaptation from Spohr, beginning:

Ex. 40

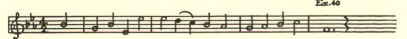

and it has also been set to an adaptation of one of Mendelssohn's *Songs Without Words*:

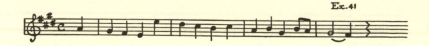

Ex. 41

"O little town of Bethlehem" is much more nearly a carol. It is a shade too poetically contrived, too self-conscious ("How still we see thee lie") to pass as a genuine carol; but the simplicity of its diction, characteristic of an author who by the end of his life was acknowledged to be one of the greatest preachers of his age, ensures for it a welcome at the Christmas season. Here is no moralising, none of that spirit of which we hear more than a whisper in Sears's lines, of "How can you be merry at Christmas with the world in such a sorry state?" The heart of its message is "Be born in us today", and if the picture of Bethlehem is a trifle romantic (for Bethlehem had never had such a rush of travellers as it had that week), and its communication of the Christmas Gospel somewhat lacking in awe, why, we can safely leave that in the hands of Charles Wesley.

Two tunes are well known in England. The senior, by a year, is that of Walford Davies, called CHRISTMAS CAROL, which first appeared, in 1905, in a setting suitable for choral rather than congregational treatment; but several hymn books now use it as a four-part tune. The next year, 1906, saw the first publication (*E.H.* 15), of Vaughan Williams's FOREST GREEN, a simple folk-song which, with its far more manageable compass and easier melodic line, is now regarded as the primary tune for these words. It is difficult to determine which of these settings the more violently offends our transatlantic visitors, for whom the words are still wedded to the original tune written by Phillips Brooks's own organist, Lewis H. Redner, in 1868. The tune, known as ST. LOUIS, runs thus:

Ex. 42

Apart from its historic priority, there is not much to be said for that.

In addition to these Christmas hymns there are two Epiphany hymns so closely associated with the Christmas season that they are almost thought of as carols. As it happens, "As with gladness men of old" and "Brightest and best" (*E.H.* 39, 41) are as widely contrasted in their styles as the two hymns we have just noticed. "As with gladness", the younger of the two, was written about 1858, by William Chatterton Dix, a Glasgow businessman who wrote several hymns and a few carols which will come under review in our next chapter. Dix wrote these words when he was hardly more than twenty years of age, and you could not have a better example of smooth, urbane hymn-writing. Nothing is over-written, nothing especially distinguished or picturesque: it sings easily, and it is made of that hard-wearing material that makes the best popular hymns. The tune is of the same kind. If you happen to know the original nineteenth-century German chorale from which it is adapted, the knowledge spoils the English version for you, for the original is a fine and dignified tune with far more "body" than the adaptation. But even if the English form, designed to be sung at a good healthy speed and not like a German chorale, conceals its virtues almost too discreetly, it makes a tune that any child can learn and enjoy, and perhaps we must not blame the editors of the original *Hymns A. & M.* too much for manhandling the original. No other tune to this hymn has found a comparable place in the affections of Englishmen.

It is far otherwise, at every point, with "Brightest and best". Its author, Bishop Heber (1783–1826) was the pioneer of the romantic style of hymn-writing, and the best expositor of that style. This is certainly romantic, in its naturalistic setting and its attention to picturesque detail. It is worlds away from Watts and Wesley. Those who could not see the point of it were taken to task by Dr. Percy Dearmer, who wrote, "Dunderheaded critics held this back from use on the ground that it involved the worshipping of a star". Perhaps the truth is, though he hardly knew or intended it, that Heber was writing a carol. The carols are not afraid of astrology. But in the end it is a matter of values. To Heber the delicate adjective and the smooth rhythm were of more value than the hard-wearing commonplace and the aptly-inserted Biblical tag, and the result is a precious devotional lyric, even if by the standards of Wesley's style or Calvin's theology it hardly reaches the dignity of being a true hymn.

"As with gladness" has one tune: "Brightest and best", to my own

knowledge, has nineteen in hymn books published since 1900. Among
the composers who have essayed a setting are S. S. Wesley, Gauntlett,
Hopkins, Walford Davies, G. Thalben Ball and W. K. Stanton. Heber
himself was not incapable of writing a tune; he wrote his own for
"From Greenland's icy mountains" (piously preserved at *E.H.* 547),
and he wrote "God that madest earth and heaven" with a tune in mind.
We cannot say what tune he had in mind for these words, but their
graceful dactyls suggest something in the Handelian style, and this
makes Goss's arrangement of "Cease thy anguish" from Handel's
Athaliah, known as a hymn tune by the name BEDE (*A. & M.* 75), a
very suitable partner. *E.H.* sets it to a Bach arrangement of a German
dance tune, LIEBSTER IMMANUEL, imparting a slightly foreign dignity
and ceremoniousness to the words. Of modern composers my own
view is that the two who have contributed new tunes for this hymn
to the *BBC Hymn Book* (No. 63) have succeeded with great distinction.

Epilogue

    For a Christmas hymn to be mentioned in a book about carols, it
must be so well known as to be in the public mind almost a carol in
its own right, or it must be of such distinction that it would be a crime
to overlook it in anything that might conceivably become an appropriate context. There are, of course, many Christmas hymns in the
appropriate sections of hymn books which though meritable do not
demand special mention here. There is the great Christmas Sequence,
Laetabundus (*E.H.* 22), which was well known to, and used by, the
medieval carol-writers. There is a choice eighteenth-century Latin
hymn variously translated as "Let sighing cease and woe" (*E.H.* 27)
and (I think far better), "God from on high hath heard" (*C.P.* 82).
There is in the *Oxford Hymn Book* a fine and ceremonious hymn
(No. 57) made out of a Christmas poem by Francis Kinwelmersh (or
Kindlemarsh), the sixteenth-century poet of whom Professor Lewis
writes that "His poems on Christmas and Whit Sunday show
'promise'"; it begins in the hymn book, "From virgin's womb this
Christmas day did spring". There is Charles Wesley's incomparable
hymn on the Incarnation, "Let earth and heaven combine" (*Methodist
Hymn Book*, 142), without which no hymn book can really be called
complete. There are Advent hymns which have almost carol-status
among modern churchgoers, like "O come, O come, Immanuel" and
(in America) Watts's "Joy to the world". But this chapter would
stretch to disproportionate length if we went into any of these in
detail. I am disposed to choose, by way of conclusion, two sets of

verses from the seventeenth century, neither of which was designed as a hymn, but which have, by the inspiration of modern editors (Dr. Dearmer and his colleagues in both cases) become very beautiful hymns for the enrichment of the season.

The first is made of lines from a poem by Henry More (1614–87), the Cambridge Platonist (*S.P.* 80), running as follows:

His robes of light he laid aside,
    Which did his majesty adorn,
And the frail state of mortals tried,
    In human flesh and figure born.

Whole choirs of angels loudly sing
    The mystery of his sacred birth,
And the blest news to shepherds bring
    Filling their watchful souls with mirth.

The Son of God thus man became,
    That men the sons of God might be,
And by their second birth regain
    A likeness to his deity.

The tune is not that set in *Songs of Praise*: it comes from a German source dated 1541 and appears in *Songs of Syon* (1910) p. 575, No. 232A.

The other hymn was taken by the same editor from lines by Sidney Godolphin (1610–43). Godolphin sat as M.P. for Helston, Cornwall, (and thus is a predecessor of our friend Davies Gilbert) in the Short and Long Parliaments, and lost his life on the Royalist side in the Civil War. He left too little to rank high among English men of letters, and is now known only for these contemplative lines. The original poem can be read at No. 138 in the *Oxford Book of Christian Verse*. Without altering any words, Dearmer took sixteen of the original thirty-six lines, and produced this:

Wise men, in tracing nature's laws,
Ascend unto the highest cause;
Though wise men better know the way,
It seems no honest heart can stray.

And since no creature comprehends
The Cause of causes, End of ends,
He who himself vouchsafes to know
Best pleases his Creator so.

There is no merit in the wise
But love, the shepherds' sacrifice;
Wise man, all ways of knowledge past,
To the shepherds' wonder come at last.

The tune given here is the tune suggested by the editor who gave us the hymn. There is a certain pathetic appropriateness in this, that the epilogue to our account of the great controversy should be provided by a young Cornish squire who lost his life fighting Cromwell. But beyond that, his verses reach over three centuries to the modern world's greatest need. This is, of all others, the scientist's carol. If that were the signature-tune of Harwell and Calder Hall, what a world might lie before us!

PART THREE

THE RETURN OF THE CAROL

The Nineteenth Century

IN any history of the arts, and in every European country, but in none more than our own, the nineteenth century presents a series of violent shocks and paradoxes. The chief paradox is that in so many ways one naturally speaks of the nineteenth century as an age of revival: we have already mentioned a carol revival and a folk-song revival; yet at the same time it is without question an age of slump in public taste.

Music and the Industrial Revolution

In every department of musical life the century shows a boom in quantity and a decline in quality. At the bottom of this, of course, is the industrial revolution. It is no disrespect to a distinguished musical publishing house to say that the foundation of the House of Novello in the year of the Regency (1811) had much to do with both aspects of the case. For once it becomes possible to print and multiply copies of music with an ease that would have at once delighted and shocked the sixteenth century, human nature can hardly resist the opportunity to write carelessly and publish uncritically. That composers declared a moratorium of three generations on self-criticism is no fault of Novello's.

But without doubt the music business boomed. That exceedingly entertaining and informative book, *Men, Women and Pianos* by A. Loesser, provides picture after picture of the rake's progress in nineteenth-century musical history, focused on that characteristically individualistic and exhibitionistic instrument, the pianoforte. From it we learn that Broadwood's produced pianos between 1782 and 1802 at the rate of 400 a year, and between 1802 and 1824 at the rate of 1,680 a year, by which time they had made 45,000 pianos; whereas the firm of Tschudi, harpsichord makers, of which John Broadwood had become director in 1782, had been producing instruments at the rate of nineteen a year in its sixty-four years of business before 1782. To quote further from this same source:

> Music, as an insignificant activity in Britain, might well have remained little influenced by the Industrial Revolution; instruments of the fiddle

or pipe series, by their relative simplicity and rarity, might never have tempted anyone to build them by factory methods. But the pianoforte, with its manifold, intricate structure—and especially with its abundance of serially repeated parts—seemed particularly suited to the new mechanical processes. Any zealot for factory production would have cast a lecherous eye upon the pianoforte's tens of identical wooden keys, its dozens of identical tuning pins and hitch pins, and its yards of identically drawn wire. The pianoforte was the factory's natural prey; purely on the basis of its structure, it was the instrument of the time (p. 233).

But the new expansion of production could not succeed without a demand. Those who could afford a piano could buy a good one for £26 in 1825, but modest though this price looks today, it ensured that the description, "Cet instrument bourgeois", given to it by the French carol-singer, Claude Balbestre, would "stick" (ib. p. 317).

For the masses of the industrialised population, seeking new forms of community agreeable to their economic situation, the musical answer was the choral society. Joseph Mainzer (1801–51), with his new technique of massed sight-singing, John Hullah (1812–84), his successor and imitator, and John Curwen (1816–80), the inventor of the tonic sol-fa system, by their zest and enterprise ensured the enduring success of the nineteenth-century choral movement in England. Here was the new popular community singing. Now natural, as it was in Wales, but organised, it came as a new notion to the ordinary man of about 1850 to hear that singing was not an activity confined to professional musicians or to select groups among the aristocracy, or to the choir in church; and whether in church or in the Town Hall, he threw himself into it with enthusiasm. The first year's issues of the *Musical Times* (1844), containing by no means a complete account of choral societies then active, mentions nineteen societies, many of which gave several performances during the year; and in 1848 hundreds of people were paying to attend congregational practices at Union Chapel, Islington, and Carr's Lane, Birmingham, in order that they might all join in the anthems as well as the hymns at the next Sunday's services. Hullah's aim was to have a million Englishmen enjoying the felicities of choral song, and Thomas Hood's amiably satirical comment on this project, written in 1842, began as follows:

MORE HULLAH-BALOO
Amongst the great inventions of our age,
    Which ev'ry other century surpasses,
Is one—just now the rage—
    Called "Singing for all classes"—

> That is, for all the British millions,
> and billions,
> and quadrillions,
> not to name *quintillions*,
>
> That now, alas! have no more ear than asses,
> To learn to warble like the birds in June,
> In time and tune,
> Correct as clocks, and musical as glasses.

Here then was the demand for choral music, secular and sacred. The churches opened their doors to anthem and oratorio, with the disastrous consequences with which historians of church music are familiar. To give one delectable example of the *cacoethes scribendi* with which the musicians of the age were afflicted, we pass on this admirable quotation from an article written by the late Charles Hylton Stewart (1884–1932) when he was organist of Chester Cathedral. Writing his monthly article in the *Chester Diocesan Gazette* he transcribes the words of a harvest anthem whose composer he does not mention. One chorus goes like this:

> The fruits of the earth, the fruits of the earth, sing praises to God most high; Have gathered the fruits of the earth, Sing praises to God most high, The fruits of the earth, Sing praises to God most high: Have gathered the fruits of the earth, sing praises to God most high, Sing praises, Grant us to gather the fruits of the Spirit; Sing praises the fruits of the Spirit, sing praises, Grant us to gather the fruits of the Spirit. Manifold are thy works O Lord, sing praises to thee be praise; Sing Hallelujah; Sing praises to God, praises to God, praises to Thee be the praise, the praise and glory: . . . For ever and ever that Thou gavest us, we gather we gather for ever and ever These wait all upon Thee, that Thou gavest us we gather, we gather for ever and ever These wait all upon Thee, that Thou gavest us we gather, we gather for ever and ever, that Thou gavest us we gather.

That is the best commentary we can offer on the music-mania of the nineteenth century.

The Oxford Movement

Into this hectic atmosphere the carol-movement entered; but a deeper note of devotion and research was being sounded by certain followers of the Oxford Movement which is also heard in the carol-revival. That Movement concerns us chiefly in that many whom it affected were brought to a new reverence for antiquity. The reverence was at first far from being critically adult, but it was at least enthusiastic.

The "Ancient" in *Hymns Ancient and Modern* and the "Old" in *Christmas Carols New and Old* express this movement of thought. Moreover, the new sympathy engendered by the Oxford Movement for the Roman Catholic Church and its institutions put certain anglicans at once in touch with the Cecilian movement on the continent for the reform of church music, and induced in this country a revival of plainsong and (later) of medieval and Counter-Reformation church music. Havergal and Helmore among priests, and Redhead and Oakeley among musicians, were pioneers of this movement. A tendency to explore again the music of the Middle Ages and all the regions of music which the Handelian ascendancy of the eighteenth century had all but cut off from common knowledge produced a climate friendly to the revival of the carol. And along with this, a tendency to look with less disfavour on the expressions and thought-forms of Catholic piety, and to take a less intransigent line with the legendary and mythological than was taken by Puritan opinion, tended even more to open the way for a new carol-technique.

But it must be remembered that the effects of the Oxford Movement, and the pressures it brought to bear on habits of thinking, were in the nineteenth century very largely confined to the clergy and (to some extent) the church musicians. Public opinion was still pseudo-Puritan, and public opinion provided the demand for published music. A priest-organist like J. B. Croft might seek to furnish the treasury of hymnody by transcribing Catholic church tunes from the seventeenth century, but outside his restricted circle nobody heard of it at the time. Public opinion was as unmedieval as it had been for two centuries until the doctrines of the Pre-Raphaelite Brotherhood began to seep into the public mind; and it was the essential puritanism of public opinion that saw to it that the carols newly composed should evince a strictly ecclesiastical idiom, and that those arranged from older sources should be dressed as far as possible like Victorians going to church. This latter requirement did us little damage in carols like THE FIRST NOWELL, whose tune is in any case some distance from the medieval folk-idiom: we sing Stainer's harmonies to it to this day, and rightly judge that beside his anybody else's seem fussy and pedantic. But it did mean that THE LORD AT FIRST DID ADAM MAKE was liable to appear without its initial sharpened sixth, and that the COVENTRY CAROL had to be harmonised in four parts throughout, and reduced to a steady triple time (compare B/S 21 with *Oxford* 1, and B/S 61 with *Oxford* 22). The fact of new carols at all was a great gain; but the style of composition showed that the heart of the middle ages had not yet been reached. The same, of

course, applies to the words. It was something to have even a reminiscence of medieval words, but that is often all that the nineteenth-century
versions amounted to.

Gilbert and Sandys, then, were heralds of a revival. But in a sense
the true carol revival waited another fifty years to be conducted on a
large scale. In between we have *Bramley and Stainer*.

Bramley and Stainer

Christmas Carols New and Old, by H. R. Bramley and John Stainer,
to which we have often referred already, is excellently described by the
Reverend C. V. Taylor as the "*Hymns A. & M.* of carols". Just as
Hymns A. & M. was the first systematic and successful attempt to
provide the Church of England with a hymn book which would
embody the best not only of its own age but of all others (other books
before it had been systematic: this alone, successful as well), so *B/S* was
the first successful attempt to present a collection of carols which would
reasonably represent all known traditions in the form. Its title might
easily have been *Christmas Carols Ancient and Modern*, and no doubt
would have been had not the hymn book arrived first. Both the new
and the old in it are in their own ways remarkable. It was published
in 1871 as a book of forty-two carols, but its most successful edition
was that of (about) 1878, when it was enlarged to carry seventy pieces.
This edition, from which all our quotations come, was reprinted many
times and is still in wide circulation. When the first edition was published, Bramley was thirty-eight and Stainer thirty-one, and both were
at Magdalen College, Oxford, Bramley as a Fellow and Stainer as
organist. Bramley's preface, printed in the second edition, was and
remains a classic on carol-history. When it originally came out, both
in its first and second editions, the book presented a pleasantly antique
appearance through its employment of long esses in the printing, and
through the stately language of Bramley's preface.

The editors had not much to work on. There were Gilbert and
Sandys; there was W. H. Husk's excellent and well-presented collection
called *Songs of the Nativity* (1868); there was *A Good Christmas Box*,
from Staffordshire (1847), from which they took three carols. There
were Helmore's *Carols for Christmas-tide Set to Ancient Melodies* (1852)
from which they took nothing, and there were Edmund Sedding's
two collections, both of 1860, *Twelve Carols for Christmas-Tide* and
Twelve Carols for Easter Tide, neither of which they used. Beyond these
there were the broadsheets on which the words of carols had been
printed for popular use from about the middle of the eighteenth

century onwards. Perhaps the most notable omission from *B/S* is the very scanty use there made of *Piae Cantiones*, the Finnish Collection which has become one of our richest sources for foreign carols, and on which we shall have something to say in our next chapter. But they were not ignorant of the French *noels*, several of which appear in translation, though not normally to their proper tunes.

But Bramley and Stainer had a market, and they had history on their side. For it was just about in the seventies that the notion of a festive Christmas as we now understand it was taking hold of the imagination of the English people at large. Reference has often been made to the influence of Charles Dickens's *A Christmas Carol* (1843) in settling the *ethos* of the modern Christmas. But even Dickens had Christmas with him. The sharp difference between the world as God made it and the world as Englishmen had disfigured it was already apparent to anybody who had eyes to see; and this gave new point to the notion that Christmas is the season of goodwill. "Goodwill towards men" began about this time to mean to most people "Goodwill between men" (which is no part of its biblical sense), and Christmas becomes a season of amnesty from the jungle-ethic of competitive industrialism. A general public consciousness of the sacredness of family ties was brought out into open expression by a rising public consciousness that the days of feudal immobility had finally gone. If the family is liable to be kept under economic pressure, we must make some occasion for recalling what the family was designed to be and mean.

Along with this go the customs which prevail in a modern Christmas. There is the curious accident of the Christmas tree, which provides a convenient focus for the Christmas family-ethos. Laurence Whistler in *The English Festivals* writes, "The Christmas Tree is not indigenous here, and was quite unknown in England till the nineteenth century. It was introduced by some German families in Manchester, and afterwards, more directly, by the Prince Consort at Windsor Castle in 1841. Within twenty years it had proliferated through the whole of society from the top downwards." Foresters say that the spruce, which is the Christmas Tree, was first planted in England about the end of the eighteenth century; but it is the English use of it at Christmas that matters here, and the Consort's patronage of it is of a piece with his high personal estimate of family life, which together with his Teutonic rectitude of character had so marked an effect on English manners.

The Christmas tree is closely linked with that Teutonic mythology of Santa Claus, with his outlandish dress and entourage, who, though ultimately he is derived from the patron saint of children, Saint Nicholas (a fourth-century Turkish bishop), appealed to the English mind chiefly through that love of the foreign which the Romantic Movement had encouraged in it. "Father Christmas" is a purely secular and naturalistic symbol of goodwill, especially goodwill towards children, and he is part of the child-cult, not necessarily exalted into worship of the Holy Child, that is inseparable from a modern English Christmas.

No doubt the modern fashion of the Christmas greeting card owes its origin to that social dispersion and that new facility of communication through the Post Office which are both consequences of the Industrial Revolution; and that peculiarly English institution, the Christmas present, provides a tangible symbol of this pervasive goodwill. Romanticism appears again in the "Christmas card" cult of deep snow and Dickensian stage-coaches. The deep snow inevitably attached itself to the Nativity story, and its pervasiveness there, transferred from its homely connotation as part of the English winter-scene, is one of the most curious and characteristic developments in the Victorian carol. The "winter" emphasis comes, like all this romantic accent, from Germany. While it does not appear in the English ballad carols, we hear it as early in Germany as the 15th century carol, "Es ist ein' Ros' entsprungen" (*Oxford* 76):

> Und hat ein Blümlein bracht
> Mittel im kalten Winter,
> Wohl zu der halben Nacht.

Snowy Christmases are always commoner in central Europe than in England; but the "White Christmas" mythology became in English use as insular as Mrs. Alexander's description in her famous hymn of Golgotha as a "green hill", and as Bishop Heber's erratic geography in "By cool Siloam's shady rill". "Good King Wenceslas" contains snow and philanthropy in just the proportions calculated to make it a favourite with the new English carol singers. The difference between the snow in that carol and the pictures of Bethlehem in the ballads is just the same as the difference between its hortatory goodwill and the cheerful begging of the wassailers.

There, then, was the market for *Bramley and Stainer*. Of its seventy carols, twenty-eight have traditional words and twenty-two traditional tunes. This includes ballad carols, a few medieval manuscript carols,

and extractions from *A Good Christmas Box*. Ten carols, with their
tunes, come from foreign sources, nearly all from southern Europe,
and nearly all translated by Bramley himself. Of authors living before
1700 we have a carol each from Ben Jonson, William Austin, Robert
Southwell, Bishop Hall, and a translation from Luther. The rest—
nearly half the collection—are carols written by authors contemporary
with the compilers; twenty authors are represented, the only ones
contributing more than one being W. Chatterton Dix with three and
Edward Caswall with two. Apart from the twenty-two traditional
tunes, plus five from foreign sources, the whole of the remainder is by
contemporaries; twenty-five composers are represented, including
J. B. Dykes with five, A. H. Brown with five, Stainer three, Barnby
three, and J. F. Bridge with two.

Old material is often ruthlessly modernised. The harmonies are by
John Stainer, who does his work for the most part with great discretion.
But although it is in a few arrangements of older carols that *B/S*
commands the respect of carol-singers of the present day, most notably
in Stainer's arrangements of THE FIRST NOWELL and GOD REST YOU MERRY,
it is the new compositions that give the book its historic character.

The most widely used of these new carols from *B/S* is almost certainly
"See amid the winter's snow", whose words are by Edward Caswall
(1814–78), and the tune by Sir John Goss (1800–80). Here indeed is a
happy marriage. The nineteenth century could achieve a certain kind
of innocent simplicity, as it does in "Once in royal David's city",
and it achieves it here without question. The tune was excluded from
Oxford (190) only because of a copyright difficulty, and the modern
tune there provided is a somewhat ponderous substitute.

But *Oxford* did not disdain Brown's setting of the medieval carol
"When Christ was born of Mary free" (*Oxford* 191, *B/S* 19), about
which, if there is little grace, there is no nonsense. Charles Steggall's
setting of "Like silver lamps in a distant shrine" (*B/S* 2) has found a
certain favour.

But although others have been reprinted, in those three you have
the only new contributions which give the lie to Edmondstoun
Duncan's judgment that "The new Christmas pieces prove how utterly
futile is all modernity in such matters". *B/S* was responsible for the
first publication of one of the most notorious, "Sleep, Holy Babe",
words by Caswall, music by J. B. Dykes (1823–76), which used to be
more popular than it is now or than it deserved to be at any time. Here
we finally drop over the edge. What connection can be traced between
the true carol and this dreadful composition?

Ex. 46
J.B.Dykes 1823-76.

B/S 9

The words of this carol run to six verses (of which *B/S* prints only four). The last two mention the Passion; the fifth is all I dare quote:

> Then must these hands
> which now so fair I see,
> Those little dainty feet of thine,
> So soft, so delicately fine,
> Be pierced and rent for me!

A wide and deep gulf separates that from the carol-culture. The medieval carols were much freer in their references to the Passion than the Victorians; but in the medieval references to our redemption there was a ruthless cheerfulness, proper to men who knew what fear and insecurity were, and how nasty, brutish and short their earthly days were likely to be. It is in the age of security, hygiene, humanitarianism and enlightenment that you have time to indulge in these bitter-sweet devotional cocktails, and, if you choose, freedom to get maudlin-drunk on them.

There is nothing else, I think, in *B/S* quite so horrifying as that.
But there is much that irresistibly suggests the demure drawing-room
ditty. There was a tendency for the words of new carols to affect
a dreary evangelical tone that brought the singer dangerously near
the error of pitying the Redeemer, like this in " 'Twas in the winter
cold" (20):

> But I have not, it makes me sigh,
>   One offering in my power;
> 'Tis winter all with me, and I
>   Have neither fruit nor flower.
> O God, O Brother, let me give
>   My worthless self to Thee;
> And that the years which I may live
>   May pure and spotless be.

Nothing but a highly artificial religion could have begotten that special
kind of doggerel. It is difficult, too, to take seriously the high emotional
content of such effusions as "When I view the Mother holding"
(No. 11), whose words are translated by Bramley (not at his best) from
the Latin, and whose music is by the incomparable Barnby. Notice
particularly the repetitions which the composer introduces at those
points where he especially wants to hold the singer's attention.

Ex. 46
J. BARNBY 1838-96.

When I view the Mother holding in her arms the heaven-ly Boy Thousand blissful
Thoughts unfolding Melt my heart with sweetest joy, with sweet-est joy - - -
With her Babe the hours beguiling Ma-ry's soul in transport lives God her Son u-pon her smiling
Thousand thousand kisses fondly gives fondly gives As the sun his ra-diance flinging
Shines up on the bright ex - panse, So the child to
Ma-ry clin-ging Doth her gen-tle heart, her gen-tle heart en - trance.

B/S 11

You don't "see" the Mother. Any such proceeding would be highly undignified. You "view" her.

Among this fantastic undergrowth of drawing-room music and pious ditties there is just one place where you can see the old path running, in No. 49, "Come let us all sweet carols sing". The words are Bramley's translation of an old Besançon noel beginning

> Come let us all sweet carols sing,
>> *Omne relicto taedio.*
> Mary, Mother of our King,
>> *Christoque Jesu Filio,*
> When she had borne that Holy Thing,
>> *Posuit in praesepio.*

Translations of the Latin lines: "Laying aside all vexatious things", "And to Christ Jesus the Son", "She laid him in a manger". The construction of the second Latin line is not such as should have commended itself to a Fellow of Magdalen; I suspect that he should have written in line 3, "To Mary, Mother of our King" and placed a semicolon at the end of line 4.

The music is by Sir Frederick Champneys (1848–1930), the distinguished obstetrician of St. Bartholomew's Hospital, whose very slight contributions to church music show him to have been a musician of singular discretion and ability, with leanings towards an earlier and healthier idiom than that affected by his immediate seniors. In this carol he writes the music of the Latin lines for unison men's voices on a four-line staff in the notation of post-Reformation plainsong. While his opening phrase, accompanied by its pedal chord, suggests the nineteenth century part-song clearly enough, there is a swing about the harmony and melody of the later phrases that comes very pleasantly after Barnby. We give here the words and music of verse 4 for the sake of the very un-Puritan fourth line.

Two eminent men of letters are represented in *B/S*. S. T. Coleridge's verses, "The shepherds went their hasty way" (63) have little distinction, even if they hardly deserved the lush anthem-setting by J. F. Barnett that they get here. But William Morris, as might be expected, catches the true medieval colour in "From far away we come to you" (40) with its interlined refrain throughout, and he is fortunate in finding J. B. Dykes in an open-air mood. One rather remarkable sight is Martin Luther's *Vom Himmel hoch* (see below, p. 198), translated in full, fifteen verses, by Bramley, but divorced from Luther's own magnificent and now celebrated tune, and set to a very Victorian hymn tune by a composer named Higgs.

Alongside these extraordinary pieces, however, so redolent of the demure religious consciousness of a society that had time to brood and croon, there are those twenty-eight traditional carols. "God rest you merry", "I saw three ships", "The Angel Gabriel" (*Oxford* 37), "The Lord at first did Adam make", "A Virgin unspotted", "A child this day is born", "The Cherry Tree" (with words somewhat abridged and modified), "The Moon shines bright", and "The Holy Well", are all there with their proper tunes, and it was *B/S* that taught these to one whole generation. Indeed, *B/S* held the popular favour for fifty-seven years, until *Oxford* appeared in 1928, in much the same way that *Hymns A. & M.*, despite serious competition, ran triumphantly for forty-five years from 1861 until the appearance in 1906 of the *English Hymnal*. Not even Woodward's great series of carol books (see below, p. 195) seriously affected the popularity of *B/S*, although the advance in taste they represented was fully as marked as that represented in *Oxford*.

CAROLS FOR USE IN CHURCH

Bramley and Stainer's chief competitor was R. R. Chope's *Carols for Use in Church*, whose first edition of 112 carols appeared in 1875, and whose second, enlarged to contain no fewer than 215, appeared in 1894. This was a more ambitious project, and its aims, as expressed in Baring-Gould's Introduction of 1875 and Chope's Preface to the 1894 edition, are more explicitly educative.

Baring-Gould had written:

We have now dethroned the Metrical Psalms, but we have hardly gone
far enough in the direction of hymnody. We want some hearty, festival
singing of carols at each of the great feasts. What are Dissenters doing now
to get congregations? They have their Services of Song, more or less
secular, with a dash of religious cant about them like a smack of garlic in a
dish. The people are becoming more musical and more to delight in music.
They seem to have a special delight in sacred music. By all means let us take
the opportunity and give them a performance of carols at the festivals.
Whilst the Dissenters are giving "Little Topsy", "Poor Joe", and
"Wandering Gyp" as Services of Song—flummery and mawkishness—
let the Church boldly produce carols and give a Service of Song at each
festival, made up of carols, teaching doctrine, and giving emphasis to the
festival. (p. xv)

And Chope wrote in 1894:

It has been an arduous, prolonged and costly work to restore the use or
Carols in Divine Service, and thus make into an act of worship what was
well-nigh considered only as a recreation at a social gathering. But now
they who have begun to love the old, old story and grow familiar with the
carol-strain at Christmas and Epiphany, go on to desire the helpful song
of Easter and Ascension triumph, and at length from victory won through
the holy Nativity, the glorious Resurrection, and Ascension of the Saviour,
long to lift the Carol of Harvest-Home, which tells not only of the
ingathered fruits of the earth, but also of the garnered store which we ourselves hope at last to be in the Home of God.

The first edition was larger than *B/S*, but contained fewer carols
for Christmas, because of its generous allowance for other feasts. It
was the first major gesture in modern times towards the celebration of
seasons other than Christmas in carols. The larger edition is almost a
hymn book, in that it provides a complete system for the whole
Christian year, except Lent and Passiontide. The larger book adds
several compositions which turn out to be hymns rather than carols,
like "O come, all ye faithful", and "Hark, the herald", no doubt for
the sake of completeness.

In the Christmas carols (of which no fewer than sixty-seven were
added in the larger edition), we have on the whole less attention to the
traditional, and more doctoring of traditional words, than we had in
B/S. The later edition added several of the older pieces, which improved
the general set of the collection, among which are "Tidings true"
(*Oxford* 36) from the medieval manuscript tradition, and "The Lord
at first did Adam make" (this time with the vital C sharp) from the

ballads. Like *B/S*, Chope sets "The Holly and the Ivy" to the triple-time D minor traditional tune which was soon to be displaced by Cecil Sharp's now familiar Gloucestershire tune.

Apart from the traditional matter there is very little in Chope of either musical or literary distinction. Like his competitors, Chope makes liberal use of the glutinous music and words fashionable in his age. He is to be commended, however, for including five specimens of George Wither, all taken from his *Hymns and Songs of the Church* (1623). Three of these are set to the tunes of Orlando Gibbons which appeared in Wither's original book: "As on the night before this blessed morn" (Song 46 in Wither) to Gibbons's SONG 1 (discreetly elongated by one of the musical editors, H. S. Irons); "Lord, with what zeal" for St. Stephen's Day (Wither 63) to SONG 4, and "That so thy blessed birth" (Wither 49) to SONG 41. The two other Wither carols, not set to Gibbons tunes, are his 64th and 65th, "Teach us by his example" (for St. John) and "That rage whereof the Psalm doth say" (for the Holy Innocents). But on the other hand Gibbons appears again in an arrangement of his SONG 18 deftly made by H. S. Irons to fit "Sleep, holy babe" and make it unnecessary to print Dykes's dreadful tune. Three of these Gibbons tunes have now passed into current use in hymn books. In *E.H.* they are—SONG 1, 384; SONG 4, 113; SONG 18, 357. SONG 41 can be found at Frost 363, or *M.C.H.*, Ex. 58.

A number of the tunes in the earlier part of the larger book (that is, of those added in the second edition) are marked "Cornish" in the index; they are clearly assignable to Methodist influence, and very much resemble the "While shepherds watched" group (see above, p. 158) in their style.

The contemporary compositions need not detain us long. The larger edition was edited jointly by A. H. Brown (1830–1926) of Brentwood, and H. S. Irons (1834–1905) of Southwell Minster. Perhaps we have to thank Irons for the fact that against his own forty-three tunes or arrangements we have fifty-one tunes, and several carols, from the hand of the Reverend R. F. Smith (*c.* 1834–1905), minor Canon of Southwell. But it is principally due to the eructations of this pious musician that the range of the composers' index in Chope is much less wide than that in the smaller collection of Bramley and Stainer. R. F. Smith is almost always quite ineffable.

Our greatest disappointment in Chope is the poor and pedestrian quality of the non-Christmas carols. In the Easter section, which has thirty-three numbers, the only one regarded as fit to sing nowadays, apart from a couple of Easter hymns, is "The world itself keeps Easter day", whose words, by Neale, survive at *Oxford* 150. *Oxford's* tune is that for which they were written. Chope's tune is, of course, by Smith. Perhaps the worst experience in the whole of Chope comes when you read no. 187: the words are by the Reverend G. P. Grantham, and begin with this unpromising couplet:

> As Mary walked in the garden green
> Of Joseph of Arimathee.

A cursory glance over the five verses suggests that we have here at least a carol based on the narrative of the Resurrection. But no. The chorus gives it all away. To feel its full effect we must have the whole verse:

> As Mary walked in the garden green
> Of Joseph of Arimathee,
> Fair shrubs and flowers she passed between,
> Tall palm and the wide plane tree.
> 'Twas early morn, as with spice and balm,
> Full laden she went, when lo!
> She thought she heard in an accent calm
> A voice which she seemed to know:
> (*Chorus*):   I am the Gardener true,
> Mine are the violets blue,
> The lily all white.
> And the rose so bright,
> And pansy of purple hue.

Canon Grantham provided his own tune; but a second—the most hair-raising in the book, but we will not waste music-type on it—is (need I say?) by Smith. It was probably only copyright difficulties which prevented the excellent Chope's setting the whole thing to the tune of "The Holy City", which it would fit very nicely.

After that the reader will be happy to take my word for it that the Easter, Ascension and other non-Christmas carols in Chope are, on the whole, worse than anything in *B/S*. Chope is reduced in the end to including one or two processional hymns of a martial and truculent nature, like "Fling out the banner" (180) and "Stand up, stand up for Jesus" (169), and several others whose words do not rise even to that level and whose music is usually made to measure. "We must not be too stiff", said the good parson of Horbury Bridge, "The church must unbend. The country people have no quarrel with the food the Church offers them, but they do not like the cooking. The meat is excellent but it is too leathery in the way it is served." It was well spiced and minced in Chope.

Other Carols of the Nineteenth Century

Those two books were the outstanding collections of the period 1870–1900, in which large numbers of carols were collected and each given its own tune. Among smaller collections there were T. W. Staniforth's *Carols, Hymns and Noels for Christmastide* (1883), containing twenty pieces with music, six of the tunes being his own. Baring-Gould published carols in *Church Songs* (1884–86), with music by H. F. Sheppard, a good deal of which found its way into the second edition of Chope. A. H. Brown was the musical editor of *In Excelsis Gloria* (1885), which again provided material for Chope. But they add nothing of consequence.

But for completeness we should mention one or two pieces from the eighteenth and nineteenth centuries which we now regard as carols. We so regard them not because they were composed as carols (except perhaps one of them), but because the musicians of the carol-revival have found or composed tunes for them and made them into "synthetic" carols.

One of these, now celebrated, is now called "Isaac Watts's Lullaby", and begins, "Hush, my dear, lie still and slumber" (*Oxford* 130). Watts wrote this as the eighth and last of his "Moral Songs" in his *Divine and Moral Songs for Children* (1715). Not to put too fine a point on it, it was a cradle song designed for harassed baby-sitters. It contains as the seventh of its fourteen verses the words

> Soft, my child, I did not chide thee,
> > Though my song might sound too hard;
> 'Tis thy mother sits beside thee
> > And her arms shall be thy guard.

Against the word "Mother" in my reprint there is an asterisk leading to a footnote which reads "Here you may sing the words, *Brother, Sister, Neighbour* etc." The *Moral Songs* sound a quaintly puritan note. The first of them is an exhortation to be up betimes in the morning, based on that very agreeable text in Proverbs 26.14. Another says "Don't be rough in your play", a third, "A thief comes to a bad end", and so on. The well known "How doth the little busy bee" and "Let dogs delight to bark and bite" are two of the thirty-odd *Divine Songs* that precede them. The best of Watts has always had to be disinterred from a heap of rubbish; you have among the *Moral Songs* this charming lullaby (or so it appears when judiciously pruned) and among the *Divine Songs* one magnificent hymn beginning "I sing the almighty power of God." Set now to a snatch of melody heard in Northumberland the carol has been rescued from the owlish moralism that broods over it in its original context.

It was not surprising that those prophets of the imagination, Dr. Dearmer and Dr. Vaughan Williams, should annex verses by William Blake. "Blake's Cradle Song", beginning "Sweet dreams form a shade" comes from his *Songs of Innocence*, and with a tune by Dr. Vaughan Williams makes a delightful meditative carol at *Oxford* 196. S. T. Coleridge, who appeared in *B/S*, gives us a tiny carol in *Dormi Jesu* (*Oxford* 175); one verse is in Latin, the other is an English verse which is simply Coleridge's translation of the Latin. He picked up the Latin verse in an old book in a German village.

Dora Greenwell, the Northumbrian poetess, has some delightful verses set to a Dutch carol tune at *Oxford* 134, beginning "If ye would hear the angels sing". The verses beginning "Rise and bake your Christmas bread" and "Rise and light your Christmas fire" sound the authentic note, although she wrote with no tune in mind. We may also mention her Christmas poem from *Carmina Crucis* (1869), used as a hymn in certain collections, which while hardly a carol has some haunting lines and makes a seasonable lyric:

> And art thou come with us to dwell,
>   Our Prince, our Guide, our Love, our Lord?
> And is thy name Immanuel,
>   God present with his world restored?
>
> The heart is glad for thee: it knows
>   None now shall bid it err or mourn,
> And o'er its desert breaks the rose
>   In triumph o'ver the grieving thorn.

Miss Greenwell, forgotten now among the flood of minor poetesses that the age produced, had more poetic insight than most of her contemporaries.

Christina Rossetti's "In the bleak midwinter" is without doubt the most popular and famous of all Christmas poems of the period. If ever there was a poem of which, with its tune, it is hard to say whether it is a hymn or a carol, it is this one, and the truth is, of course, that in its author's mind it was neither. It is Gustav Holst's tune (*Oxford* 187) that has made it what it is. Its wayward metre makes it difficult to sing, but nobody seems to mind. We may mention, although it is our rule not to mention anthem-settings, the very charming choral setting by Dr. Harold Darke, published in 1911 by Stainer and Bell, Ltd. This setting has a certain interest apart from its delightful music in that it alters one slightly embarrassing line in the original, so that one couplet reads

A heart full of mirth
And a manger-full of hay.

For general use that alteration is commendable. Christina Rossetti also comes into the Christmas season with her tiny lyric, "Love came down at Christmas"; this has not been so fortunate in finding its inevitable tune, and in consequence settings are in currency by Basil Harwood, Sidney Hann, R. O. Morris, Edgar Pettman and Eric Thiman, not to mention one arrangement of an Irish folk song. It is perhaps for this reason that the anglican hymn books have fought shy of the words but seldom has so much theological insight been packed into sixty-three words. Thirdly, there is her "The shepherds had an angel", another carol which has never found its tune, but which could have wide success if it did. I believe that the most promising and worthwhile is that written for the words in the 1926 edition of *Songs of Praise* by Imogen Holst, the daughter of the composer of "In the bleak mid-winter". The tune was dropped from the enlarged edition of that book (which became the best-seller), and is now undeservedly neglected. The words are set to a Béarnais noel at *U.C.B.* XII, 83.

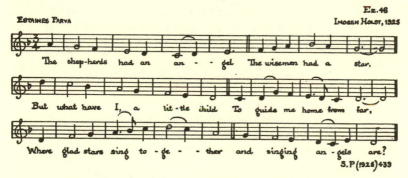

ESTAINES PARVA

Ex.48

IMOGEN HOLST, 1925

The shep-herds had an an - - gel The wisemen had a star,
But what have I, a lit-tle child To guide me home from far,
Where glad stars sing to-ge - - ther and singing an-gels are?

S.P.(1925)439

Attractive though Christina Rossetti's verses always are, they are not in any sense medieval in their diction. There is often a brooding, evangelical colour in them, as in that dark, expressive, highly-wrought and almost unsingable poem of hers, "None other Lamb", which is of her own age, not of the carol age.

For real carols in the nineteenth century you go, as we have already seen, to William Morris. Like these others, he did not write for music; but his lines easily find their tune. Gustav Holst found a magnificent French tune for Morris's "Masters in this Hall" (*Oxford* 137), which has made it nearly as popular as "In the bleak midwinter", and in the judgment of some even more worth singing. This is a real resurrection of the ballad-style:

> This is Christ the Lord,
>   Masters be ye glad!
> Christmas is come in
>   And no folk should be sad.
>   Nowell, Nowell, Nowell!
>   Nowell, sing we clear!
>   Holpen are all folk on earth,
>   Born is God's Son so dear:
>   Nowell, Nowell, Nowell!
>   Nowell sing we loud,
>   God to-day hath poor folk raised,
>   And cast a-down the proud.

Morris is a latter-day urban medieval, but there is one even more medieval mind than his—that of the rustic Robert Stephen Hawker of Morwenstow, whom in another connection we have already met. Verses of his written about 1836 which are little known, and have no tune, and which have probably never been sung because we are not yet quite ready for his quaint and naïve "Aunt Mary", make a fitting conclusion to this chapter. The verses are accessible in Rickert (p. 287) and are too good to miss: so once again we end in Cornwall.

> Now of all the trees by the King's highway,
>   Which do you love the best?
> O! the one that is green upon Christmas Day,
>   The bush with the bleeding breast.
> Now the holly with her drops of blood for me:
> For that is our dear Aunt Mary's tree.
>
> Its leaves are sweet with our Saviour's Name,
>   'Tis a plant that loves the poor:
> Summer and winter it shines the same
>   Beside the cottage door.
> O! the holly with her drops of blood for me:
> For that is our kind Aunt Mary's tree.

'Tis a bush that the birds will never leave:
  They sing in it all day long;
But sweetest of all upon Christmas Eve
  Is to hear the Robin's song.
'Tis the merriest sound upon earth and sea:
For it comes from our own Aunt Mary's tree.

So of all that grow by the King's highway,
  I love that tree the best;
'Tis a bower for the birds upon Christmas Day
  The bush of the bleeding breast.
O! the holly with her drops of blood for me;
For that is our sweet Aunt Mary's tree.

Carols from Other Countries

WHILE the modern repertory of carols uses the English tradition as its chief source, the reader must have noticed that many very well-known carols have so far gone without mention in these pages. This is because it is with carols as it is with hymns: our carol-books, like the hymn books, are now full of translations from foreign carols and anglicisations of foreign tunes. We have still not strayed beyond Europe and America for our carols; but from the continent of Europe, especially from Germany and France, we have taken many of our modern favourites.

One thing strikes an observer of these matters at once, and calls for comment before we go further. This is virtually a one-way traffic. Consider for example Germany, which of all foreign countries has a religious and social culture most like our own. Pick up a German hymn book: how many English hymns translated will you find in it, and how many English tunes imported? In the preparation of the dissertation on which my book, *The Music of Christian Hymnody* is based, I analysed the contents of the *Deutsches Evangelisches Gesangbuch* (1926), and I found that of the 342 hymns in its First Part, no fewer than forty-five are familiar in our own country in translation: but not a single English author is translated in that series of hymns. Indeed, there is hardly an author from outside Lutheran Germany. Similarly, in the whole book of well over 500 hymns there are but two English tunes, and those in the *Volkslieder*, or Second Part. I wager that the reader who comes fresh to the subject would never guess which two they are. In fact they are Dykes's PAX DEI (*A. & M.* 31) and F. C. Atkinson's MORECAMBE (*Methodist Hymn Book* 688), two very mournful examples of the English style. It hardly needs saying, on the other hand, that at least half the chorales printed in that book are known, in some form, in this country.

Various reasons account for this. Up to the middle of the nineteenth century this country was as self-supporting in the matter of church music as were other European countries. In, say, 1800, England was as firmly Protestant and as insularly English as it ever became in church matters. The demand for popular church music or for religious folk-song was supplied, where it was not flatly suppressed, by the hymn-writers. Similarly in Lutheran Germany the same demand was supplied by the writers of religious *lieder* and chorales. The only difference was that while Protestant England, having thrown overboard the whole system of Tudor church music, was only beginning to learn, under indifferent tuition, the techniques of modern religious folk-song, Lutheran Germany has, from the beginning of the Reformation, a tradition of first-rate religious poetry and musicianship running from Luther to Paul Gerhardt in words, and from Luther to Cruger in music which had formed a solid tradition of good hymnody before the age of English hymnody had begun; so that even though there was a notable slump in the years following 1715, it hit Germany less hard than it hit the less well-prepared English musical tradition.

The English tradition was inextricably involved with a puritanism that would have horrified Luther. The stream of popular music for the pious was artificially reduced in the seventeenth century, and diverted away from the popular style in the eighteenth; so that by 1850 those Englishmen whom the Romantic Movement had taught to become less insular in their habits and whom the Oxford Movement had taught to value order and beauty wherever they might originate (even among papists) were looking out for material to enrich the depleted and corrupted store.

England badly needed a new and freshening stream in church music, and the hymnologists of the years following 1845 found it in the Genevan psalters and the Lutheran chorale-books. The early editions of *Hymns A. & M.* are packed with the results of their researches. In a manner characteristic of an England filled with a romantic approval of the exotic, they searched the chorale-books of the continent, and in a manner characteristic of empire-building England they adapted what they found to the strait-laced requirements of the hymn-metres.

Piae Cantiones

In the matter of carols, however, the eager scholars had a stroke of pure luck in the year 1853. About the beginning of that year G. J. R. Gordon, Her Majesty's Envoy and Minister at Stockholm, brought to England a copy of a rare and ancient book, at the time entirely unknown in this country, whose short title, now venerated throughout the English carol-singing world, is *Piae Cantiones*. The book had been printed in Finland in 1582, and was a collection of seventy-three Latin hymns and carols, set to their proper melodies, edited by Theodoric Petri of Abo. The object of the original work seems to have been twofold: to make a collection of the best European religious folk songs available at the time, and to set them to words whose sentiments should be conformable to the rugged intellectual Protestantism prevalent in Germany and Scandinavia. The words are doctrinally much more erratic than their innocently medieval originals: but it is the tunes that matter.

Few of Her Majesty's envoys have done the country such signal service as did this Mr. Gordon. After all, the man who was primarily responsible for our singing "Good King Wenceslas" deserves mention as one of our more conspicuous national benefactors. Mr. Gordon, who was interested in church matters and who believed in the possibilities that lay in the precious book, handed the book to the Rev. J. M. Neale, Warden of Sackville College, East Grinstead, Sussex. Neale had already made his name as a translator of Greek and Latin hymns and as a liturgist; and his name is now one of those which appear with the greatest frequency in our hymn books. It was he who translated hymns into English versions that have become firm favourites in England, such as "Jerusalem the golden", "Blessed city, heavenly Salem", "O happy band of pilgrims", and "Christian, dost thou see them?". Neale, who was no musician, called in Thomas Helmore, Vice-Principal of St. Mark's College, Chelsea, a priest-musician with a lively interest in antiquities, and invited him to interpret the music of *Piae Cantiones* while he himself set about writing words to fit some of the tunes. This was virtually the beginning of what has become a full flow of foreign carols towards these islands.

We have many tunes, but few words, from *Piae Cantiones*. Of the carols in which both tune and words (translated) come from this source, the best known is "Unto us a boy is born" (*Oxford* 92). Here is a very characteristic example. Both tune and words are older than *Piae Cantiones*; they appear in a manuscript preserved at Trier and dating from the fifteenth century. But they come to us through *Piae Cantiones*, and it is that form of the tune that is now most widely known. Another form of the tune, arranged by M. Praetorius in 1599, in triple time, will be found at *E.H.* 14, ii; it is nothing like so effective, having lost its *melisma* at the end. The carol is not one that Neale translated. The *Oxford* translation is by Dearmer, the *Cowley* one, also well known, beginning "Unto us is born a Son", and retaining Latin words in the last verse, is by Woodward. "In dulci jubilo" (see below, p. 195) was also in *Piae Cantiones*, but was known in England long before that book was brought over.

It is, of course, "Good King Wenceslas" that has at a stroke "naturalised" *Piae Cantiones* in this country. The words of this carol are blown

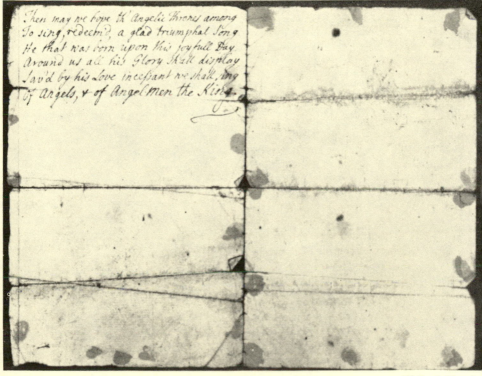

"CHRISTIANS, AWAKE"

(Chetham's Library)

The original Manuscript by John Byrom, now in Chetham's Library, Manchester

CAROL SINGING IN THE EARLY NINETEENTH CENTURY
(showing the characteristic broadsheets)

"The London Carol Singers" by Robert Seymour (d. 1836), the first illustrator of the
Pickwick Papers

on by the editors of *Oxford* and by other respectable authorities. "This rather confused narrative", says Dearmer in his most donnish style: "Doggerel", snorts Duncan, and "poor and commonplace to the last degree" sighed A. H. Bullen. Poor Neale! He wanted a carol for St. Stephen's day, and he had heard of the Bohemian legend of St. Wenceslaus; so he writes what is to most ears a picturesque and agreeable narrative with a cosy moral that meant business in the nineteenth century. Myself, I am unable to see what is wrong with "Good King Wenceslas" as a sociable carol. It lacks pious unction, and looking at the nineteenth-century productions that have it, we may be thankful for that; it is nothing like a hymn. But Neale knew what he was doing: had he meant to write a hymn he would have done so, and done it better than most of his contemporaries. What he did do, indeed, was to discard the original, *Tempus adest floridum*, a spring carol which, had he lived forty years later, he might have been content to translate (see *Oxford* 99).

Whatever its merits, we have in "Good King Wenceslas" one of the earliest examples of the modern synthetic carol; and in the other carols of Neale which introduce *Piae Cantiones* we see this new technique applied with skill and grace.

A noble dance-like tune from this source, which Neale set to Christmas words, is the tune DIVINUM MYSTERIUM. Here Neale again ignores the original in *Piae Cantiones* and gives us a translation of a hymn by the medieval Latin poet Venantius Fortunatus, beginning in translation, "Of the Father's heart begotten" (*E.H.* 613). This was one of the tunes that caught Helmore's eye, and Helmore's original arrangement of it happens to be an excellent example of the limitations of knowledge that attended his zeal for antiquity. When he looked at the diamond-shaped neums in which the tune was originally noted, some instinct within him prompted him to translate them into a hymn-like duple rhythm which made the tune, at its opening, look reasonably like a possible English hymn tune, but which broke down as the tune progressed, leaving a melody in irregular and somewhat unmanageable bars. "Never mind," says Helmore, "plainsong is not metrical; we must make the best of it." To Helmore the traditional anglican, the ordinary English psalm-tune was respectable: to Helmore the antiquarian, plainsong was respectable. It simply did not occur to him that there was a third form—the dance—to be reckoned with by church musicians. The tune is not plainsong, but a dance—a dance gracefully extended beyond strict four-bar rhythm, but no less a dance for that, written in the most popular of the dance-modes of the late middle ages, and in a rhythm which would not have been tolerated for a moment in a composition designed for church use. It was all very well for *Piae Cantiones* to set the tune to serious-looking words. Neale's inspiration was much happier, in translating the gay and light-hearted words of Fortunatus. The following examples show how Helmore's stiff ecclesiastical presuppositions misled him. They quote simply the fifth and sixth phrases of the tune, first as noted in *Piae Cantiones*, then as transcribed by Helmore, and finally as first transcribed in the 1904 edition of *Hymns A. & M.* and as later taken over in other books. (*E.H.* in 1906 has a nearly, but not quite, correct form of the tune, extending the melismas at the end of each even line beyond the intention of the original composer. This was brought back into line in the 1933 edition.)

A very delightful carol has been made at *Oxford* 120 by associating the medieval English carol, "In Bethlehem that fair city" (*G. 21*) with a *Piae Cantiones* tune. The Finnish book took the tune from two earlier German sources, Klug's *Geistliche Lieder* of 1543, and Lossius's *Psalmodia* of 1553. In the two sources the tune appears in quite different forms: but it is clear that the 1553 form is a descant to the 1543 form, and they can be seen side by side in *Oxford*. Yet another form can be found at *Oxford* 85. Although English hymn books have used the tune in its 1543 form (*E.H.* 34), the descant is much more attractive. This is another FIRST NOWELL situation, and it can be paralleled in German chorale books at other places.

Even these few examples show that *Piae Cantiones* has an atmosphere all its own. Although there are a few very simple and rudimentary tunes in it, few of them can resist the occasional decoration or *melisma*, such as we hear in the last line of UNTO US A BOY IS BORN, in the fifth of OF THE FATHER'S LOVE BEGOTTEN, and even on the last syllable but one of GOOD KING WENCESLAS. But although it was Neale who first attempted to leaven the lump of English sacred music by setting words to a dozen or so of its tunes, it was G. R. Woodward (1848–1934) who really taught us to use it on a large scale. He produced a series of distinguished carol books, entirely devoted to "synthetic" carols designed to bring these and other melodies back into use. The first of his books were *Carols for Christmastide* (1892) and *Carols for Easter and Ascensiontide* (1894), each containing twelve hand-picked melodies with new words by Woodward himself. These were the forerunners of the *Cowley Carol Book* (first published in two sections, 1901 and 1902, and finally in an enlarged edition of 100 carols in 1919), which remains, with its pleasantly antique words and the beautiful harmonisations of the tunes, chiefly by Charles Wood, a classic in the literature. Dr. Woodward produced also the *Cambridge Carol Book*, containing fifty-one carols chiefly to English and French tunes, and the *Italian Carol Book*, which explores southern Europe. Woodward saw to it that at least half the tunes in *Piae Cantiones* were made available for English singers, and he goes well beyond the modest nine included in *Oxford*. And beyond *Piae Cantiones*, it is to Woodward that we owe our present-day enthusiasm for foreign folk-carols which, collected and arranged by him and various other editors after his day, have greatly enriched our repertory.

GERMANY

Beginning in Germany and Austria, we may first do homage to "In dulci Jubilo". This is the most famous of the macaronic carols, in which Latin and vernacular words are used in alternate lines, the sense running straight through. There is a legend that Henry Suso (d. 1366), the mystic, wrote the German/Latin original at the dictation of an angel, having dreamt that he was invited to join in an angelic dance. The first written copies of words and tune come from German sources dated about 1500 onwards, and from its frequent appearances we gather that it was exceedingly popular by that time. The first English version was made in John Wedderburn's *Gude and Godly Ballates* of about 1540. Many English versions have been made since then. The old English psalm-book, *Lyra Davidica* (1708), to which we owe the Easter hymn, "Jesus Christ is risen to-day" with its tune, has a translation. Another was made in 1825 by the distinguished diplomat, traveller and hymn-writer, Sir John Bowring. Yet another is in the delightful part-song arrangement of the carol made by R. L. da Pearsall (1795–1856). The version we know best (*Oxford* 86) is by Dearmer. The text from which all these translations, save only that of Wedderburn, are made is that which contains a third verse altered from the fifteenth-century original by Martin Luther when he had it included in Babst's *Gesangbuch* of 1545.

Apart from the *Oxford* translation, however, the form of the carol most popular in England, and first popular on the grand scale, was Neale's "Good Christian men, rejoice" (*B/S* 8). This is not a translation, but a freely written three-verse carol interpreting the general sense of the original. As the reader will be aware, it interpolates a two-syllable ejaculatory line in the middle of the verse, and this conceals another curious piece of misreading on the part of Helmore. Neale and Helmore were taking "In dulci jubilo" from *Piae Cantiones*, which means that they were looking at it in Swedish, not in German. The old German in the first verse ran, in lines 3 and 4:

> Unsers herzens wonne
> Leyt *in praesepio,*

and there is no difficulty in seeing how that fits the music. In 6/4 time, *leyt* goes to a sixth-beat crotchet. The Swedish in *Piae Cantiones* runs:

> Then all tingh för oss Förmo
> Ligger *in praesepio.*

Ligger (="lies") had to divide that crotchet into two quavers, and therefore at this point in the Finnish book there appear two diamond-shaped notes with tails, representing a quarter of the oblong note (breve) and half the untailed diamond-shaped note (semibreve). Helmore thought these two notes were "longs" or double breves, which are printed oblong with tails. In the following Example, (A) shows how it ran in *Piae Cantiones*, (B) shows what Helmore made of it, and (C) shows the true value of the notes. This makes it clear why Neale thought it necessary to provide weighty words for these emphatic notes.

A   Ex.50

The carol often sung in Woodward's version, "Christ was born on Christmas Day", comes also from medieval Germany through *Piae Cantiones*. The tune is at *Oxford* 77, there set to a translation of its original words which formed part of a German mystery play, and were first written down in the manuscript which also gives us our first version of "In dulci jubilo". *Piae Cantiones,* of course, set the tune to different words, being uninterested in the legendary material that formed the plot of the play; hence the tune is often called RESONET IN LAUDIBUS, its Finnish title, in modern hymn-books. It is thought by some that it is closely related to the great chorale of Philipp Nicolai (1597), WIE SCHON LEUCHTET DER MORGENSTERN (*Oxford* 104). There are only two points, at the beginning and near the end, where the tunes seem to meet, but it is possible that when Nicolai wrote his hymn he had the carol tune somewhere in the back of his mind.

"*Quem pastores laudavere*" (*Oxford* 79), whose tune became very well known in English hymn books (*E.H.* 598) before it became associated with English versions of the original words which *Oxford* leaves in Latin, is another late medieval German carol tune, dance-like and gracious, like so many. Words and tune were first written down in 1555. "Es ist ein' Ros' entsprungen" (*Oxford* 76), another carol which *Oxford* was shy of translating, was no doubt of the same period, but its first written source was about 1600. Christmas words to the former tune have been written by Principal George Caird (*Congregational Praise* 708) beginning "Shepherds came, their praises bringing", and the most familiar English version of the other is that of Woodward, "The noble Stem of Jesse". But Neale provided other words for the first appearance of ES IST EIN' ROS' in England, in his translation of a Greek original, "A great and mighty wonder" (*E.H.* 19).

From the same period in Germany we have also "There stood in heaven a linden tree" (*Cambridge* 37), a gracious legendary carol of the Annunciation. Many other German carol tunes have been used in "synthetic" carols in our own time, of which the most interesting both in quality and in collocation is ALS ICH BE MEINEN SCHAFEN WACHT, set in *Oxford* (122) to words by Herrick, "What sweeter music can we sing?". This tune, with its haunting "echo" motif throughout, was part of a sixteenth-century German nativity play, sung as a solo by a shepherd, with the angels joining in the "chorus" off-stage.

Perhaps the most dramatic of the German carols in our repertory is "Marias Wanderschaft", which appears twice in *Oxford*. The carol tells a story of our Lady, as it were in a dream, searching the streets of Jerusalem looking for her Son, and suddenly seeing him bearing the cross: another version tells of her meeting St. Peter, who tells her that Jesus has just been sentenced to death. This seems to be a dream-like conflation of the Passion story with the incident narrated in Luke

2.41–52. The original folk-song, with an editorial version of the words, is at *Oxford* 93. *Oxford* 179 gives us Johannes Brahms's very beautiful setting, from his *Marienlieder*, op. 22 (1859), there called "Marias Wallfahrt"; the English version here is by Professor H. T. Wade-Gery of Oxford. This is the only time in our story when we shall mention the name of a musician of the first rank in the classical humanist succession (for Bach comes just before it, and Vaughan Williams after it), and we may mention here that among Brahms's settings of German folk songs for unaccompanied voices are several carol-like compositions, including one of the tune IN EINEM KRIPPLEIN (*E.H.* 338)—a strange, exotic melody which would surely have appealed to him. "Marias Wanderschaft" has that slightly fantastic quality which we have noted in many of the English ballads but which, as a matter of fact, we do not encounter very much in the German carols that have come into our use.

Martin Luther's celebrated carol, *Vom Himmel hoch*, is better known in England as a hymn than as a carol. This is partly because its tune came into this country through the Bach version as a serviceable Long Metre hymn tune before we were aware of its true association. The fact that the Englishman has learnt it in this way, and through Bach's version, has tended to make him think of it as a solemn and ponderous piece, suitable for weighty words and hardly suggestive of Christmas domesticity. But Luther's original was written for his own family. The first five of its fifteen verses were to be sung by a child, representing the announcement of the angel, the rest by the whole family. Two verses, the 13th and 14th, in the translation of the later Wedderburn book, *A Compendious Buik of Godly and Spirituall Songs* (1567), appear at *Oxford* 181, "O my dear heart", to music by Peter Warlock. But probably the carol will not find its way into the English popular repertory until we begin to see its tune again in the light and simple version in which Luther wrote it. Bach is magnificent: but he has no contact with the carol-technique.

Ex.51

Vom Himmel hoch da komm ich her, ich bring euch gute neu-e mär, der gu-ter mär bring ich so viel da-von ich singen und sa-gen will.

A group of German tunes from Catholic sources of the seventeenth century has become popular in English use during the last two generations. The best known of these is probably "O Jesulein Süss", which appears at *Oxford* 109 with a translation of its original words beginning "O little one sweet". It first appeared in a Catholic song book published at Cologne in 1623 in the following form:

Ex.52

In the slightly smoother, but no more attractive form that we know, it first appeared in 1650, and later J. S. Bach harmonised it. During the seventeenth century in Germany it was familiar to both Protestants and Catholics: but in words and music it is a lullaby-carol very characteristic of the Catholic culture of the time, with its tender, Mary-centred piety. The other tune of this kind, from another Catholic collection of 1649, is "Ein Kindlein in der Wiegen", known to us as "He smiles within his cradle" (*Oxford* 84) or "I heard an infant weeping" (*Cowley* 90). Another, in gayer mood, is "To us in Bethlem city" (*Oxford* 112), and yet another for the Easter season, is "The whole bright world rejoices now" (*Oxford* 96), from the same source as "O Jesulein Süss".

The student of hymnology will know that the hymns of Catholic piety in seventeenth-century Germany are all of a carol-like, informal kind, and that not a few very attractive English hymn tunes have been made of them. Of these the most universally popular nowadays is what we now call EASTER ALLELUIA, and was called in Germany LASST UNS ERFREUEN, set in *E.H.* at No. 519 to "Ye watchers and ye holy ones" and in other books to "All creatures of our God and King". Here is an excellent example of a carol-like tune which is regarded in England with a solemnity foreign to its nature. While one must admire Dr. Vaughan Williams's arrangement of the tune in *E.H.* as a most admirable piece of music, one realises how it was originally meant to sound if one has the chance to sing the hymn "All creatures . . ." in the version at No. 2 in *Cantate Domino* (1951); there the tune is given in its original version, with one Alleluia after each of the first three lines, and three at the end, and it suddenly seems to be as light as a feather. On German Catholic hymnody, see *M.C.H.*, Chapter 21.

The only carol, or Christmas hymn, from the culture of Protestant pietism of the seventeenth century which is familiar here is "All my heart this night rejoices", a translation of a hymn by Paul Gerhardt (1607–76) associated with a charming tune that was not originally written for it. Curiously enough, it is not in *Oxford* or in any of the standard anglican hymn books, but all the Free Church standard books have it. Pietism, which produced the magnificent treasury of Gerhardt's hymns, and has given us many English hymns of great beauty, came very near the borders of Catholicism in some of its religious habits, and not a few pietists were received into the Roman Catholic Church in the years following the Thirty Years' War. (For the hymnody of pietism, see *M.C.H.*, Chapter 10.)

Eighteenth-century Germany has given us nothing. This was a period of decadence in German church music, and, as in England, of the gradual extinction of popular music. But from the Germany of the nineteenth century we have a unique and precious legacy in one or two of the songs of Peter Cornelius (1824–74). These are carols only in the sense that Brahms's *Marias Wallfahrt* is a carol, but they cannot be left out of consideration because one of them has become a great favourite in England. Cornelius was a great friend of both Liszt and Wagner, but most of his work was written for voices. He wrote two operas (one unfinished), several choral works, and some song-cycles. It is from his *Weihnachtslieder* that we have the fascinating song, "The Three Kings" (*Oxford* 193). This is now well known as an unaccompanied choral piece, and has been sung in the King's College Festival in Sir Ivor Atkins's arrangement for solo baritone and eight-part choir; but originally it was a solo song with accompaniment for piano or organ, just as *Oxford* gives it. The accompaniment consists simply of Nicolai's chorale, WIE SCHON LEUCHTET (*Oxford* 104), and the solo part is a recitative woven round the chorale. The words are lyrical, hymn-like, and slightly pietistic (with their final "Offer thy heart"). It may be said that the choral arrangement, though not by Cornelius himself, is exactly in the style of his own choral works, and that it forms a tribute to one of the very few composers of his age who attempted *a cappella* choral writing on any considerable scale. His anthem for eight-part choir, "Liebe, die du mich zum Bilde", still occasionally performed by very capable choirs, is a memorable piece of rich choral writing. Cornelius was one of those humbler journeymen of music who move about in the circles of the great; the kind of person who became secretary of some musical society. But his lyrical gifts, though slight by the standards of the greatest, are far beyond anything in church music that his country was producing at the time. He is represented in *Oxford* a second time by another of the *Weihnachtslieder* at No. 191, "The holly's up", a piece whose words are far more carol-like than the other.

From Austria we have two carols. One is only a tune—but what a delicious breath of Tyrolean air it is! It is set to "Down in the valley" at *Oxford* 161, and its melody suggests at once the Alpine yodelling technique:

Ex. 53

That phrase is essentially of the countryside; but even if "Stille nacht", known to us as "Silent night" or "Still the night", has a rustic origin, its idiom is urban to the last comma. "Silent night" has in our own time very nearly taken the place of "Good King Wenceslas" as the most popular of all foreign carols among English singers. At no point has it anything whatever in common with the true carol: it is even marked off from the carol category in this, that behind it lies the kind of anecdote that lies behind certain well known hymns. Unlike the apocryphal legends that have grown up round "Rock of Ages", the "Silent Night" story is well attested. It appears that on Christmas Eve, 1818, the organ broke down in the church of St. Nicholas, Oberndorf, in Upper Austria; this was a major crisis in the church and upset all the plans for the next day's music: for those were not the days of unaccompanied singing. The assistant priest of the church, whose name was Joseph Mohr, had written this carol, and he handed it to the acting organist, Franz Gruber, suggesting that he might set it to music that could be accompanied on a guitar, the only musical instrument available. This he did at once, setting it to music for two solo voices and the guitar, and it was sung the same evening. That might have been the end of it, had not the organ-builder, who came speedily after Christmas to repair the organ, been given a special performance of the carol that had saved the church from a musically silent Christmas. The organ builder was so impressed with the carol that he immediately spread it through the district, and after that nothing could stop it. In 1840 it was published in Austria in printed copies; but by that time it was already well known in the district where it was first sung.

"Silent night", then, is a homogeneous carol, in that its words and music, though written by different hands, were indissolubly wedded from the beginning. Its words form a lullaby-carol in the direct

Catholic tradition. Its tune is typical of its age and environment. Music of that kind, moving entirely in parallel thirds and sixths and suitable for singing in duet, was extremely popular in Catholic churches on the Continent. It recalls the hymn tunes of Bortniansky and Tcherlitzky, and the slightly later tunes (like STELLA, *E.H.*, Appendix 54) of the English Catholic revival, operatic and highly sentimental in their style, most of which go best as duets for soprano and alto (see *M.C.H.*, Chapter 21).

The first English translation of these words was made by Miss Emily E. S. Elliott about 1858 for the choir of St. Mark's Church, Brighton. The translation beginning "Silent night, holy night" is anonymous, having first appeared in the *Sunday School Hymnal* (1871). Other translations have been made, including that beginning "Still the night" by Stopford Brooke, which has been used in several English hymn books. Miss Elliott was also the author of the hymn, "Thou didst leave thy throne and thy kingly crown" (*E.H.* 585), which deserves at least this mention among carols. It is an evangelical hymn of the Incarnation and Atonement, and it is at least as much a carol of the nineteenth-century revival movement as "Hark the herald" was of the Wesleyan.

The popularity of this carol in England is independent of the romantic story of its origin. It happened to be the kind of tune that appealed widely in its own age—the kind of tune which in our time becomes a folk-song among the urbanised population. It will be noted, however, that it was not included in *Bramley and Stainer*; neither Woodward's books nor *Oxford* would touch it, and the only hymn books which include it are books of Dissenting ethos from the *Church Hymnary* (1927) onwards. In my own youth, say thirty years ago, it was not, I think, regarded as so indispensable a part of an English Christmas as it it now. I first learnt it not at Sunday school or in church but from an ancient gramophone record made by Ernestine Schumann-Heink in the early 1920s. Its popularity in this country in more recent years was materially assisted by the patronage of Mr. Bing Crosby, whose performance of it in a film, *The Bells of St. Mary's*, distributed about 1946, gave it a certain special status in public estimate. The real force in "Stille nacht" is, without doubt, the manner in which historically and stylistically it epitomises the German Christmas, cosy and child-centred, which was first becoming part of the English scene just when it was being composed. Christmas music nowadays extends along a long line, from "O come, all ye faithful" to "Jingle Bells", and, examining the opinions and presuppositions of the carol-book editors on the one hand and the ordinary singing populace on the other, one comes to the conclusion that "Silent Night" stands exactly half-way between those two.

POLAND AND CZECHOSLOVAKIA

The modest contributions of Poland and Czechoslovakia to the English repertory all sound the happier and more gracious note, and help to leaven the lump of our Protestant piety. The "Rocking Carol", or "Little Jesus, sweetly sleep" (*Oxford* 87) provokes three comments: first, that in its own right it is delightful, second that it has a dreadfully embarrassing final line, and third that its tune is of more than passing interest. In regard to our second comment, "Darling, darling little man" seems to have touched a protestant snag in your author's not very faithfully protestant mind, but he is not alone in finding it difficult to sing. When Dr. Geoffrey Bush was preparing his *Christmas Cantata* (Novello, 1949) he applied for, and was refused, permission to alter the line to "Gentle Jesus, God made man": a rejected, but none the less a very felicitous emendation, even though it departs from the last line of the original. (The only time the carol was used in the King's College Festival (in 1928), the last line appeared in the printed copy, "Little Jesus, God and Man".) The interesting thing about the tune is that it is clearly a variant of an almost universal nursery-rhyme, associated in England with "Twinkle, twinkle, little star". In the nursery-rhyme it is bare, in the carol charmingly decorated: but they are certainly the same. On the connexion between carols and nursery rhymes we shall say something in the final chapter.

The other Czech carol for which we have to thank the editors of *Oxford* is the Carol of the Birds, "From out of a wood did a cuckoo fly" (*Oxford* 103), a merry naturalistic folk-song, more carol-like than anything we have taken from Germany. I do not think Sullivan can have known it when he wrote the opening bars of the "Tit-willow" song (another bird-carol, to be sure) in *The Mikado*, even if he did have an unexpected knowledge of English folk music. But there is nothing else in the literature quite like "The Birds", and we are very glad to have it.

From Poland comes "Infant holy" (*C.P.* 696), which escaped the *Oxford* editors, but which at the present time is gaining ground. The tune appears in England as early as the *Hymnal Companion* (edition of 1877: dropped from the later edition), set in straight common time to "Angels from the realms of glory" at No. 80; but the carol in its proper form does not seem to have come into use before Miss E. M. G. Reed translated the words as we now have them; these were first printed in a periodical called *Music and Youth* and the first hymn book to include them with the tune was *School Worship* (1926). I am disposed to relate a dreadful story that exposes the fallibility of editors, if I may assume Christmas goodwill in the reader. When we sought to include the carol in *Congregational Praise* (1951), we looked at the author's ascription in the book from which we took it, which read "W Zlobie Lezy", and said, "Quite so: the English translator is Miss Reed, and the Polish author, no doubt, is Mr. Lezy." To our unlinguistic minds this seemed not improbable, so we noted it as by one W. Zlobie Lezy, with a full point after the W. It was only some years later that a distinguished man of science, who knew Polish, wrote and gently told us that "w zlobie lezy" is Polish for "He lies in the cradle". What we had done was as if we had written, of "O come, O come, Immanuel" that its translator was J. M. Neale, and its original author, V. Immanuel. Had we read our Edmundstone Duncan we should have been delivered, for on p. 53 of his book he prints the tune, ascribing it rather optimistically to the thirteenth century, with the original Polish words. Whoever wrote it, it was not a Mr. Lezy. I am sure this would not have happened to the *Oxford* editors: but then, they did not print it at all.

HOLLAND

We have several carols, and several tunes for synthetic carols, from Holland. We should be much the poorer without that little gem, *Jesus's Bloemhof*, variously translated in English with first lines in the form "Lord Jesus hath a garden" (*Oxford* 105, *Cowley* 67). One of the earliest translations, and one of the most attractive, was that of Woodward in *Cowley*, whose refrain to all verses but the last runs:

> There nought is heard but Paradise bird,
> Harp, dulcimer, lute and cymbal,
> Trump and tymbal,
> And the tender soothing flute.

There is a truculent and un-Christmassy note in the version printed in the *University Carol Books*, Book II, No. 10, which disparages Woodward's version as full of "grievous error"; it seems that the paradisebird cannot sing, and that the orchestra in the original contains no percussion section or brass, but only harp, flute and clarinet (like Ravel's *Introduction and Allegro*). By the time they have done with him, poor Woodward sounds as immoral as Respighi arranging Bach; the version above this testy criticism was written by the Bishop of Southwell,

Dr. F. R. Barry, who keeps near the Dutch, but writes "Imperial Crown for Woodward's "Crown Imperial", which is certainly a pity. However all this may be, nobody can deny the imaginative appeal of the lyric, which is not a carol for any church season, but a sacred song about the Christian virtues. It leavens and lightens any collection that includes it: and we may note that English editors were not slow to do this, for it was first translated by S. S. Greatheed as early as 1856, and was included in E. Sedding's *Christmas Carols* (1860) and in his *People's Hymnal* (1867); but it was not in *Bramley and Stainer*. The tune, which with the original words is dated 1633 from its first publication, but may well be older, appears in many different versions, all rhythmically different at the end. That of the *University Carol Book* is the nearest to the original, but that in *Oxford* is the most familiar in England.

The other Dutch carol well known in England is that which has given its tune to "This joyful Eastertide" (*Cowley* 51). The tune was introduced to this country with those words by G. R. Woodward as No. 8 in *Carols for Easter and Ascensiontide* (1894), where it was harmonised by W. H. (later Bishop) Frere. It went into *Cowley*, there harmonised by Charles Wood, and then into *Oxford*, arranged by Geoffrey Shaw, with new words by Dearmer ("How great the harvest is", No. 152). It is a magnificent tune, but appropriate though it is to Easter (since Woodward made it so), it was originally a harvest song, "Hoo groot die Vreuchten zijh", in a seventeenth-century Amsterdam psalter. That original first line has actually been kept in the *Oxford* carol set to this tune, but the rest of the carol refers to Whitsuntide and Trinity Sunday, not to the natural harvest. *Oxford* says that in the seventeenth century the tune was very popular in Holland, but it appears to be hardly known there at the present time. I have shown it to several Dutch friends, including the eminent hymnologist, Dr. G. J. Hoenderdaal of Amsterdam: none had seen it before. Dr. Frank Fletcher (1870–1954), sometime Head Master of Charterhouse, wrote Christmas words for the tune in the *Clarendon Hymn Book* (No. 53), whose first verse runs:

> Let joy your carols fill:
> Away with sin and sadness!
> To men of gentle will
> Be peace on earth and gladness!
> O man with sorrow worn,
> Your chains the Lord has riven,
> To you a Child is born,
> To you a Son is given.

Other Dutch carols are at *Oxford* 73 (obviously a cousin of *Puer natus in Bethlehem*, 85 and 120), 89, another of the same general character, and 100, *De Boodschap*, a spacious lyric of obviously later date and of haunting phrase. Dutch tunes to other words are at No. 134, in merry triple time, and No. 153, which one feels would have been popular in eighteenth-century Cornwall had it been known there. No. 100 apart, there is nothing of marked individuality here; but then they come from the pre-individualistic age, and preserve much more of the workaday folk-song idiom than do most of the carols that we have taken from the neighbouring countries.

FRANCE

The other country to which we owe a great deal is, of course, France. Here more than in any of the other countries of Europe that have supplied us with carols we see the lively survivals of a catholic peasant culture. There is nothing in music so childlike as the French *noel*, with its short and often repetitive phrases, and its absolutely unsophisticated grace. Take for example the best known of all French carol tunes, that which we know as IRIS, and which we have already mentioned as a tune commonly sung to Montgomery's "Angels from the realms of glory" (*Oxford* 119). Every carol-singer now knows it, with its almost monotonous opening phrases and its delightful sequential "Gloria". The French noel which carried this tune began "Les anges dans nos campagnes", and the first appearance of the tune in an English book carried an English translation of that carol by the Rev. G. Grantham beginning "When the crimson sun had set", and setting the opening lines in this form:

When the crimson sun had set Low be-hind the win-try sea.

This was in the 1875 edition of Chope, and another translation of the original French, "Angels we have heard on high", appears at No. 42 in the *Hymnal* (1941) of the Episcopal Church of the U.S.A., with the tune as Chope had it. Yet another variant of the tune, described as a "Bavarian Air", appears with Grantham's words at *U.C.B.*, V, 32. *U.C.B.*, II, 15, has the more familiar form of the tune and calls it "Old French". But more commonly Englishmen sing the tune in the less sophisticated form either to Montgomery's hymn or to words beginning "Shepherds in the field abiding", by Woodward (*Cowley* 68).

CAROLS FROM OTHER COUNTRIES 207

The repetitive opening phrases offer much scope to the ingenuity of the harmoniser, and Charles Wood's setting in *Cowley* is a very delightful but never oppressive adornment.

The other famous "Gloria" tune is that associated with Woodward's "Ding dong, merrily on high" (*Cambridge* 2), so long associated with the King's College Festival. This tune, more developed and dramatic than the other, comes as one might expect from a more learned source. It is in an old French book published in 1588 entitled *Orchésographie*, which is a fanciful classicism for "A Book of dances". Its editor styled himself Thoinot Arbeau, but this is an anagram of his real name, Johan Tabourot. Tabourot (1519–93) was a canon of Langres, and the *Orchésographie* immortalises his name, not only because of the treasure of delightful tunes it contains, but also because of the pleasure to be had from reading his text. Three quotations from it, translated by Cyril W. Beaumont, are given in Dr. Percy Scholes's *Oxford Companion to Music*, first edition, 1938, p. 248, of which we may be allowed to reproduce one:

> When you dance in company, never look down to examine your steps and ascertain if you dance correctly. Hold your head and body upright, with a confident mien, and do not spit or blow your nose much. And if necessity obliges you to do so, turn your head away, and use a fair white handkerchief.

There is nothing world-denying or unduly cloistered about the good Canon's perception of the decencies of the ballroom. DING DONG, MERRILY was originally a *Branle*, that is, a round dance of rustic origin which found its way into aristocratic circles in the seventeenth century, chiefly through Tabourot's work, and which, like the *Gavotte* and the *Bourrée*, was originally accompanied by singing. That is to say, its origin is just where carols themselves have their origin, and nothing could be more appropriate than to find carol words for such a tune. Another *Branle* is similarly treated at *Cambridge* 6, and yet another, a very dramatic fragment in which you can hear, as it were, the stamp of feet and the clapping of hands, at *Cambridge* 45. At *Cambridge* 7 there is a Gavotte with carol words. Tabourot is revived for modern ears in Peter Warlock's *Capriol* Suite for orchestra, founded on dances all of which come from Tabourot; on the other hand, some enterprising souls have attempted to make a hymn tune of Tabourot's *Pavane*, which is also heard as one of the movements in the Warlock.

Sandys preserves in his collection a few French dialect carols. A popular and amusing one is *Guillô, pran ton tambourin*, translated in

Oxford, "Willie take your little drum" (No. 82), and rendered by Woodward "Hob and Colin, Yule is come" (*Cambridge* 15). Here is the first verse of the original:

> Guillô, pran ton tambourin;
> Toi, pran ton fleûte, Robin.
> Au son de cés instruman,
> Turelurelu, patapatapan;
> Au son de cés instruman
> Je diron Noei gaiman.

Carols from Besançon and Béarnais sources are, as we have seen, found in *Bramley and Stainer*, usually set to unsuitable tunes, but they missed one French folk carol which Woodward rescued in *Cambridge* (No. 12), namely QUITTEZ PASTEURS. *Oxford* (144) sets it to words appropriate to Lent, but a serviceable translation of the original beginning "Now leave your sheep" will be found at *Congregational Praise* 720. This is a typically gay and cheerful melody, running up and down the scale like a child trying out the stairs in a new house.

All these are uninhibited, cheerful melodies. But the most interesting thing about French carols is the strange ambivalence of mood we encounter in many of them. It is very broadly safe to say that if you hear a carol sung to a tune in the minor mode, it is likely to be a French carol. That will not hold water all the way, of course; GOD REST YOU MERRY and THE LORD AT FIRST DID ADAM MAKE and the COVENTRY CAROL come at once to mind. Yet there is, among the tunes we have so far dealt with, a striking preponderance of the major mode. This is historically to be explained by the fact that by the fifteenth century the Ionian mode (our major scale) was becoming accepted for popular music, and while popular music would tolerate any of the other church modes, for some reason the church was shy for many generations of the Ionian; in consequence tunes of great antiquity but of popular origin (like SUMER IS ICUMEN IN) sound much less outlandish to the key-conditioned modern ear then church tunes that may be a couple of centuries later. Therefore most carol tunes from England and abroad use the Ionian mode, which, apart from the matter of modulation, sounds like a modern major scale. It is further to be observed that there is a rather higher proportion of minor-mode carols in England than in Germany, which corresponds with a reluctance in England until a late date to accept the distinction between sacred and secular in music which was allowed to prevail on the Continent.

But there are many French carols, some of quite late date, that use

CAROL SINGING IN THE TWENTIETH CENTURY
Students of King's College, London, singing at Lincoln's Inn

CAROLS IN WESTMINSTER HALL

minor keys freely, and use them not with any solemn intention, still less to produce a mournful effect (it is only a romantic fashion that leads people into the error that minor keys are sad), but simply to imply innocent pathos. Since French is the one foreign language that remains inescapable in English education, a few French carols are known untranslated over here, and many children delight in them. Is not there something quite unlike any other kind of carol in the atmosphere of this?

Ex. 55

Entre le bœuf et l'â - ne gris   Dort, dort, dort le petit fils

Mille anges divins Mille seraphins Volent à l'entour de ce Dieu d'amour.

That is innocent pathos: pathos, I mean, without gluey pity. There is tragedy as well as comedy in the Nativity; a comedy of incongruity, a tragedy of human unreadiness and blindness nowhere better summed up than in the simple words of a great Christmas hymn:

> Haste with the shepherds, see
> The mystery of grace:
> A manger-bed, a child
> Is all the eye can trace.
>
> Is this the eternal Son,
> Who on the starry throne
> Before the worlds began
> Was with the Father one?

"Is this . . .?" That is the question which the French touch can put more subtly than any other. That is why the tune of the French carol, "Jésus Christ s'habille en pauvre" can, without the alteration of a single note, become one of the most solemn of English hymn tunes. Yet that tune, PICARDY, which we sing to "Let all mortal flesh keep silence" or to "Sing, my tongue, the glorious battle", has a virility, almost a ferocity, that never descends to typical minor-key introspection of the kind we get in music like Tchaikovsky's LEGEND.

Another French tune that has found its way all over the continent as well as to England is what we call JESU DULCIS MEMORIA (*E.H.* 238,ii), set in English books to "Jesu the very thought is sweet", but known in many parts of France and in the Basque country as a carol (see *U.C.B.*, II, 11). Then there is that fascinating Dorian-mode tune,

Noel Nouvelet, to be found with Easter words at *Oxford* 149, which has also achieved fame by becoming the subject of one of Marcel Dupré's best known organ pieces, *Variations on a French Noel:*

Ex.56

"Je sais, Vierge Marie" (*Oxford* 162) and "Un nouveaux présent des Cieux", whose tune appears in Wales as the hymn tune ARFON, are both well known to Englishmen. But there is one French carol, "Promptement levez-vous, mon voisin" (a first line which suggests "Dame, get up and bake your pies") which seems to have been known to them three or four centuries ago. It furnishes an example of that interchange of folk-songs between this country and the Continent in the sixteenth century on which an extended comment in the field of hymnody will be found in *M.C.H.*. pp. 23f. The French tune appears at *Oxford* 166 in this form:

Ex.57

This clearly has something to do with the maypole dance given in Playford's *Dancing Master* (1651) and Chappell's *Popular Music of Olden Time* in the following form:

Ex.58

Whether this is originally an English or a French tune is impossible to determine at this time of day; but the English form of the tune

has certainly taken to itself something of the typically French ambivalence, in as much as it has been used by the editors of modern hymn
books as well as of carol books. Woodward put it in *Cowley*. The Public
School Book sets it to "Come, O come, in pious lays", the *Methodist
Hymn Book* to "Sinners, turn, why will ye die?" and *E.H.* (89) to "Soul
of Jesus", a very solemn and intimate meditation on the prayer *Anima
Christi*. The simplified form in which (arranged first in *E.H.*) it appears
in all these places seems to go equally well in the context of praise and
in that of penitence. Like PICARDY, it changes its character quite radically
when the speed of singing is altered. It is only when one recalls the
rhythmic urge and festive associations of the original that one finds
it difficult to sing as a penitential tune. This is the hymn form:

Ex. 59

How different all this is from the suave German and Austrian style,
from the tenderness of QUEM PASTORES and the heavenly lilt of IN
DULCI JUBILO. When you have become aware of the pawkiness of the
typical French carol with its short phrases and abrupt rhythms, it
becomes the more impressive and remarkable that the French psalters
of 1542–62, whose publication was presided over by John Calvin,
and whose music up to 1551 was edited by that great genius Louis
Bourgeois, contain so many tunes of long, spacious phrase and of
large-scale harmonic architecture. These melodies, composed for the
Genevan metrical psalters, were often founded on popular tunes, but
their style is as unmistakably ecclesiastical as the carol style is secular.
They are indeed symbolic of the church tradition of Calvinism, of all
Reformed traditions the most austere in its distinction between sacred
and secular. One or two of the Genevan psalm tunes are set to carol
words by Woodward (see for example, *Cambridge* 30, and other places),
and many more are set to hymns in his great hymn collection, *Songs of
Syon* (1904 and 1910). On the whole the hymn is their proper association, just because they have abandoned so decisively the popular carol
style.

One or two French carols of later vintage retain the popular accent.
We may reasonably class with the carols the splendid Easter tune
O FILII ET FILIAE (*E.H.* 626), which goes with the words translated by
Neale, "O sons and daughters, let us sing". The carol narrates the

Resurrection story in a simple style, and the tune in its earlier form is more truly festive than the flamboyant form in which Webbe introduced it into this country at the end of the eighteenth century. Both forms are at *E.H.* 626, but there is little point nowadays in using the later. Neither words or tune is probably older than the Reformation. Even later, but certainly festive and in the true carol tradition, is "Dans cet étable" (*Oxford* 75), familiar in Gounod's amusing arrangement. (How horrid a static bass is in four-part hymns, and how light and appropriate it can be in a carol!)

BASQUE CAROLS

A fruitful source for the English repertory has been the Basque country. We owe it chiefly to the *University Carol Books* that so many Basque carols are now known here; the author whose settings of Basque tunes are most celebrated is Baring-Gould himself. One of the finest tunes for which he provided words is "The Angel Gabriel":

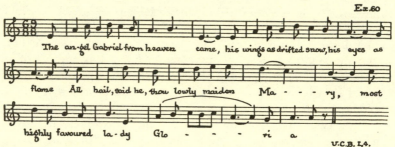

Ex.60

The an-gel Gabriel from heaven came, his wings as drifted snow, his eyes as flame All hail, said he, thou lowly maiden Ma - - - ry, most highly favoured la - dy Glo - - - ri a

U.C.B. L.4.

Equally well known, especially since it has been included in the King's College Festival for some ten years up to 1956, is "The Infant King", or "Sing Lullaby", also by Baring-Gould (*U.C.B.* 9), which recently made its first appearance in a hymn book as No. 385 in *Christian Praise* (1957). The words of this carol are somewhat along the lines of Caswall's "Sleep, holy Babe", but the music lightens them, and they lead in their last verse to an Easter climax. The other Basque lullaby, adapted by Edgar Pettman to the ancient words, "I saw a maiden sitting and sing" (*U.C.B.* 12) has also been honoured by King's College, and worthily. In this carol only the first two lines are traditional; the refrain, with its delightful change of rhythm, is the work of Edgar Pettman himself.

Many others of these carols can be studied in the same accessible source. The variety of styles which they display leads us to a feeling of regret that those who communicated them did not leave any record of their original versions. If indeed we have authentic versions in the carols we know, then it is obvious that the melodies come from different periods of musical history. "The Infant King" (*U.C.B.* 9), with its shapely and continuous melody, suggests a quite different period of culture from that of "The Angel Gabriel", and both are different from "Hasten to Bethlehem" (*U.C.B.* 13). They seem to have been somewhat drastically anglicised in the versions that we know; that is not to say that they are not, as we have them, tunes of great beauty. The most English of them all, two-thirds of which is by Edgar Pettman —"I saw a maiden"—is perhaps the most beautiful. But their beauty is not now always of the folk-song kind.

OTHER EUROPEAN COUNTRIES

Carols from many other countries will be found in various English collections. The *Italian Carol Book*, for example, has added some delightful things to our repertory, the best known of which is "Hail, blessed Virgin Mary", which is often sung at the King's College Festival. *Oxford* has nothing from Italy, but one or two interesting things from Spain (No. 81 is a very extraordinary piece indeed), and further search among the many books now available often brings unexpected treasures to light. In a book of less than three-volume size we can handle only what is well known or easily accessible to the reader, and it is fair to say that nothing from these countries has become well known yet, although you never know when some enterprising conductor of a carolare will produce something delectable that has never been heard in England before. We have said enough to illustrate the European folk traditions in the Teutonic and the Latin contexts, but it remains to mention one country, namely Russia, which has given us a few scraps of Slavonic music that add a special colour to the repertory.

Neither of the Russian folk-carols in *Oxford* is, in its own right, of great importance. No. 94, "Easter eggs", is a carol of benevolence, and No. 107, "Praise to God in the highest" is a general song of social goodwill which would be quite safe in modern Russia, being in no explicit sense Christian. "Praise to God" has a tune that has become celebrated in being used here and there in classical music. Rimsky-Korsakov used it in a cantata, Liapunov uses it in one of his *Christmas pieces* for piano, and Beethoven, as a compliment to his patron, includes the tune in the trio of the third movement of his String Quartet in E minor, Op. 59, No. 2, one of the three dedicated to Count Rasumovsky.

Both these folk-carols are very fragmentary and primitive in their music; but the carol for which most of us have to thank Russia is that which is called *Tschaikovsky's Legend* (*Oxford* 197). This is No. 5 of his Op. 54 (1883), *Sixteen Songs for Children*, all of whose words are by the Russian poet, Plechtcheyev. It was (like Cornelius's carols) originally a solo, but is familiar to us as a choral piece. Arensky used it as the theme of his *Variations for String Orchestra on a Theme of Tchaikovsky*. The tune is, of course, far from the traditional Russian style; all Tchaikovsky's work was directed towards a breaking through the nationalistic musical barrier which in generations before him had surrounded Russian musicians. Tchaikovsky's music is never typically Russian, but it is always, of course, typical Tchaikovsky, cosmopolitan if you will, but intensely personal. This tune, with its dying fall, is highly characteristic, and the rather gruesome story told by the words is, one feels, the sort of story that a Russian versifier of the period would choose, and that Tchaikovsky would choose to set to music. The origin of the legend of the disagreeable playmates of Jesus is entirely obscure. It fits in plausibly enough with the story recounted in "The Holy Well" (see above, p. 53), but what it most looks like is a Sunday School address of a pious but slightly morbid kind. It would not surprise us to find the origin of this unpleasant but popular libretto in the Apocryphal Gospels, but as a matter of fact it is not in any that have survived.

THE BRITISH ISLES (EXCLUDING ENGLAND)

There are few carols, as foreign to modern English protestant culture as any from farther away, that come from nearer home. *Oxford* has an interesting handful of Welsh carols of a somewhat sophisticated kind. The simplest and perhaps the oldest of Welsh carols is "Suo-Gân", described in *Welsh Bards* (1793) as "the lullaby song which the Welsh nurses sing to compose the children to sleep". Its melody could hardly be more rudimentary, consisting as it does of three notes in four bars :

Ex. 61

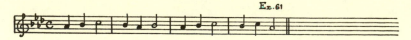

But most of the Welsh carols now in English currency have commended themselves because of the peculiarly haunting qualities of Welsh music. Welsh hymn tunes of the kind now very well known in England were mostly composed under the inspiration of the Welsh Evangelical Revival, and the golden age of their composition was about 1770–1870 (see *M.C.H.*, Chapter 20). Some of the tunes of the Welsh carols have close affinity with the hymn tunes of that period. The glorious tune OLWEN, set at *Oxford* 34 to "All poor men and humble", from the Welsh "O Deued pob Cristion" is one of this kind, with its anapaestic rhythm and that insistence on the notes of the common chord which is so marked a feature of the major-mode Welsh hymn tunes (the translation in *Oxford* is by Miss K. E. Roberts. A translation of the original second verse by Principal Pennar Davies will be found at *C.P.* 721). Some, on the other hand, are older. NOS GALAN, for example (*Oxford* 50), looks much less like an evangelical Welsh hymn tune than SEREN BETHLEHEM (*Oxford* 9), which we know to have been composed by a Welsh anglican clergyman. But few traditional Welsh carols have come into English use, and it is only natural that Welsh carols should have been largely assimilated to the hymn form, seeing that the Welsh sacred lyric and music were affected by the Evangelical Revival even more profoundly than the English.

In Scotland puritanism laid a heavy hand on carol singing. It is, indeed, a clearer picture than that of England; for Scotland has never had the kind of feudal agricultural system that formed the backbone of English medieval life. There never was such rich soil in Scotland as in England for the carol to grow in, and puritanism, when it came, affected radically just those parts of Scotland which might have nurtured a carol-culture, the Lowland, while the districts it left unaffected were as destitute of a carol-culture (for the same reason) as Cumberland. It was something more fierce than carols that formed the singing material of the Highland clans.

Scottish minstrelsy, however, has its finest flower in the songs of the mountains and the love-ballads of Gaelic minstrels. A remarkable collection of these was recently published by Dr. Arthur Geddes, which contains besides much interesting material of a secular kind one carol entitled "The World's Light". Translated from the Gaelic by Dr. Geddes, it runs as follows:

> The world, ere came the Son of God
>   Was dark, a bog forlorn,
> Void of sun, of moon or star,
>   Void of body, heart or form.
> 'Twas Mary, Mother tender, kneeled,
>   The inmost Being brought to birth,
> Darkness and tears were driven afar,
>   The guiding star rose o'er the earth.
>
> Light on the Land the Deep illumed
>   From sullen gloom to ocean stream:
> Grief was laid and joy was raised,
>   With praise and hail and harping free.

Illumined hills, illumined plains,
  Illumed the ocean, sea and firth;
Illumed the whole wide world as one,
  The hour God's Son came down to earth.

Light o'er the land from hills to plain,
  Light o'er grey-green deep and first,
Light o'er all the world as one,
  The hour God's Son came here on earth.

Dr. Geddes' accompanying note contains these sentences: "With the Old Style calendar, Christmas Day—Noel—came after our New Year. Thus Noel, and the following twelve days of Christmastide, brought lengthening days and strengthening cold, snow on the hills and light on land and sea." The lines, uncouth though the translation may be, evoke the grey Scottish winter light quite unmistakably.

Duncan preserves one Scottish carol, from a late edition (1621) of *Ane Compendious Buik of Godly and Spirituall Songs*, beginning

I come from hevin to tell
The best nowellis that ever befell;
To yow this tythings trew I bring
And I will of them say and sing.

It is crude stuff, contrived by a very rusty minstrel. Beyond these there is little of interest from Scotland; the words "Scottish traditional" have no place in the authors' or composers' indexes of *Oxford*, even though one tune, that set to *Rorate caeli* (125) could be so described.

Ireland is another matter. Here we have an ancient Catholic civilisation delighting in community and friendly chatter, and here minstrels could flourish. Three really notable examples are preserved in *Oxford*. The earliest is an ecclesiastical composition, corresponding in context (but not in form) with the English manuscript carols. It is *Angelus ad Virginem* (*Oxford* 52), which appears in a Dublin Troper dated about 1300 now preserved in Cambridge. It is a ceremonious carol of the Annunciation, originally written to do duty as a Sequence, that is, to adorn the Mass at its special season by adding a composed lyric to the regular "Alleluias" of the rite. Its words and tune are of great dignity and grace. (*Oxford* does not translate these words, but gives a specimen verse of the original English translation in a footnote. A modern translation by Gabriel Gillett (b. 1873) will be found at No. 3 in the *English Carol Book*, and another by Canon J. M. C. Crum (b. 1872) in *Hymns A. & M.* (*Revised*) at No. 547, where the tune is given in a different version, arranged by Sir Sydney Nicholson.)

Most of the Irish folk-carols now sung we owe to the researches of Dr. Grattan Flood (1859–1928), an Irish Catholic organist and musicologist. He is acknowledged at several points in *Oxford*, and especially for the contribution of No. 14, "The Wexford Carol", and No. 6, "Christmas Day is come". The former of these, beginning, "Good people all", is an unusually interesting composition. The words were noted from an Irish singer, but they share at least four lines with the unequivocally English carol, "All ye who are to mirth inclined" (*Oxford* 51). Which country had it originally we cannot tell; we have before noted examples of Irish tunes being found also in England, and this will be another example of such interchange, possibly indicating that it was a two-way traffic. Of the tune given in *Oxford* there can be no doubt at all. It is one of the most remarkable carol tunes that have been preserved to us. Its first half is in the mixolydian mode (G major without the F sharp)—and we may note once again how infrequently we have had to mention the ecclesiastical modes in this book. But in its second half the tonality shifts down a whole tone. There is what in modern music would be called a modulation: but it is the one modulation (a whole tone up or down) which is hardly ever found in music of the style that depends for its form on modulations. In all the carol tunes we have encountered, this is unique in modulating at all, except for the conventional half-close in the dominant at the half-way point. The secret of what strikes the modern ear as a strange and outlandish melody is that it is indeed pure melody. It sounds more natural and is easier to sing without harmony than with it. Although *Oxford* prints it, it is remarkable enough to quote again here:

Ex.62

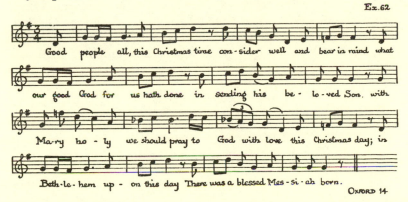

Good people all, this Christmas time con-sider well and bear in mind what our good God for us hath done in sending his be-lo-ved Son. with Mary ho-ly we should pray to God with love this Christmas day; in Beth-le-hem up-on this day There was a blessed Mes-si-ah born.

OXFORD 14

The other Irish-carol, *Oxford* 6, introduces the name of Bishop Luke Wadding (1588–1657) of Ferns, whose book of songs, *A Pious Garland*

of Godly Songs, was published in 1680, and forms the primary collection
of Irish folk-carols. In many cases he wrote words for traditional tunes,
much in the manner of G. R. Woodward, and the original of *Oxford* 6
was his. The modernised version makes a vigorous companion for the
tune in *Oxford*, but I am glad to be allowed to quote the following
carol, written recently for the same words by Anne Scott:

> Come, ye thankful people, and welcome Christ to earth
> With songs of joy and gladness at this amazing birth.
> For now within the manger the new-born Baby lies;
> For him the angels' music is ringing through the skies.
> They hail with adoration the one eternal Word
> That has to earth descended to be by all men heard.
>
> A maiden and a baby, a stable cold and bare,
> Yet never was there palace that could with this compare.
> For here the Queen of angels her son and God adores
> While he his heavenly Father for all mankind implores.
> He comes from highest heaven to end our woe and strife,
> That we may live for ever with his celestial life.
>
> "Holy, Holy, Holy" the glorious angels cry,
> And "Holy, Holy, Holy" let Christians now reply.
> Gold and myrrh and incense are gifts from Eastern kings,
> But prayer and adoration the poorest of us brings,
> As singing with the angels "Nowell, nowell, nowell",
> We worship in the manger our Lord, Emmanuel.

Duncan (pp. 236 ff) prints two other Irish carols of excellent quality
one from Luke Wadding and the other from P. W. Joyce's *Old Irish
Folk Music and Songs* (1909). Wadding's carol is a song for St. Stephen's
day, a verse from which gives some idea of its forthright diction:

> This champion of the Cross
> To conquer death did die,
> Sufferings are his triumphs,
> Death is his victory.
> The stones like showers of hail
> Which Jews on him did cast
> Became pure crowns of pearls
> And palms which ever last.

The tune of the other, "The Leading of the star" is altogether too good
to miss:

Ex. 63.

Grattan Flood says that this is originally a secular song, "The captivating youth"; but it was worth baptizing.

It may be observed that these few examples of Irish carol music provide an excellent epitome of the rich variety of styles to be found in Irish music. It is tempting to offer to identify some tune already known to be Irish as Irish on the ground of its style; it is sometimes said that you can always tell an Irish tune because of the double repetition of the keynote at the cadence (as in Ex. 62 or SLANE or DANIEL or THE WEARING OF THE GREEN). But as a matter of fact there is no single feature that you can rely on an Irish tune to produce, and no corpus of music so rich in surprises as the Irish. Anything from the rollicking high spirits of the tune last quoted to the most sombre lament is within the compass of the Irish minstrels, and our carol books and hymn books are very greatly enriched by their compositions.

The Isle of Man has contributed one tune to *Oxford*, at No. 167. Others are preserved in *JFSS*. While the tunes are often of considerable interest, the words are not worth much attention. They are collected in A. W. Moore's *Carvalyn Gailckagh* (1891) without music, and these *carvals*, or ballads on sacred subjects, are rightly dismissed by Duncan as largely trivial. They were chiefly written after the publication of the Manx Bible in 1772. George Borrow wrote romantically about them, but one passage of his is worth repeating:

"These carols were formerly sung in the parish churches on Christmas Eve ... though many of them, both from their contents and their enormous length, were quite unsuitable for such an occasion. ... After the prayers were read and a hymn sung, the parson usually went home, leaving the clerk in charge. Then each one who had a carol to sing would do so in turn, so that the proceedings were continued until a very late hour, and sometimes also, unfortunately, became of a rather riotous character, as it was a custom for the female part of the congregation to provide themselves with peas, which they flung at their bachelor friends."

This sounds rather like a horrid parody of I Corinthians 14.26. The quality of the words of these songs was such that they were rendered little worse by this profane treatment. Nothing is to be gained by quoting them in the Manx tongue, but Duncan says that, "for the most part didactic, they lack the picturesque imagery and the quaint rustic melody of the best of our English carols". Some indication of their trend can be gathered from the fact that one of the best of them is a Manx version of "Jacob's Ladder" (*Oxford* 58).

AMERICA

Finally, we must turn to America, which has enriched the popular carol repertory with two pieces that have become irreplaceable. America's true carols are, of course, the negro spiritual, and even these are the sacred folk-songs of an immigrant people. In the nature of things, America has not lived long enough as a nation to find a folk-song of its own, unless we are to judge that ragtime and its descendants are indeed the folk-song of America. But two modern carols from America are among the very first Christmas carols learnt by English children. One is "We three kings of orient are", whose words and music were both written, in true minstrel-tradition, by Dr. J. H. Hopkins, Rector of Christ's Church, Williamsport, Pennsylvania, about 1857. It was immediately successful, and was printed in *Bramley and Stainer* as its solitary American example. The effective dramatic form of the verses and the very simple tune made it at once a favourite among children.

The other, also for children, is "Away in a manger", first printed anonymously in Philadelphia in 1885. It has had many tunes in its time; one American scholar has collected forty-one. But one tune is inseparable from it in this country, and it is the work of an energetic Gospel-song composer, W. J. Kirkpatrick, who was musical director at Grace Church, Philadelphia. This, published in 1895, is the only piece of music by which the editor of sixty Gospel song-books is remembered. There used to be a superstition that Luther wrote both words and tune; the best we can do for that is to say that conceivably the words were suggested to their author by the sight of some verses of *Vom Himmel hoch*; but the tune would have seemed as strange to Luther as the music of Herbert Howells would have seemed to Scarlatti.

It remains only to say, in closing this chapter, that in one respect we have everything to learn. What will happen when we begin to hear indigenous carols from those regions of the world in which the traditional date of Christmas falls in midsummer? How will it be when the very European mythology of the modern carol collides head-on with utterly different mythologies from the younger churches? The ordinary English repertory has not yet begun to touch that apprehension of the Nativity theme which is represented in our illustration from Ceylon. What folk-songs of the Passion and of Eastertide will come when that East-country from which the Faith came to the West, and in which it has been all but obliterated for twelve centuries by Islam, returns to the Faith? It is too early yet even to speculate; for Christian song in the African and Asiatic communities is still very largely Western by imposition or imitation. It is early to speculate, but hardly too early, perhaps, to hope.

Carols Today

ALL the familiar carols have now passed under review. The most recent compositions to become folk-songs of present-day Christendom have now been before us: I take it that they are "Away in a manger" and "In the bleak midwinter". Carols are, of course, still being written, but nothing less than two generations old has had time to be tested in popular use and found sound or wanting.

Carols are still being written, and both in words and in music they are being written at a higher standard than at any time since the seventeenth century. The final section of *Oxford* has some exquisite specimens, and at other places in the same collection modern authors have been called on for translations or for new words to old tunes. But we have to remember that what is happening now is more like what happened in the early seventeenth century than what happened in the sixteenth. Nearly all modern carols are designed for singing not in the market-place but somewhere where there is either a good choir or a domestic gathering of singers who enjoy an intimate singing party. *Oxford* itself, in its modern sections, resembles the carols of Byrd and the lutenists more than those of the minstrels.

Subject to that, we can find much beautiful work among contemporary writers. A modern carol that has very nearly become a folk-song in its own right is Frances Chesterton's "How far is it to Bethlehem?" (*Oxford* 142), so felicitously mated with its West Country tune. Mrs. Chesterton's distinguished husband would have been the last man in the world to describe himself as a minstrel, but he has achieved something like minstrelsy in his lines beginning "The Christ child lay in Mary's lap" (*Oxford* 143). What an inspiration it was, again, when the *Oxford* editors turned to A. A. Milne, that master of wit and innocence, for words to carry a French carol tune (No. 106). Milne is as right for the French idiom as he would be wrong for the German:

> Poor Satan, you can hear him,
> Is raging down in hell,
> For now there's none to fear him,
> And none to wish him well.

The fires that he was keeping
Are on his footsteps creeping,
So brother! laugh and sing
That Christ the Lord is King!

Selwyn Image is another who catches the modern carol idiom to perfection. Two of his compositions are in *Oxford*, "The snow lies thick upon the earth" (192) and "Three Kings in great glory" (194); a third was No. 4 in the *English Carol Book*:

As up the wood I took my way
   The oaks were brown and bare,
And all about the snow was white,
      The snow was white,
      The snow was white,
And all about the snow was white
      And bitter blew the air. . . .

And suddenly grew the snow to rose,
   The bare oaks grew to green,
The bitter wind was a gentle air,
      And I felt not fear or teen.

For golden Gabriel took my hand,
   And brought me to the shed,
Where 'mid the cattle sat Queen Mary
      And rocked Lord Jesus' bed.

Then hie! good shepherds and masters mine,
   We'll cease to moil and grieve;
For this brave Babe is the Lord of all,
      And this is Christmas Eve!

There is the dedicated imagination, there the delicate-coloured adjective and the bold choice of words. But for sheer narrative sweep nothing comes near that wonderful carol of Walter de la Mare (*Oxford* 163), "The Three Traitors". *Oxford* sets it to the tune THE THREE KNIGHTS, the dance-tune found at the end of Sandys's collection. They are verses which would stand a weight of commentary, but they had better speak for themselves. Note how the uncanny silence of a snowy walk is evoked in a word or two, and the biting irony with which the three traitors are shown as impressive figures, and one of them is named only in the very last line. I do not know where you will find the old carol-style more bravely integrated with the harsh complexity of modern life than here:

A BALLAD OF CHRISTMAS

It was about the deep of night,
  And still was earth and sky,
When 'neath the moonlight shining bright
  Three ghosts came riding by.

Beyond the sea, beyond the sea,
  Lie kingdoms for them all:
I wot their steeds trod wearily—
  Their journey was not small.

By rock and desert, sand and stream
  They footsore late did go:
Now like a sweet and blessed dream
  Their path was deep with snow.

Shining like hoar-frost rode they on,
  Three ghosts in earth's array;
It was about the hour when wan
  Night turns at hint of day.

O, but their hearts with woe distraught
  Hailed not the wane of night,
Only for Jesu still they sought
  To wash them clean and white.

For bloody was each hand, and dark
  With death each orbless eye;
It was three Traitors mute and stark
  Came riding silent by.

Silver their raiment and their spurs,
  And silver-shod their feet,
And silver-pale each face that stares
  Into the moonlight sweet.

And he upon the left that rode
  Was Pilate, Prince of Rome,
Whose journey once lay far abroad,
  And now was nearing home.

And he upon the right that rode,
  Herod of Salem sate,
Whose mantle dipped in children's blood
  Shone clear as Heaven's gate.

And he these twain betwixt that rode,
  Was clad as white as wool,
Dyed in the Mercy of his God,
  White was he crown to sole.

Throned mid a myriad Saints in bliss
  Rise shall the Babe of Heaven
To shine on these three ghosts, I wis,
  Smit through with sorrows seven.

Babe of the Blessed Trinity
  Shall smile their steeds to see:
Herod and Pilate riding by,
  And Judas one of three.

Elsewhere in the modern poets you will find Nativity poems which might, given the right tunes, become carols. And certainly there are modern composers who have shown the way towards a modern carol idiom in music. *Oxford* has, of course, a hand-picked selection of those available in 1928. Dr. Vaughan Williams himself contributed a few noble tunes. There are but four of his tunes in the book—he was always modest about the inclusion of his own music in books he edited—but of these two are pure vulgar carol. "*The Golden Carol*" (173) was an old manuscript carol that had lost both its burden and its tune. But Vaughan Williams's setting could easily have come from the late fifteenth century. And his tune to William Morris's "From far away" (186), though more elaborate, is in the same tradition. Wither's Carol (185) and Blake's Cradle Song (196) are both in the song-style rather than that of the popular carol, but no less delightful for that.

Dr. Martin Shaw has five original tunes in the same book; they are more clearly "modern" tunes, usually depending for their effectiveness on a vivid accompaniment; "In Excelsis Gloria" (178) alone is a strictly unaccompanied setting, but even this depends on choral effects foreign to the ballad style. Armstrong Gibbs catches a true breath of the sixteenth century in "Herrick's Ode" (176), but Rutland Boughton, in "Ben Jonson's Carol" (168) achieves, in a very fine tune, a surprising affinity with the German chorale rather than the English folk-song; for it is in the chorales that you find more frequently the particular rhythmical device that he has used there. John Ireland in "New Prince, New Pomp" (170) writes in a burden-stanza form a tune that might well pass for one of the more austere examples in *Musica Britannica*; Gustav Holst's settings of "Lullay, my liking" and "In the bleak midwinter" (182, 187) have already come under review; in the first he produces a choral favourite, and in the second he most success-fully gives ground to modern popular opinion. Peter Warlock's contributions (169, 180, 181) are always effective and exciting, but altogether too elaborate to be called modern vulgar carols.

It may well be because *Oxford* has had such prodigious success, and has remained for thirty years the only available carol book that is at the same time capacious and comprehensive, that almost all serious carol-publishing since its day has been through separate leaflets. That has had its own effect on the carol technique of our time. The leaflet-carol, the logical successor in more sophisticated times of the broadside, has been popular for about a hundred years. It was about 1850 that Novello's began to publish separate carol settings; by Edmonstoune Duncan's day (1911) the number of these had reached 350; at the time of writing these pages (Christmas 1957) it has passed 600. Most of these have been settings on too ambitious a choral scale to have appeared in a book like *Oxford* (though as we saw, *Bramley and Stainer* did not disdain some of the earlier numbers). Other publishers have since swelled the stream, and the consequence has been a fashion for writing choral carols which has turned away the attention of the composers from the popular technique. What is published separately tends to be composed for a choir; what goes into a book of wide circulation may well be required to be "popular". Church congregations or carol-singing assemblies can handle a book, or a broadsheet, but do not take kindly to separate copies. It is more than conceivable that if a carol book were produced today that were assured of a circulation comparable with that of *Oxford*, some of our modern composers would produce some real-folk tunes of our time, just as when a new hymn book is composed it usually contains several new and serviceable tunes.

The choral settings of carols available today fall outside the proper scope of this book. The time is ripe for a comprehensive bibliography of carol-settings available at present, and the massiveness of such a compilation would be an indication of the way in which choral carols have proliferated during the past two generations. Such a compilation would include Gustav Holst's dramatic setting of "My dancing Day" from thirty years ago, and John Joubert's "Torches" (1955) and "Welcome Yule" (1957) from our own day, and those, with a few others, would show that in a crowded market there is still room for deep musicianship and boldness of expression. Beyond these choral settings again we have the modern Christmas Cantatas, such as Ben-jamin Britten's *A Ceremony of Carols*, Bruce Montgomery's *Christ's*

Birthday, and Geoffrey Bush's *Christmas Cantata*, all of which use traditional words and to some extent traditional music as well. Christmas celebrations are worthily adorned in such works, but the place for critical consideration of them is not here.

Other carol books exist, of course, and have been in wide use, besides *Oxford*, and many carol books have been published since its time, some of which, like the *University Carol Book* (whose later numbers are later than *Oxford*) have made notable additions to the repertory, while others, containing nothing new and bad versions of what is old, are clearly little more than attempts to take advantage of the "Christmas market". If *Oxford* is your only carol book, you will miss entirely certain beauties, such as all the carols of Woodward's books, and some also of Sir Richard Terry. But on the whole the present position may be summed up in saying that while the composition of choral carols and the compilation of small collections shows no sign at all of falling off, the production of modern folk carols is no nearer a renaissance than it was a hundred years ago.

CAROL SINGING AND CAROL SERVICES

Our folk-song idiom may be in jeopardy, but there is no doubt that carol-singing is more popular and more widespread an activity in this country at the present time than it ever was before. In any considerable town during the week before Christmas it would be possible, by assiduous use of the radio and zealous attendances at carol assemblies, to be singing Christmas carols continuously for a large proportion of each day. Carols will no doubt be sung in church on the Sunday before Christmas; there will be children's services, a rally round the Christmas tree in the public square, a carolare in the Town Hall. Carols will be sung and played at home, and the radio will provide everything from "Jingle Bells" to King's College. If there is a little spare time you can play a long-playing record of carols on the gramophone. There never was such a diversity of carol-singing as there is at present.

The custom of small children singing carols outside the street-door for pennies dies hard. My own impression at the time of writing is that it is on the way out. Before 1948 I lived on a busy street in an industrial town, and the carol-singers appeared regularly about three weeks before Christmas. In 1948 I came to live in this university City, and carol-singers were heard outside our door as early as the 26th of November in that year. These might have been young children hoping for a Christmas gratuity or organised choirs collecting for a charity. In 1956 two groups appeared; in 1957, in our street at all events, none at all.

Television probably accounts in part for the decline of street-singing: the television set makes householders inhospitable to any kind of social interruption; but I must add that of the thirty-seven houses in our street only two displayed television aerials at Christmas 1957. On the other hand, the custom among churches of sending their choirs to sing carols in hospitals and old people's homes is certainly growing at present, and as for the holding of special carol services in church, this is at the present time in the very height of fashion.

There can be no doubt that the most powerful force in bringing carols back into the worship of the church has been the Festival of Nine Lessons and Carols at King's College, Cambridge. This has done a hundred times more than Chope or Bramley and Stainer were able to do. For over thirty years that service has been attended, through the radio, by millions of listeners, and it has become a national occasion hardly less assiduously attended than the Queen's Speech on Christmas Day.

The first service of this kind in modern times was held at Truro as long ago as 1880. The diocese of Truro was established in 1877, and its first bishop was Edward White Benson (1829–96), who in 1883 became Archbishop of Canterbury. At the time of the creation of the diocese there was, of course, no cathedral, and while St. Mary's Church was being pulled down to make way for the new cathedral (which was opened in 1910), worship was carried on in a temporary wooden building. This building has now completely disappeared; when it was no longer in use at Truro it was removed to Redruth and housed a boot factory (called locally "the cathedral boot factory"), but no trace of it now remains there.

Before 1878 it had been the practice of the cathedral choir to sing carols from house to house in the city, but in 1878 the custom began of singing carols at a service in the temporary church on Christmas Eve at 10 p.m. The announcement in the "West Briton" was in the following form:

> The choir of the Cathedral will sing a number of carols in the Cathedral to-morrow evening (Christmas Eve), the service commencing at ten o'clock. We understand that this is at the wish of many of the leading parishioners and others. A like service has been instituted in other cathedral and large towns, and has been much appreciated. It is the intention of the choir to no longer continue the custom of singing carols at the residences of members of the congregation.

The service included two lessons, prayers and a sermon, with carols conducted by the Vicar-Choral, the Reverend G. H. S. Walpole; the organist was William Mitchell. The "other services" referred to in the newspaper were, no doubt, services of this kind—abbreviated evensong adorned with carols.

When it came to Christmas Eve, 1880, we learn from the "West Briton" that "the usual festal service" is to be held, but that this time a pamphlet with the order of service is to be issued. The service was "usual" in that it was a carol service held at the accustomed time. But more history was here being made than anybody knew at the time, for this was the inauguration of the Festival of Nine Lessons and Carols. The Lessons tell the story of our Redemption in the manner with which we have become familiar; but a glance at the order transcribed in Appendix I (p. 245) will show that the order is at certain important points different from that which we hear from King's College.

In 1911, when the service had already been running over thirty years, an elaborate book of full words and music was issued for the Truro service, with a Preface by the then bishop (C. W. Stubbs, 1845–1923). In this book the words of the carols are largely written by Stubbs himself, and the music composed or arranged by T. Tertius Noble (1867–1950). Noble, who spent the last forty years of his life as an organist in New York, was organist at York Minster from 1897 to 1913, and for five years before 1897 was organist at Ely, where Stubbs was Dean. Noble became Stubbs's son-in-law. Stubbs has a ponderous, declamatory style and tends to write in large verses which are hardly suitable to the carol style. The opening carol of the 1911 service is a hymn in seven verses, each of six tens, on the Great O's of Advent. But one remarkable discovery is among the carols, taken from Cynewulf's *Christ* (about A.D. 750), beginning in its modern version:

> They came three Kings who rode apace
> To Bethlem town by God's good grace,
>   Hail, Earendel!
>   Brightest of angels.
>
> Foudre! it was a duteous thing
> Wise men to worship childe King;
>   God-light be with us,
>   Hail, Earendel!

"Earendel" is a fanciful name for the Star which guided the wise men.

Noble's music is indifferent material—hardly a notch above *Bramley and Stainer*. Originally the service included carols of a simpler and more congregational kind.

The general dispersion of this rite was begun when Bishop Benson became Archbishop of Canterbury in 1883. He was the last Archbishop to reside at Addington Palace, which building, after nearly sixty years of secular employment, became by a most felicitous series of chances the headquarters of the Royal School of Church Music in 1954. Benson, on his arrival, imported the carol service to the parish church at Addington, which stands near the Palace. The service was altered to meet the needs of a small parish church, and all the carols are of the simple kind that can be sung by everybody present. All but one are taken from *Bramley and Stainer*, and that one (the last) is the only one that did not appear in the original order of 1883. The service has continued unaltered to the present day—except, of course, that now the final lesson is not read by the Archbishop. Mr. W. H. Still (b. 1867), who was appointed organist not long after the institution of the service, has at the time of writing completed a heroic record of sixty-five years' service, and has furnished much useful information from his store of memories. The order is transcribed in the Appendix, p. 247, and it is at Addington that the early tradition is now most faithfully preserved.

The King's College rite was devised by Dr. E. A. Milner-White, who was appointed Dean of the College in 1918. In that year the service was used at King's for the first time, in a form closely following that used at Truro (see p. 248). He kept the benedictions before the Lessons, added short explanatory prefaces, altered the series of readers to conform with the context of a college chapel, and entirely revised the music. At once he included not two congregational hymns but five, and from the first he saw to it that the carols should be carols and not pious Victorian lyrics. The metrical Magnificat at the end of the service was sung by the choir at the altar, to which they moved while the congregation sang alone the final verse of "The first Nowell".

With this experiment the Dean of King's was not wholly satisfied. The reasons which led him to make radical alterations in it the following year (1919) are set out in his statement, which is reproduced on p. 249 below. For the 1919 service he composed the King's College Bidding-prayer, which is perhaps the finest thing of its kind in the language since Cranmer. The benedictions were compressed into two sentences spoken after the Lord's Prayer:

> God the Son of God vouchsafe to bless and aid us; and unto the fellowship of the citizens above may the King of Angels bring us all. Amen.

The longer form, still based on the Truro benedictions, was brought into use in 1930:

The Almighty God bless us with his grace: Christ give us the joys of everlasting life: and unto the fellowship of the citizens above may the King of Angels bring us all. Amen.

In 1919 the first notes of music to be heard are not the invitatory carol but "Once in royal David's city", and "God rest you merry", which ran uninterrupted until 1957, comes in as a congregational carol after the third Lesson.

At the time of the inception of the service the College organist was Dr. A. H. Mann (1850–1929), who had already held the post for forty-two years. Mann ranks low among church composers, but he lives still in his remarkable harmonisation of "Once in royal David's city", which remains peculiar to King's and was described by Mann's successor as a "closely guarded secret"; with subtle art that arrangement turns the homely children's hymn into a processional of immense spaciousness.

From 1929 to 1957 the organist at King's was Mr. Boris Ord, who in 1957 was appointed Director of Music. During the years of the Second World War, when Mr. Ord was serving in the R.A.F., his place was taken by Dr. Harold Darke. Since Mr. Ord took over the organistship the custom has been, at the broadcast service, for the organ to be played throughout the service by the organ-scholar of the college. This made possible the agreeable custom, which persisted from 1930 to 1956, by which the third Lesson was read by the Organist. Since 1945 the organ-scholars who have played the service have been Mr. David Willcocks, Mr. Garth Benson, Mr. Hugh Maclean, and Mr. Hugh Popplewell. From 1957 Mr. Willcocks was appointed organist of the college, and in that year for the first time for twenty-seven years (war apart) the service was played by a senior musician.

Orders of service for 1938 and 1957 are reproduced in the Appendix (p. 250), and it will be seen from them that from the beginning the King's service has been planned on a pattern dictated by the value of tradition. Of the carols sung by the choir in 1919, only one was sung in 1957. "In dulci jubilo" is the one carol (in Pearsall's arrangement) that has remained immovable. But from year to year changes are made slowly, not more than one or two alterations being made in any one year. By this means a sense of tradition has been built up, and the King's rite has become a religious gesture of first-rate national importance.

But popular though the King's College Festival of Nine Lessons has become, the Advent Procession held in the same Chapel on Advent

Sunday is a more impressive and liturgically interesting rite. In this we have a revival of significant movement as part of a liturgy, which takes us straight back to the processional-dance origin of the carol. I am allowed to quote from the opening rubric:

> In the old English liturgies, the Advent Offices made a more vivid preparation for the coming of our Lord to earth than those of the Prayer Book. This Carol service is designed to include many of these older features.
>
> Throughout the service, the Choir will be moving in procession from west to east, "from darkness to light". First, from the west, the Responsory of ancient Mattins on Advent Sunday announces the hope of the Messiah, and is followed by the hymn of St. Ambrose, "Veni, Redemptor gentium". As the procession passes into the Choir, prophetic lections alternate with carols. Finally, in the Sanctuary, the Gospel replaces the Prophets.

The prophetic Lessons in the 1957 order are from Isaiah 6, Isaiah 40 and Malachi 3–4; the Gospel Lessons are the Annunciation in St. Luke 1, and the Birth of Jesus in St. Matthew 1. The final hymn in the rite is "O come, O come, Immanuel", and the recessional hymn, "O come, all ye faithful", ending at "Sing, choirs of angels".

A similar procession is enacted at York Minster at Epiphany, in which three choirs converge from different parts of the Minster to join in adoration in the Sanctuary. Again, at various "stations", carols and hymns are sung.

These are both liturgical developments of medieval techniques, and are appropriate to their august settings. The more familiar Festival of Nine Lessons is now imitated in other churches, and in churches beyond the Anglican Communion; and sometimes, of course, the imitation has been sentimental and ineffective. The processional, "Once in royal David's city", for example, is useless except in the kind of building and the kind of religious culture that accommodates processions. On the other hand there is room for services of readings and carols which develop the Truro and King's principle beyond the season of Christmas. The service described in Appendix II, although its symbolism is still largely conceptual, and there is in it none of the ceremonious movement of the Processions, is an attempt in a non-anglican setting to use the pattern of Lessons and Carols for another season, and to use it in order to "say" something that is quite certainly not said in the course of ordinary Free Church worship.

Note: The medieval origin of the Festival of Nine Lessons is by no means clear. But there may well be a distant relation between the ninefold division of the service and the Nine Odes which were introduced into the Byzantine Office of Lauds some time in the early sixth century. In earlier Byzantine use selections were made from fourteen lyrical passages from the Old 'and New Testaments; but some time before 550 the following Nine Odes became the rule: (1) Exodus 15. 1–19; (2) Deut. 32. 1–43; (3) I Sam. 2. 1–10; (4) Hab. 3. 2–19; (5) Isa. 26. 9–19; (6) Jon. 2. 3–10; (7) Dan. 3. 26–45 and 52–6; (8) Dan. (Apoc.) 3. 57–88 (i.e. the *Benedicite*); (9) St. Luke 1. 46–55 and 68–79 (i.e. the *Magnificat* and *Benedictus*). The Odes were chosen for their lyrical character rather than for their aptness for a Gospel-sequence; but in the time of St. John of Damascus (d. 750) it became the custom for *Canons*, or composed hymns, to form a commentary on the Ode-sequence on Easter day (and later during the whole Easter season). Dr. Wellesz says (and this is interesting in view of Appendix II below) that the original use of the *Canons* was not at Easter but in Lent. (Wellesz, *Byzantine Music and Hymnography* (Clarendon Press, 1949), pp. 30 ff. and 168 ff.)

WHERE IS THE CAROL NOW?

It would be agreeable to end in the delightful and august surroundings of King's College chapel; but we must not be tempted to by-pass the question, What has happened to the technique of the folk-carol now? Our story has shown how English culture has passed from an age in which carols were popular by design and destination to one in which carols are largely confined to Christmas and are only in a restricted sense to be called "folk-song". Perhaps they really are folk-song for about one week in the year. Perhaps during that season they really do run in the minds of the people at large. But are they anything like what they werè to the English countryman of the sixteenth century? If not, what is it that does for us in modern life what the carols did for him?

The reader must have observed how pervasive in the Christmas numbers, not only of religious papers but of the secular weeklies as well, is a nagging note of condemnation of the modern commercial Christmas. Christmas, say the prophets of our day, has been bedevilled by the businessmen. Christmas is an orgy of spending and eating and (far worse) drinking. Christmas crowds the trains and the streets and makes the children sick with sweets.

Much of that is cant. I am reminded of one of the hundred and one wise remarks in a book by the Dean of King's to which I have referred before in these pages, where he refers to the "extraordinary collective asceticism of our society—the clocking in, the commuting, the tax-paying, the heroic fortitude of the queues." The asceticism is worldly enough, and Dr. Vidler wants it redeemed. If the fast is worldly, so will the feast be. If the social life of our country from which the most religious of us cannot contract out is regimented in this post-puritan fashion, then its relaxations will be to the sensitive mind pedestrian and even brutish. There is nothing shocking or dreadful about this, though there is material here for the spiritual pastors and directors who ought to have something better to do than, in Dr. Vidler's words (in the same place), "thinking up fresh little bits of religiosity for us".

It is not of much consequence even to express anxiety about the abysmal vulgarity of the popular music that is disseminated about Christmas time through the sellers of music and gramophone records. The other day, trying over a L/P record in a gramophone shop before buying it (it happened to be of music by that bourgeois character, Mozart), my eye fell on an advertisement stuck to the wall of the audition-cubicle calling attention to the following selection on a new L/P Christmas record:

> Jingle Bells
> The Christmas Song
> Mistletoe and Holly
> I'll be home for Christmas,
> Christmas Waltz
> Have yourself a merry little Christmas

(here you turn over and the tone comes higher:)

> The First Nowell
> Hark the herald angels sing
> O little town of Bethlehem
> O come all ye faithful.
> It came upon the midnight clear
> Silent night.

In those first six titles you have the carol-story in modern dress. The pagan fertility rite, the Nordic legend, the dance, the home (plus the nostalgia created by modern mobility), and, in its blandest form, as a kind of beaming Master of Ceremonies or Butlin Barker, the over-arching influence of transatlantic culture:

Have yourself a merry *little* Christmas.

It is all there: and who is a Mozart-lover to say that this is the end of the world because the religious and the secular are getting so inextricably mixed up?

There is no doubt that in a post-Christian society, where the religious are becoming increasingly marked off from the rest in respect of their whole culture and many of their interests, as well as of their outward habits, you normally must not look to religious circles for the survival of a carol-habit. Nothing so self-conscious as modern religious society can produce naïve folk-song of that kind. It happens that at Christmas the barriers are still almost down, people gather round the public Christmas Tree to sing carols who never go to church, and people spare a thought for the Birth of Christ to whom His Death and Resurrection are no more than a fable. But otherwise than at Christmas you find no folk-song in the modern religious context.

Do we then say that jazz and ragtime are the folk-song of our age? No, for they are still specialised interests. The ephemera of the light-music market have not the staying power to become folk-song. That may be the point at which the argument lying behind Father Geoffrey Beaumont's highly controversial *Folk Mass* (Weinberger 1956) goes astray. Folk-song does not "date" as do the ephemera.

No, in looking for real folk-song, we must above all look for the world-affirming, not the world-denying. World-denial may lead to a puritan silence, but it may equally lead to that escapism which is the most notable feature of the modern "light" repertory. The world-affirming will contain those bold juxtapositions of incongruous things, those impudent parodies of the sacred, those uncompromising affirmations about the terrifying and the sinister which crop up again and again in the folk-songs and to some extent even in the carols. Where shall we find the precipitous contrasts of gracious and sombre that we find in "All under the leaves of life"? I believe we may look for them in two places.

The first is the nursery-rhyme. Much background information on this can be read in that fascinating reference-book, the *Oxford Dictionary of Nursery-rhymes*. Consider in what ways the nursery-rhyme exhibits the qualities we are looking for.

(1) The text of a nursery rhyme does not matter, and it is rarely read from a book. It is still traditionally taught by parents to children before the children can read. It rests on oral tradition, even though (like the carol) written sources for it may go back to the eighteenth century. But that does not signify. Neither tune nor words are exactly the same from one family to another, or from one book to the next. In "Sing a Song of sixpence", sung in C major, is the note on "Birds" in the third phrase A or B? Editions differ; children taught from different traditions differ almost to blows. What is the authentic last line of "Humpty-Dumpty"? Who cares, anyway?

(2) There is among nursery-rhymes a marked community of tunes

parallel to that which we find in the ballad carols. Normally it is one rhyme, one tune; but as a matter of fact the tune of "There was a crooked man" is the same as that of "Little Bo-peep." We noticed a relation between the "Rocking Carol" and "Twinkle, twinkle, little star", which tune is also used for other rhymes. There is even a parallel in nursery-rhymes to the invasion of the carol-repertory by the "Agincourt Song", in as much as the tune of "Rock-a-bye-Baby" is derived from the seventeenth-century political song, LILLIBULERO.

(3) But more important than either of these is the uninhibited quality of the sentiments of many nursery-rhymes—a quality which has given pause to certain sociologically sensitive editors in our own time. Not a few of us are hesitant about "Ding dong bell", even if in the end justice triumphs in a condemnation of the boy who threw the cat in the well, and in a rescue of the cat. In "Baa-baa, black sheep" (whose tune, a correspondent has reminded me, is used by the composer of an infants' hymn beginning "Praise him, Praise him, all ye little children") we have a sharp social comment in "none for the little boy who lives down the lane". "One for the little boy" satisfies both arith-metic and social justice, but can we doubt that "None" is authentic? Jack and Jill fetch a pail of water from a strangely-situated well and break their crowns on the way back: very funny. The crooked man probably had rheumatism—why poke fun at him? The old woman who lived in a shoe is a type of a very sorry social problem. The lion and the unicorn ill-treated each other and suffered at the hands of an in-human mob. Tom, the piper's son, was a thief. There is nothing sinister about "Hey diddle-diddle, the cat and the fiddle", but it is quite dreadfully irrational. There is another song about a girl who fell in love with a pig. Nursery-rhymes are everything that would horrify a puritan did not their domestic associations make them honourable in his eyes. It is all very crude and reactionary, and attempts have been made to clean up the nursery-rhymes, one of the more elegant of which is the streamlined version of "Cock Robin", which converts the whole story from a murder to a wedding, with the refrain:

> All the birds in the air
> Fell a singing and a throbbing
> When they heard of the love
> Of dear Cock Robin.

What is staggering is that the editors of that version kept, for their new nuptial poem, the gloriously doleful dirge that goes with the original. A new tune, of course, is wanted.

The matter of nursery-rhyme reform has been taken up in a pamphlet by Geoffrey Handley-Taylor entitled *A Selected Bibliography of Literature Relating to Nursery-Rhyme Reform* (Manchester 1953). It is all very hygienic and progressive. The crudest thing in nursery rhymes, and the first target of the reformers, is death: but at all points they are vigilant for references to the unkind and the disagreeable.

This is all very well; but folk-song does not lie that way, because that is world-denying, not world-affirming. This zeal for reform, which has brought modern civilisation untold benefits for which the bills are beginning to come in, is itself a product of a climate in which neither nursery-rhyme nor carol can flourish. This is the climate of hymns and uplift. Nursery-rhymes and carols are both, in Sir Arthur Quiller-Couch's word, "youthful", and the youthful is crude as well as natural. In youth there is an innocence which attracts side by side with a gaucherie in delicate things that repels. Youth makes us blush and smile by turns. It made the puritans blush with embarrassing frequency. What is natural can be uncomely and embarrassing, and all ceremony, all protocol and etiquette and even in the end liturgical rubric, is devised as a safeguard against the unseasonable embarrassment caused by the uninhibitedly "natural".

However this may be, the nursery-rhyme stands on the very border of the carol country. We noticed an example of this in "I saw three ships" (p. 60 above), from the shipbuilding country of Tyneside. The carol is far, and the nursery-rhyme (*D.N.R.* 471) farther, from the legend of the Three Kings of Cologne. But the carol has certain other relationships. The nursery-rhyme "Dame, get up and bake your pies" (*D.N.R.* 126) comes also from Tyneside, and its second verse in Sharpe's collection began "See the ships all sailing by". Its tune, which looks like the first half of the eighteenth-century version of GREENSLEEVES (see Ex. 32, p. 102) is not unlike a minor-mode version of THREE SHIPS; another related tune is LONDON BRIDGE IS BROKEN DOWN, which, oddly enough, comes also from Tyneside (*D.N.R.* 306).

Again, "Old King Cole" has several tunes which have become at various stages associated with carols. The "Bellman's Carol", otherwise called HITCHIN CAROL (*Oxford* 46), is one, and the tune used by Woodward for his very entertaining carol on the Exodus (*Cambridge* 43) is another.

On the border between nursery rhyme and carol is a Christmas song which is exceedingly popular just now, and full of points for the assiduous commentator or student of folklore—"The Twelve days of Christmas"; with its french hens and colly birds and all the rest of the

Noah's ark-like collection of livestock which the suitor pressed on his true-love, it is about half way between "A New Dial" and "The Animals went in two by two". The familiar version will be found in *Carols*, 1400–1950 (ed. R. Nettel), p. 52; a slightly different form of the tune, designated "Northumbrian", is at *U.C.B.* X, 69. The editors of *D.N.R.* quote Greene 8, "The first Day of Yule", which links the rhyme at once with the more familiar "Welcome Yule" (see above, p. 74). The secular rhyme, first printed in 1780 in a form we should hardly recognise, is nothing more than a fanciful and festive community song.

But the upshot of all this is that the nursery-rhyme is folklore and folk-song. The pervasive Christmas pantomime, conventionally based on folklore of this kind, proves how truly the nursery-rhyme is folklore. This is where we find the old carol-technique still prevailing. The potent fact in the survival of these songs is not that they are printed but that they are still sung to a hearer who cannot read but can join in a chorus, and can enjoy a story, and has a sense of humour, and is not unduly frightened by the facts of life. Disinfected nursery-rhymes and jazz ephemera are equally, through different kinds of breach of the carol-code, disqualified from truly vulgar popularity and therefore from survival through the three or more centuries which have in past history marked the life of many carols and most nursery-rhymes. A clamorous appeal to a passing fashion is not, in our sense, true vulgar popularity.

The other context in which we do not look entirely in vain for a carol technique is in what I call, for want of a better or more official designation, the social song. We had a clue to this in our opening pages where we referred to sea-shanties. Here are community songs of a specialised group, led by a minstrel and joined in by all who are at work with him. Their "naturalness" led, in consequence of their being the songs of an all-male group, to an inevitable bawdiness here and there which will not stand print. Terry records that the bawdy lines were never in the choruses, but were always sung by the minstrel in such a way as to be audible only to the other singers, not to the bystander. In their context they were witty, and they were not designed to be heard where they would prove offensive. Sea-shanties are work-songs, and are far too world-affirming to be romantic or high-falutin, They are always topical, humorous, intimate and improvised. Printed editions give a fair idea of their tunes but, in the nature of the case, communicate little of the real salt in the words.

This "salt" lies precisely in the intimate and topical nature of what the words say. What is topical is removed from the printed edition because it means nothing to the general reader; what is intimate, because perhaps it may shock him. But it was these matters that really anchored the shanty into real life for its singers. The topical reference might well be a good-humoured salutation to the ship-owner for whom the sailors are working—like "Mr. Tapscott" in "We're all bound to go", or a dig at some national enemy like Napoleon, as in "Boney was a warrior". "There is nothing funny about Hitler *now*", said Professor C. S. Lewis, and that is precisely the point. Napoleon had his terrifying aspects, and therefore his humorous aspects, *then*: so did Mr. Tapscott. As for the bawdiness—embarrassing in cold print, there is nothing embarrassing or squalid about it in the context of hard physical labour in a society which has no other way of healthily protesting against its isolation from women: any other kind of protest would be less healthy.

The atmosphere in which this kind of song thrives is that in which the fundamental controversies of human life are not obscured; in which men work and are not ashamed of admitting the temptation to be lazy; in which men face danger and are not ashamed of admitting fear; in which they face privation and are not ashamed to admit their desire of what is, or may be, taken away. The modern contempt of the Middle Ages is rooted principally in the modern contempt for the admission of these fundamental controversies. If it is naughty to admit you would rather not work, to admit you might be afraid, to admit your natural need of women or your homesickness, there is no chance of your joining in a social song that presupposes these natural matters.

This is obviously what has happened to the folk-song of the army. The shanty went with the sailing-ship. "Tipperary" and "Pack up your Troubles" are equally "dated" by the passing away of the age in which the army was still an organisation designed to fight a personal enemy, healthily if unregenerately hated, in circumstances of extreme privation and protracted discomfort. The physical emphasis of "marching" has gone with mechanisation, and as for the enemy, in our own time everybody agrees that the thing to be feared is a weapon of destruction which, whoever uses it, will do far more damage than can ever be done by a personal enemy acting in a personal fashion on any country. In Napoleon's time we really feared Napoleon: in the Kaiser's time we feared and laughed at the Kaiser. In the first few months of Hitler's war we feared and lampooned Hitler. It was perhaps only in 1940 that we learned to fear the weapon rather than the man. To be honest, there is nothing funny about any of the leaders of the countries with which we are at odds *now*; and there is nothing funny about the nuclear bomb either.

There was more than a trace of the folk-song atmosphere at one time in student life. The atmosphere of "Gaudeamus", though a thing of the past, is something which could be commercially distilled in such publications as the *Student Song Book*. But that too has gone. Modern university life has lost it for the same reasons that modern economic life, with which it is now irretrievably involved, has lost the "Cherry Tree" atmosphere. The student of the present day will play the 'cello at the music club or listen to records of Bartok, or sing hymns in church, but he has no folk-song; he is too unsociable and at the same time too serious-minded and anxious about himself and his future to achieve that.

For the carol to prosper, you must have world-affirming assumptions. Two things, then, will kill it at once. One is anxiety, the other romance. The middle ages were interested in neither, if we interpret "romance" as meaning "modern romanticism". The middle ages knew fear, they knew danger. But what they did not know is that "anxiety of being" which Paul Tillich has rightly attributed to our own time, that sense of futility and "futurelessness" at the centre of things with which our rich and brilliant modern civilisation is burdened. That was the secret of their unshockableness, of that singing in the dark which one hears within and around Dunbar's superb *"Rorate caeli desuper"*. Neither did they know romanticism. Death to them was death, not a kind of sleep. The Incarnation to them was God made flesh, not a pretty baby. The Blessed Trinity to them was the Blessed Trinity, not a religious lyric set to a tune by Doctor Dykes. I verily believe that the carol was killed not by puritanism, under which it might have survived, and indeed under which in England it never wholly died, but by that Teutonic romanticism which overtook the English Christmas and brought in *Bramley and Stainer*. For with that romanticism, that whole universe of imagery which includes the snow and the baby and the Mother and the Christmas Tree and the Dickensian stage-coach, came the triumph of the world-denying mind more decisively than it could ever have come under puritanism. The puritan onslaught on the world, the flesh and the devil was a straight fight compared with the allusive, insinuating, indirect penetration of the romantic idea which threw the whole Christmas story out of focus and made it more of an "entertainment" and an evasion of reality than the medieval mystery plays could ever have been.

If we look for the carol-atmosphere now, we shall find it where there are people who produce a natural song with sound popular melody whose words have, in the medieval sense, a world-affirming accent. If you can find a company of people who for a season are carefree enough to sing so, and yet whose singing is informed by a religious profession that enables them to resist the temptation to evade the world, you will find something surprisingly like carols on their lips. You are the more likely to find it in those companies of people which are bound together in some enterprise that presents some hazard and some sense of achievement, without presenting them so oppressively as to suffocate the singing instinct altogether. You have not the breath for carols when you have climbed Everest; but (to my personal knowledge) you have it when you have climbed Scafell.

I am tempted to particularise, and to offer examples. But the songs I have in mind are songs that would be murdered by print. In circles of this reasonably mature and convivial kind, however, a folk-song tradition persists which excludes the erotic and escapist, but which includes much that is unexpected, intimate, topical, and (not under the law) unprintable. There are songs which deal light-heartedly with the Bible, and with death; songs which make fun of Communism (which no modern youngster can fail to regard as a major threat to his happiness); there are even songs which take a light-hearted line with drink and drugs which is more certain to evoke a healthy attitude to them than any movement of alleged "temperance". Any of these, were I to print them here, would be likely to go where they would appear offensive. But they would appear offensive only to those who have overlooked one crucial point.

This point is that where you find religious people singing songs that take the Bible lightly (without ever making light of it), like "The Darkies' Sunday School", or songs that make light of the sting of death, you have religious people who have abandoned their right to take themselves seriously. We are now at last at the heart of it. You could put it also by saying that in any repertory that contains songs of that kind you will also find many songs that are nothing more than magnificent nonsense—mature versions of "The cow jumped over the moon". The "shocks" of the carols, and likewise of these social songs, constitute a direct affront to the human but entirely unregenerate urge to take oneself seriously. It is often a chastening and painful business to disentangle that seriousness which is selfish and fugitive from that which is truly of faith; but it must be done, because, to put it at its most obvious, if you take yourself seriously, then you have no hope of taking seriously the truths of your faith.

Here then we have the real enemy of the carol, the poison which will assuredly kill it. Puritanism is not the enemy, except in so far as it is the truth to say that it contains this poison of self-seriousness; historically and dogmatically it can be demonstrated that not all puritanism is of that kind. Commercialism is not the enemy, except in so far as it breeds a false seriousness about secondary things, and especially about personal security and reputation. It need not always do that. Pride is the only enemy. The shockable person, or the shockable ethical tradition, is entirely informed by this false seriousness. G. K. Chesterton did no better thing for the defence of the Christian Faith than he did when he wrote a series of detective stories on the theme that all moral mysteries yield their defences to humility; not only is Father Brown somewhat ridiculous to the casual observer: he means something profound when he says in the end, "I committed all those crimes myself." He means that not one of them *shocked* him, because he took not himself, but ultimate Goodness, seriously.

If Christmas is the season especially of the putting down of the mighty from their seat, then Christmas is the archetypal carol season. A whole tradition of heresy is based on the notion that the Incarnation is a humiliation unworthy of the Eternal God. It survives today in that tight-lipped stoicism that cannot admit the ridiculous into life because it dare not admit the redeemability of life. "The genius of the present age requires work and not play." Work is what you do in the firm's time. Work is good, it is good for you, it is not to be treated lightly.

And what was the *work* of God? To create the world in all its majestic design, and then to rescue it from frustration and grievance by an undignified act that begins with an impromptu cradle in a cowshed and ends with the gross horror of a crucifixion. Where that becomes not remote dogma but a texture of life, where men see that reality is as terrible and as triumphant as that, there you lose at once the cautious speech of the man of worldly weight, the portentous demeanour of the reputable and respected, and you get something like a "general dance". In a word, you get carols.

Appendices

APPENDIX I

The Service of Nine Lessons and Carols

THE TRURO ORDER

The Lord's Prayer

The Preces

Preface: *With perpetual blessing may the Father everlasting bless us.* Amen.

FIRST LESSON: Genesis 3. 8–16 (A senior Chorister)

> CAROL

Preface: *God the Son vouchsafe to bless and aid us.* Amen.

SECOND LESSON: Genesis 22. 15–19 (A lay Choirman)

> CAROL

Preface: *May the grace of the Holy Ghost enlighten us heart and body.* Amen.

THIRD LESSON: Numbers 24. 15–18 (A lay Reader)

> CAROL

Preface: *The Almighty Lord bless us with his Grace.* Amen.

FOURTH LESSON: Isaiah 9. 6–8 (A deacon)

> CAROL, or "For unto us a child is born" (*Messiah*)

Preface: *Christ give us the joys of everlasting life.* Amen.

FIFTH LESSON: Micah 5. 2–5 (A Vicar Decani)

> CAROL

Preface: *By the words of the Lord's Gospel be our sins blotted out.* Amen.

SIXTH LESSON: St. Luke 2. 8–16 (A Vicar Cantoris)

> CAROL, or "There were shepherds" (*Messiah*)

Preface (all standing): *May the fountain of the Gospel fill us with the Doctrine of Heaven.* Amen.

SEVENTH LESSON: St. John 1. 1–15 (A senior Canon Decani)

> CAROL or HYMN

Preface: *The Creator of all things give us his blessing.* Amen.

EIGHTH LESSON: Galatians 4. 4–8 (A senior Canon Cantoris)

> CAROL

Preface: *Unto the fellowship of the citizens above may the King of Angels bring us all.* Amen.

NINTH LESSON: I John 5. 1–5 (The Bishop)

> (all standing) CAROL, or the Hallelujah Chorus (*Messiah*)

The Magnificat

The Salutation

Collect for Christmas Day

The Blessing.

For identification of the carols, see the Addington Order on page 247. The congregation at Truro sang from a book of twelve well-known carols, the selection from year to year being slightly varied.

Mr. W. A. J. Davey writes: "To-day the service is basically the same, save that the choristers carry lighted lanterns on the end of thorn-sticks during the opening procession, when "Once in royal David's city" is sung. A recent order follows:

TRURO 1955

Processional: Once in royal David's city

Bidding Prayer (in the form used at King's College, slightly adapted)

The Lord's Prayer

Invitatory: "Behold, the great Creator makes"   (A. & M. 69)

FIRST BENEDICTION AND LESSON: Gen. 1. 1 & 27 and 3. 8–15 (A Chorister) "O loving wisdom", the 2nd verse of "Praise to the Holiest" (A. & M. 185) "O little town of Bethlehem"

SECOND BENEDICTION AND LESSON: Micah 5. 2–4 (A lay Vicar)
CAROL (by All): "I saw three ships"

THIRD BENEDICTION AND LESSON: Isaiah 9. 2–7 (A lay Assistant)
HYMN (by All): "A great and mighty wonder"   (A. & M. 68)

FOURTH BENEDICTION AND LESSON: St. Luke 1. 26–35 (A lay Reader)
CAROL: "The angel Gabriel" (Basque)

FIFTH BENEDICTION AND LESSON: St. Luke 1. 46–55 (A Deacon)
CAROL: "I saw a fair maiden"   (Terry)

SIXTH BENEDICTION AND LESSON: St. Luke 2. 1–7 (A Priest-Vicar)
CAROL: "Sing Lullaby"   (Basque)

SEVENTH BENEDICTION AND LESSON: St. Luke 2. 8–16 (An honorary Canon)
HYMN (by All): "While shepherds watched"   (A. & M. 62)

EIGHTH BENEDICTION AND LESSON: St. Matthew 2. 1–11 (A Residentiary Canon)
CAROL: "Ye shepherds leave" (French)

NINTH BENEDICTION AND LESSON: St. John 1. 1–14 (The Bishop)
HYMN (by All): "O come, all ye faithful"   (A. & M. 59)

The Bishop: God is the Lord who hath shewed us light
          Blessed is he that cometh in the name of the Lord!

People: Hosanna in the highest!

Collect for Christmas Day

The Blessing

THE ADDINGTON ORDER

The Lessons and Benedictions are the same as those in the Truro Order

Opening Sentences

The Lord's Prayer

The Preces

FIRST BENEDICTION AND LESSON (A Choir-boy, Cantoris)
CAROL: "As Joseph with travel was weary"   (B/S 35)

SECOND BENEDICTION AND LESSON (A Choir-boy, Decani)
CAROL: "A Virgin unspotted"   (B/S 3)

THIRD BENEDICTION AND LESSON (A Choir-boy Cantoris)
CAROL: "Like silver lamps"   (B/S 2)

FOURTH BENEDICTION AND LESSON (A Choir-man, Decani)
CAROL: "The holly and the ivy"   (B/S 5)

FIFTH BENEDICTION AND LESSON (A Choir-man, Cantoris)
CAROL: "The First Nowell"   (B/S 6)

SIXTH BENEDICTION AND LESSON (An Assistant Priest)
CAROL: "The Seven Joys of Mary"   (B/S 12)

SEVENTH BENEDICTION AND LESSON (An Assistant Priest)
CAROL: "When Christ was born of Mary free"   (B/S 19)

EIGHTH BENEDICTION AND LESSON (The Vicar)
CAROL: "Good Christian men, rejoice"   (B/S 8)

NINTH BENEDICTION AND LESSON (The Archbishop)
CAROL: "Angels we have heard on high"

The Magnificat

Salutation

Collect for Christmas Day

The Blessing

At a later stage the hymn, "O come, all ye faithful" was added after the Collect and before the Blessing.

I am informed by Mr. W. H. Still, who was appointed organist at Addington by the Vicar, the Rev. W. M. Townshend, at the Archbishop's request in 1892, that the carols in the above order, with the exception of No. 9, were all in the original Truro order.

KING'S COLLEGE, CHRISTMAS EVE, 1918

From the opening rubrics:

This service was drawn up from sources ancient and modern by Archbishop Benson[1] for Cathedral use, the Lessons, which tell us the whole story of our Redemption, being read in order by the Cathedral ministers from chorister to Bishop. In this Chapel it is adapted also to symbolise the loving bond between the two foundations of King Henry VI here and at Eton, the good-will between University and Town, and peace within the whole Church of the Lord Jesus, as well as the joy and worship of us all at the coming of our Christ.

The congregation should stand for the Benedictions and Carols, and also for the Sixth Lesson. Its members should join heartily in the singing of the hymns and verses specially marked for that purpose.

INVITATORY CAROL: "Up good Christen folk"   (*Cowley* 29)

HYMN: "Once in royal David's city"   (*E.H.* 605)
    (in procession, the congregation joining in the last two verses)

The Bidding Prayer

The Lord's Prayer

HYMN: "A great and mighty wonder"   (*E.H.* 19)
    (the following Lessons are preceded by a Benediction in the form used at Truro and then by the explanatory Preface)

FIRST LESSON: Genesis 3. 8–15 (A Chorister)
CAROL: "A virgin most pure"   (*Cowley* 69)

SECOND LESSON: Genesis 22. 15–18 (A Chapel-clerk)
CAROL: "Blessed be that Maid Marie"   (*Cowley* 2)

THIRD LESSON: Isaiah 9. 2, 6, 7 (An undergraduate member of the College)
CAROL: "As up the wood I took my way"   (*English* 4)

FOURTH LESSON: Micah 5. 2–4 (A Fellow)
HYMN: "While shepherds watched their flocks by night"   (*E.H.* 30)

FIFTH LESSON: St. Luke 1. 26–33 and 38 (The Vice-provost)
CAROL: "Unto us is born a Son"   (*Cowley* 25)

SIXTH LESSON: St. John 1. 1–14 (A Free Church Minister)
HYMN: "O come, all ye faithful" (four verses)   (*E.H.* 28)

SEVENTH LESSON: St. Luke 2. 8–16 (The Mayor's Chaplain)
CAROLS: "O night peaceful and blest"
       "Childing of a maiden bright"   (*Cowley* 3)

EIGHTH LESSON: St. Matthew 1. 1–11 (The Provost of Eton)
CAROL: "*In dulci jubilo*"   (arr. Pearsall)

---

[1] In strict truth, the inspiration came from the Rev. G. H. S. Walpole; see above p. 229 and Bullock, *op. cit.*, pp. 121–2.

NINTH LESSON: Galatians 4. 4–7 (The Provost)
CAROL: "The first Nowell"
 (The congregation sang the last verse)

THE MAGNIFICAT   (Charles Wood: metrical)
      Salutation
     Collect for Christmas Day
      The Blessing

RECESSIONAL HYMN: "Hark, the herald angels sing"   (E.H. 24)

("While shepherds watched" and "O come, all ye faithful" are described in the Order of Service as Carols.)

An explanatory statement by the Very Reverend E. A. Milner-White, Dean of York, on the development of the King's College Festival.

In his *Life of Edward White Benson*, Archbishop of Canterbury, Vol. 1 (1900), pp. 483–484, A. C. Benson wrote as follows:

"My father arranged from ancient sources a little service for Christmas Eve— nine carols and nine tiny lessons, which were read by various officers of the church, beginning with a chorister, and ending, through the different grades, with the Bishop."

This Service was first performed on Christmas Eve at 10 p.m. in 1880 in the wooden cathedral of Truro. Its structure consisted of the nine lessons (not those now usual) read by the nine readers mentioned above. Between the lessons were two hymns, four carols and three choruses from the Messiah, with the Magnificat as the climax.

In 1918 the Rev. E. Milner-White tried out the devotion in the Chapel of King's College, Cambridge, of which he was then Dean. Excellent on paper, it did not transfer at all well into a service. Extracts from the Messiah were wholly out of place, and for these the Dean substituted carols. The movement was continually held up by a series of ancient but arbitrary Benedictions between each lection; there was next-to-no prayer; and, unexpectedly, after so metrical and "naïve" a succession of carols, the Magnificat proved wholly unsatisfactory as a climax.

Next year the Dean re-ordered the service by prefacing it with an act of prayer, a Christmas Bidding and the Our Father; by cutting out the Magnificat and the Benedictions—except after the Lord's Prayer and at the end—and by making the Ninth Lesson, the Gospel of the Incarnation from the first chapter of St. John, the supreme climax, for which everybody stood. We need not concern ourselves with small changes of detail; Archbishop Benson's imaginative succession of Readers remained. The beauty of the singing in King's Chapel did the rest. The "Nine Lessons and Carols" attracted vast crowds to Cambridge: and even before the B.B.C. made it a world institution, it had spread throughout England (including non-Anglican churches and chapels) and to all the Dominions.

There are now many minor variations (some regrettable) in different places to suit local conditions: the *Textus Receptus*, so to speak, is kept steady by King's Chapel and York Minster acting in conjunction. And this is necessary. For its liturgical order and pattern is the strength of the services; the main theme is the development of the loving purpose of God from Creation to the Incarnation through the windows and words of the Bible: the scriptures, not the carols, are the backbone. It is fatally easy to ruin the devotion, to make it mere "community carol-singing", by reducing the number of lessons and doubling the number of carols. As it stands the service is a fruitful example of the use of ancient liturgical form in a new combination to create, what the Church to-day finds so difficult, a "Special Service"—a devotion of Christmas, with dignity of order, development, mood, colour, action and variety of parts, all appropriately concentrated upon the coming of our Lord Jesus Christ.

I am permitted by the Provost and Fellows of King's College, Cambridge, to reproduce here the orders of service for the Festival of Nine Lessons and Carols in 1918, 1937 and 1957. As is indicated in the Dean's statement, the order was radically revised in 1919, the year after the institution of the Festival at King's. From then to the present time the service has been varied only slightly from year to year. From 1919 to 1939 inclusive the Lessons remained unvaried. In later years the Fourth Lesson alone has been varied: verses from Isaiah 60 and (in 1957) from Isaiah 11 have been substituted for those from Micah. The only year in which the previous year's service was used with no variation whatever in Lessons or Carols was 1925. In all other years at least one carol (but not often more than one) has been varied. The congregational hymns remained unchanged from 1919 to 1956 inclusive; in 1957 for the first time "O Little Town of Bethlehem" (which had for some years been replaced by the Bach chorus at the Invitatory) was sung to the tune FOREST GREEN, in place of "God rest you merry". The form of the Blessing which is now invariable was instituted in 1920. At the 1919 service the Aaronic Blessing was used.

It may be observed that at several points the present-day Truro order has conceded the wisdom of the Dean's criticism. (See Truro 1955 above, p. 246.)

KING'S COLLEGE, CHRISTMAS EVE, 1937

PROCESSIONAL HYMN: "Once in royal David's city"

Bidding Prayer

The Lord's Prayer

Benediction

INVITATORY CAROL: "O little town of Bethlehem"   (Walford Davies)
("After this the Congregation shall sit for all the Carols, except those following the third, sixth and ninth Lessons, in which they are asked to join heartily.")

FIRST LESSON: Genesis 8. 1–15 (A Chorister)
CAROLS: "Ding dong merrily on high"   (*Cambridge* 8)
      "I saw three ships"   (*English* 18)

SECOND LESSON: Genesis 22. 15–18 (A Choral Scholar)
CAROL: "The holly and the ivy"   (arr. Walford Davies)

THIRD LESSON: Isaiah 9. 2, 6, 7 (The Organist)
CAROL: "God rest you merry" (Choir and Congregation)

FOURTH LESSON: Micah 5. 2–4 (A Fellow)
CAROL: "*In dulci jubilo*"   (arr. Pearsall)

FIFTH LESSON: St. Luke 1. 26–33 and 38 (The Vice-provost)
CAROL: "The Angel Gabriel"   (Basque: arr. Pettman)

SIXTH LESSON: St. Matthew 1. 18–23 (A Free Church Minister)
HYMN: "While shepherds watched"

SEVENTH LESSON: St. Luke 2. 8–16 (The Mayor's Chaplain)
CAROLS: "Shepherds in the field abiding"   (*Cowley* 68)
      "Hail, Holy Child"   (*Cambridge* 12)

EIGHTH LESSON: St. Matthew 2. 1–11 (A Representative of the Sister College at Eton)
CAROL: "The Three Kings."   (Cornelius, arr. Atkins)

NINTH LESSON: St. John 1. 1–14 (The Provost)
HYMN: "O come, all ye faithful"   (*E.H.* 614, omit v. 4)

The Salutation

Collect for Christmas Day

The Blessing

RECESSIONAL HYMN: "Hark, the herald angels sing"

KING'S COLLEGE, CHRISTMAS EVE, 1957

PROCESSIONAL HYMN: "Once in royal David's city"

The Bidding Prayer

The Lord's Prayer

Benediction

INVOCATORY: "There were Shepherds" and "Break forth", from the *Christmas Oratorio*   J. S. Bach

FIRST LESSON: Genesis 3. 8–15 (A Chorister)
CAROLS: "Adam lay ybounden"   B. Ord
      "Ding dong, merrily on high"   (*Cambridge* 8)

SECOND LESSON: Genesis 22. 15–18 (A Choral Scholar)
CAROL: "On Christmas night all Christians sing"   (*Oxford* 24)

THIRD LESSON: Isaiah 9. vv. 2, 6, 7 (An Eton Scholar)
HYMN: "O little town of Bethlehem" (choir and congregation)   (*E.H.* 15)
FOURTH LESSON: Isaiah 11. 1–9 (A Fellow)
CAROL: *In dulci jubilo*   (arr. Pearsall)
FIFTH LESSON: St. Luke 1. 26–33 and 38 (The Lay Dean)
CAROL: "Hail, blessed Virgin Mary"   (*Italian*)
SIXTH LESSON: St. Matthew 1. 18–23 (The Vice-provost)
CAROL: "A Virgin most pure"   (*Cowley* 69)
SEVENTH LESSON: St. Luke 2. 8–16 (A representative of the Cambridge Churches)
HYMN: "While shepherds watched"   (*E.H.* 30)
CAROL: "I saw a maiden"   (*University* 12)
EIGHTH LESSON: St. Matthew 2. 1–11 (A Representative of the City of Cambridge)
CAROLS: "Rejoice and be merry"   (*Oxford* 25)
        "A Babe is born"   (F. Bainton)
NINTH LESSON: St. John 1. 1–14 (The Provost)
HYMN: "O come, all ye faithful"   (*E.H.* 614, the whole)

Salutation

The Collect for Christmas Day

The Blessing

RECESSIONAL HYMN: "Hark, the herald angels sing"

It is perhaps worth observing that in R. R. Chope's *Carols for Use in Church*, (Complete edition, 1894), patterns for services of lessons and carols are appended to the carols. There are six for Christmas, two for Easter and three for Harvest. The first order for Christmas prescribes ten Lessons of length varying from one verse to twenty as follows: (i) Phil. 2. 5–12, (ii) Matt. 1. 18–end, (iii) Luke 1. 26–34 and 2. 1–8, (iv) I Cor. 1. 26–30, 2. 7–11 and Luke 2. 8–12, (v) Luke 2. 12–15, (vi) Heb. 12. 18–25 and I Pet. 1. 1–12, (vii) Psalm 95. 6–7, 96. 9 and 27. 8, (viii) Luke 2. 15–17, (ix) Luke 2. 17–18, (x) Luke 2. 20. The second order prescribes two Lessons and an address; so do the third, fourth and fifth, following slightly different patterns. The sixth, a short order, prescribes three Lessons and no address. In the second form for Easter the Lessons are (i) Ex. 14. 13–31, (ii) John 20. 11–19, (iii) Dan. 7. 13–14, (iv) Heb. 1. 1–13 or 4. 14–end. The first form has two Lessons only, Ex. 12. 21–8 and Matt. 28. 2–10. Of the harvest orders, the first has one Lesson, the other two, two each. The carols are, of course, all taken from the book in which the orders appear. There is no historical or liturgical connection between these orders (which are after all nothing more than suggestions of ways of using the book) and the Truro tradition.

APPENDIX II

A Service of Lessons and Music for Lent, in a non-anglican tradition

In 1952 in the chapel of Mansfield College, Oxford, a form of carol service was experimentally held, and this has since become an annual tradition. The order that follows is that which was used in 1957. Since there was no tradition to build on, the organisers of the service had to feel their way, and alterations from year to year are more radical than those made in the Advent carol service which is also held in that Chapel. The chief liturgical problem is, of course, what should be done and said at this time of year. About half the Trinity Term normally falls within the Easter season, but the last Sunday of Hilary Term (on which this service is always held) invariably falls in Lent. It would therefore be inappropriate to hold a service of Passion music or of Easter carols.

The Lessons, then, seven in number and read alternately by two readers, are designed to form a meditation on the Life and Work of Christ. Each New Testament Lesson (except one) is ushered in by a passage of Old Testament prophecy. At the sixth Lesson we deliberately move from the synoptic Gospels to St. John. This is quite deliberate. In the King's rite the Lesson from St. John makes a unique impression not merely because it is the last Lesson (it was not in 1918, nor at Truro), but because it is from St. John. The same principle holds here. It would be unseemly at this season to read the historic accounts of the Passion and Resurrection: on the other hand, it would be unseemly also to leave the service without any reference to the Atonement and Victory of Christ. St. John meets the case exactly because from him we have two utterances of our Lord spoken, as it were, in the timeless accents of prophecy: spoken before the events took place and yet providing an ultimate comment on them, and ending with the words, "I have overcome the world". The Passion and Victory are there, not only foretold but in principle accomplished, and in telling of them we have done no violence to the traditions of the Church's Year.

At the end of the Organ Voluntary, the Congregation rises with the Ministers, while the Presiding minister says:

The Crucified is risen from the dead, and hath redeemed us. Alleluia!
Tell it out among the nations that the Lord reigneth from the tree.
Christ being raised from the dead dieth no more; death hath no more dominion over him.
For in that he died, he died unto sin once, but in that he liveth, he liveth unto God.

HYMN: "O love, how deep, how broad, how high"   (*E.H.* 459, tune 215)

Prayers, leading to
The Lord's Prayer

253

FIRST LESSON: *The Beginning of the Gospel*. Isaiah 49. 1–4
St. Mark 1. 1–11

CAROL: "All ye who are to mirth inclined"   (*Oxford* 51, vv. 1, 2, 7)

SECOND LESSON: *The Temptation*. Psalm 107. 1–9
St. Matthew 4. 1–11

HYMN: "With joy we meditate the grace"   (*C.P.* 97)

THIRD LESSON: *"The Fast that I have chosen"*. Isaiah 58. 1–8
St. Matthew 5. 1–12

CAROL: "King Jesus hath a garden"   (*Cowley* 67)

FOURTH LESSON: *"The Messiah"*. Isaiah 42. 1–4
St. Mark 8. 27–34

CAROL: "Saint Mary goes a seeking"   (*Oxford* 179)

FIFTH LESSON: *The Way*. Isaiah 50. 4–7
St. Mark 10. 28–34

ANTHEM: "Vox Ultima Crucis" (W. H. Harris)

HYMN: "Ride on, ride on in majesty"   (*E.H.* 620)

SIXTH LESSON: *The Judgment*. St. John 12. 23–33

CHORALE: "It is finished"   (*E.H.* 118)

ANTHEM: "Come, my Way" (Alexander Brent Smith)

SEVENTH LESSON: *The Victory*. Isaiah 52. 13–53. 6
St. John 16. 25–33

HYMN: "The head that once was crowned with thorns"   (*E.H.* 147)
The Collect for Good Friday
The Blessing

In this service the prayer at the beginning is taken from page 97 of Dr. Nathaniel Micklem's *Prayers and Praises* (Independent Press, second edition 1954), using the first personal plural throughout. References to the hymns are given in *E.H.* for the reader's convenience, but the second hymn is not in that book. "Shepherd divine, our wants relieve" (*A. & M.* 317) is sometimes substituted. For users of *E.H.* "Forty days and forty nights" would no doubt be acceptable.

At two points during the service, as well as before and after it, organ music was played. The sequence of four pieces was taken from Herbert Howell's 1951 set, published by Novello. Before the service the choice was "Praeludio Sine Nomine"; after the second hymn, "Sarabande in Modo Elegiaco"; between the chorale and the anthem following the Sixth Lesson, "Master Tallis's Testament", and after the Blessing, "Sarabande for the Morning of Easter". In one other order (that of 1955) a similar sequence of pieces from Bach's "48" was played: (1) Prelude in B flat minor, (2) Fugue in B flat minor, (3) Prelude in E flat minor (all from Book I), and (4) Fugue in E (Book II). But organ music is not always played in the service. Alternative opening hymns have been "Come, let us to the Lord our God", "Sing, my tongue, the glorious battle", and "Praise to the Holiest". The final hymn is invariable (apart from one occasion when it had been requested for the morning service on the same day). "Ride on" is almost always used, but in one order which took a different turn at that point "Ah, holy Jesu" (*E.H.* 70) was sung. For the opening carol "Remember, O thou man" (*Oxford* 42) and the "Sussex Mummers' Carol" (*Oxford* 45) have both been used, and will be again. Other carols at various points in the service have been "The Decree" (*Oxford* 65) and (in 1952, but never again) "Tchaikovsky's Legend" (*Oxford* 197). In 1958 "My dancing day" was added. The presence of two anthems makes the service not quite a true "carol service", but none the less it is a development of the Truro technique which may have something to commend it.

Annotated Bibliography

The references are arranged as they appear in the text of the book.

Page

17 *Sandys, William* (1792–1874), one of the first modern collectors of traditional carols. The quotation is from his *Christmas Carols, Ancient and Modern*, page fifty (roman figures) of Preface.

17 Greene, R. L., *Early English Carols* (Clarendon Press, 1935).

17 *Musica Britannica*, ed. J. Stevens (Stainer & Bell, 1952).

18 Duncan, E., *The Story of the Carol*, one of the series under the general title, *The Music Story* (Walter Scott publishing Co., in America, Scribners, 1911).

19 Terry, R. R. (1865–1938), *A Forgotten Psalter and other Essays* (O.U.P., 1929), chapter on "Sailor Shanties", pp. 141–169.

19 *English County Songs*, ed. Lucy Broadwood (d. 1929) and J. A. Fuller-Maitland (1856–1936) (J. B. Cramer, no date), p. iv of Preface.

19 Terry, *op. cit.*, pp. 162 ff.

25 Dearmer, Percy (1867–1936), *A Parson's Handbook*, first published 1899; I here refer to the Preface to the 5th and subsequent editions.

26 Bramley, The Rev. H. R. (1833–1917), Fellow of Magdalen College, Oxford, and co-editor with Sir John Stainer (1840–1901) of *Christmas Carols New and Old*, referred to in this book as "Bramley & Stainer" or B/S; the quotation is from the first paragraph of his Preface.

26 Greene, *op. cit.*, p. xxiii.

27 Greene, *op. cit.*, p. cxxxi and xcv.

28 Greene, *op. cit.*, pp. cvii f. *et al.*

29 Manuscripts: the collection in *M.B.* comprises six mss., details of which can be read on p. 125 of *M.B.* They are: (1) British Museum, Add. Ms. 5665, (2) British Museum, Add. Ms. 5666, (3) British Museum, Egerton 3307, (4) Trinity College, Cambridge, Ms. 0.3.58, (4) Bodleian Library, Oxford, Ms. Arch. Selden. b. 26. and (6) Bodleian, Ms. Ashmole 1393.

30 *Piers Plowman*, ed. Wells (Sheed & Ward, 1936), xv 609–11; cf. xv 537.

35 Greene, *op. cit.* p. cxi note 2.

36 *Oxford Dictionary of Nursery Rhymes*, ed. I. and P. Opie (Clarendon Press, 1951), p. 171, no. 167.

40 *The Boar's Head*: "Be gladde . . ." is from G. 132 *b*. The version in *Oxford* is relatively late, from Magrath's *The Queen's College* (1921), II 240 f.

Page

43   *Oxford Book of Carols*, ed. P. Dearmer, M. Shaw and R. Vaughan Williams, p. 484 and p. xii of Preface.

44   Greene, *op. cit.*, p. cxxxi.

     " . . . not born Christian"; this is the governing proposition of my own book, *The Church and Music* (Duckworth, 1950), and is made on p. 9.

44   Chambers, G. B.; *Folksong-Plainsong* (Merlin Press, 1956).

44   Greene, *op. cit.*, pp. xxiv ff.

45   *Noel:* Sometimes the word is said to derive from the Latin *novellae* (= "news" and therefore "Gospel"). Plausibility is added to this theory by the frequent conjunction in medieval carols of the word *nowell* with the word *tidings* (as in *Oxford* 21, 36 *et al.*). But the difficulty is that *novellae* is not good Latin, even good medieval Latin, for "news", and the resemblance between the two words is only superficial.

46   Mellers, W., *Music and Society* (Dobson, 1946), p. 20.

47   *Oxford Book of Ballads*, ed. A. Quiller-Couch (O.U.P., 1910), p. x of Preface.

47   *Oxford Book of Ballads:* quotations—"They sought her . . .", no. 113 st. 14–15; "This began . . .", no. 218, st. 4–5; "When captains . . .", no. 165, st. 1.

48   Sternhold's 23rd Psalm. Keen observers will note how George Herbert borrowed a phrase or two for his exquisite version in *E.H.* 93.

49   Tye, "Then sayde. . . ." Quoted in Frost, *English and Scottish Psalm Tu..es, c.* 1543–1677 (S.P.C.K. and O.U.P., 1953), p. 358.

49   Chappell, W. (1809–88), musical antiquary and song-collector. *Old English Ditties* (our quotations are from pp. xii f. of its Preface) is a selection from his larger and more celebrated work, *Popular Music of Olden Time (c.* 1850). It may be remarked that the legislation on which he adversely commented 100 years ago is still active.

50   Baring-Gould, The Rev. S. (1834–1924), Rector of Horbury Bridge in the W. Riding of Yorks, best known as the author of *Lives of the Saints* and the hymns "Onward, Christian soldiers" and "Now the day is over". His biography was published (1957) under the title *Onward, Christian Soldier*, by W. Purcell. Our quotation is from p. xi of his Preface to Chope's *Carols for Use in Church.*

51f   *New Testament Apocrypha.* Several quotations are here taken from M. R. James, *The Apocryphal New Testament* (O.U.P., 1926). *Pseudo-Matthew* is on pp. 75 ff. of that book; the *Gospel of Thomas* on p. 50; *The Acts of Thomas*, p. 63, and the passage (p. 57) from the *Protevangelium of James*, p. 42.

53   Terry, R. R., *Gilbert and Sandys' Christmas Carols* (Curwen, no date), p. 38.

Page

56 Dives and Lazarus in *St. Luke:* see J. M. Creed, *The Gospel according to St. Luke* (Macmillan, 1930), pp. 208 ff.

60 *The Three Ships.* Mr. Richard Nettel in his excellent introduction to his *Carols, 1400–1950* (Gordon Fraser, 1956), p. 18, gives a tradition different in details. I think that if it is Constantine's mother who brought the relics from the East, the city to which they were brought must be called Byzantium: the transport from there to Milan is, in his tradition, ascribed to St. Eustathius; both the historic persons of this name were bishops in the East (of Antioch, and of Sebaste), and the reason for such a pilgrimage to Milan is very obscure; the transport from Milan to Cologne is ascribed to Bishop Renaldus. Nobody has made it clear why Barbarossa (if it was indeed he, as O.D.C.C. says) took the sea-route.

73 Trevelyan, G. M., *English Social History* (1942), p. 65.

75 *Green grow the rushes–O:* for a detailed exposition, see *English County Songs* (as above), pp. 158 ff.

78 *Song of Solomon:* see Commentary by G. A. F. Knight in the Torch Bible Commentaries (S.C.M. Press, 1955).

78 Charles Williams (1886–1945), *The Descent of the Dove* (1941), a Church History whose ground-bass is Ignatius' "My *eros* is crucified".

78 *Holy Worldliness*—see chapter of that title in A. R. Vidler, *Essays in Liberality* (S.C.M. Press, 1957).

81 Richard Hill, sixteenth century London grocer, in his *Commonplace Book*, gives us versions of *Oxford* 36, 39, 118, 120, 169 and 172.

81 Gilbert, Davies (1767–1839), born Davies Giddy, High Sheriff of Cornwall, 1794; M.P. for Helston, 1804, and for Bodmin, 1806–32; President of the Royal Society, 1827–30. His collection, together with the tunes in Sandys, is reprinted in R. R. Terry *Gilbert and Sandys* (as above).

84 Lucy Broadwood (d. 1929), great-granddaughter of John Broadwood, pioneer piano-manufacturer. Cecil Sharp (1859–1935), editor of many collections of folk dances and songs. J. A. Fuller-Maitland (1856–1936), folk-song collector and editor of *English Carols of the Fifteenth Century* (1891), a collection of thirteen manuscript carols of the "Greene" period. R. Vaughan Williams, O.M. (1872–1958) doyen of English composers, part-editor of *E.H.* and *Oxford.*

87 Sampson, George, *Seven Essays* (Cambridge University Press, 1947), esp. that entitled "The Century of Divine Songs". Quotation from p. 216.

92 Davies, H. Walford, *The Pursuit of Music* (Nelson, n.d.) p. 73.

93 WAS LEBET: The two forms of the tune will be found at *E.H.* 42 and *A.M.* (S) 746; they are commented on in *M.C.H.*, p. 103, and in K. L. Parry (ed.), *Companion to Congregational Praise* (Independent Press, 1953), p. 147 at hymn 275.

Page

99   THE FIRST NOWELL: An ingenious and agreeable organ piece by Mr. J. B.
     Rooper was published about twenty-five years ago by J. B. Cramer,
     called "Prelude on Two Christmas Carols", which introduces this as
     a counterpoint to "A Virgin Unspotted".

100 Terry, *Gilbert and Sandys* (as above), p. ix.

108 Dunlop, Colin, *Procession* (Alcuin Club Tracts, O.U.P., no. 20, 1932).

111 The Lord of Misrule: see Sandys, *op. cit.*, pp. xviii ff.

113 Blake, Nicholas, *Thou Shell of Death* (Collins), ch. 1.

115 Guardini, R.; *The Spirit of the Liturgy* (Sheed & Ward, 1930), p. 115.

120 Neal, Daniel, *The History of the Puritans* (1732), ed. Toulmin (1837);
     "This day . . ." from ii 284 ff.; "The changing . . ." and "during
     the space . . ." from ii 458 ff.

123 Scholes, *The Puritans and Music* (O.U.P., 1936).

123 Reed, E. B. (ed.), *Christmas Carols Printed in the Sixteenth Century* (Harvard
     University Press, 1932,) p. iii of Preface.

131 Lewis, C. S., *English Literature in the Sixteenth Century Excluding Drama*
     (Oxford History of English Literature, O.U.P., 1954), pp. 94 f.

134 Rickert, E., *Ancient English Christmas Carols* (Chatto & Windus, 1914).

134 Lewis, C. S., *op. cit.*, p. 540.

138 Wither, G.: Both books here mentioned are accessible in editions by
     Edward Farr; that of the 1623 book is dated 1856, that of the 1641
     book, 1857. The quotation "For so innumerable . . ." is from
     The Hallelujah, ed. Farr, p. xxv. "Nurses usually sing . . ." from the
     same book, p. 67.

141 *Hymns*. See C. S. Phillips, *Hymnody Past and Present* (S.P.C.K., 1937),
     or Bishop Frere's Introduction to the Historical Edition (1909) of
     Hymns A. & M., or perhaps my own book, *Hymns and Human Life*
     (Murray, 1952).

143 Baxter, R. (1615–91): his liturgy is appended to *A Petition for Peace with
     the Reformation of the Liturgy* (London, 1661). A good discussion of
     it will be found in chapter VI of Horton Davies, *The Worship of the
     English Puritans* (Dacre Press, 1948).

143 Watts, Isaac: see A. P. Davis, *Isaac Watts* (Independent Press, 1948), p. 19.

145 Manning, B. L., *The Hymns of Wesley & Watts* (Epworth Press, 1942),
     ch. IV.

147 Stéphan, J.: *Adeste Fideles*, published at Buckfast Abbey, 1947.

152 Butts, T., *Harmonia Sacra*. Its date is usually quoted as 1753, but the
     reasons for preferring the later date are given by Dr. Maurice Frost
     in the *Bulletin of the Hymn Society*, vol. III, no. 5, pp. 73–9. For
     Frere's note, see Historical *A. & M.* (1909), p. 82.

155 Wainwright, J.: he was appointed organist of Manchester Collegiate
     Church (now Cathedral) in 1764. This whole story is based on
     entries in Byrom's diary, but in H. Talon's edition of the *Journal and*

Page

Papers of John Byrom (Rockliff, 1951) neither John Wainwright nor the incident of Dolly's birthday are mentioned.

157 Moffatt, J. (with Millar Patrick), *Handbook to the Church Hymnary* (O.U.P., 1935), p. 514.

159 Mayo, C. H. (ed.): *Traditional Carols*. . . . This small book of 32 pages, containing twelve carols, was collected by the Reverend C. H. Mayo, Vicar of Long Burton with Holnest, Dorset, and printed at Sherborne by J. C. and A. T. Sawtell. The Preface is dated 1893, and in it the editor writes that the tunes have been collected from ms. books of "the old band of singers". The tune to "While shepherds . . ." is described as locally current. All the harmonies are by Miss Edith C. Howorth. The words of the carols, though described as traditional and rightly regarded by the editor as the work of unskilled hands, display to a marked degree the effect of the Evangelical Revival, being rarely narrative, always cast in the form of short hymns, and usually hortatory in tone.

162 CHRISTMAS CAROL (Walford Davies): Sir Walford Davies wrote two tunes for these words. The other, known as WENGEN, has appeared in *Hymns A. & M.* since the Second Supplement of 1916.

164 Lewis, C. S., *op. cit.*, p. 267. Kinwelmershe's original may be read in English Religious Verse (Everyman's Library 937), p. 21, or in Rickert, *op. cit.*, p. 269. William Byrd's setting of this poem may be seen in R. Nettel, *Carols, 1400–1950*, p. 71.

169 Loesser, A., *Men, Women and Pianos* (Gollancz, 1955), esp. ch. 13. "Music, as an insignificant activity . . ." from p. 233; "Cet instrument bourgeois", p. 317.

170 *Musical Times*. See Percy Scholes, *The Mirror of Music* (Novello, 1947), Vol. I, p. 23. "Hullah-baloo" from p. 13.

171 Hylton Stewart, C., *Posthumous Papers*, ed. E. H. Fellowes (O.U.P., 48 pp., 1933), p. 13. Dr. Hylton Stewart remarks that he has preserved the punctuation in this extract with great care.

172 Croft, J. B.: for the work of this school of editors, see C. E. Pocknee, *The French Diocesan Hymns and their Melodies* (Faith Press, 1954).

173 The Rev. C. V. Taylor, in the Preface to *Christmas Carols* (Batsford, 1957).

173 Husk, W. H., *Songs of the Nativity*: undated; the book was deposited at the British Museum in the spring of 1868.

174 Whistler, L. M.: *The English Festivals* (Heinemann, 1947), pp. 20 f.

176 Duncan, E., *op. cit.*, p. 242.

182 Baring-Gould, S., Preface to Chope, *op. cit.*, p. xv.

188 Rickert, E., *op. cit.*, p. 287.

190 *Deutsches Evangelisches Gesangbuch*. Lutheran practice in Germany is to have a common hymn book throughout the churches, with local supplements. The book I refer to is that in use in Schleswig-Holstein.

Page

Its first 342 hymns constituted the common stock. The details of these researches can be read by the persevering reader in the original version of my dissertation, deposited in the Bodleian Library, Oxford, under the title *Music in Christian Hymnody*.

191   *Piae Cantiones.* An edition was published in 1910 by the Plainsong and Medieval Music Society, edited by G. R. Woodward, who wrote an excellent preface to it. A short account of it can be read at *M.C.H.*, pp. 21 ff.

194   Descant. Three other examples from Germany are given at *M.C.H.*, pp. 19 f. The great chorale at the end of the *St. John Passion* of Bach is the most distinguished tune to have had such a history.

201   *Stille Nacht:* Full information about this carol can be read in Mary Flager Cary's *Stille Nacht* (New York, 1933), which is quoted in the article on it in *The Hymnal* (1904) *Companion* (New York, 1949), pp. 27 f.

213   Liapunov, Sergei Mikhailovitch (1859–1924) is an inconsiderable composer, but he was a member of the Imperial Geographical Society's folk-song commission in Russia, which published in 1897 a collection of 275 Russian folk-songs and carols.

215   Geddes, A., *The Songs of Craig and Ben* (Serif Books, Edinburgh, 1951), p. 2. The Gaelic original of these lines is in *Carmina Gadelica* (Oliver & Boyd).

226   Novello's: see Scholes, *A Mirror of Music*, II, 558.

227   Terry, R. R.: *Twelve Christmas Carols* (Curwen, 1912).

228   Truro: I have this information partly from Canon F. W. B. Bullock's book, *A History of the Parish Church of St. Mary, Truro* (A. W. Jordan, Truro, 1948), and partly from documents in the Colles Library of the R.S.C.M.

228   "The choir . . ."; quoted from the *West Briton* for 23 December 1878, in Bullock, *op. cit.*, p. 122.

229   Stubbs: Hymnologists must beware of confusing C. W. Stubbs wth William Stubbs, Bishop of Oxford (1825–1901), who also wrote hymns, and who also was partial to the 6 × 10 metre: see *Oxford Hymn Book* 237.

236   *Cock-Robin:* Newly edited by Geoffrey Hall and Edith Bathurst, Hinrichsen, Edition No. 317 a. The full text of "Who'll wed Cock Robin" appears in Hinrichsen's *Ninth Music Book* (1957); the pages are (surprisingly) unnumbered, but the verses appear on the next page but one following section 915 h.

238   *Shanties:* see Terry, *A Forgotten Psalter* (as above), p. 168.

Index

First lines and titles are printed in *italic*. Where either begins with the definite or indefinite article, first lines are indexed thus: 'The Angel Gabriel', while titles are indexed thus: 'Holy Well, the'.

The sign * preceding a title indicates that it is the title not of a carol but of a book or article.

The sign † following a page reference means that a *tune* is there referred to.

INDEX TO CAROLS IN THE OXFORD BOOK OF CAROLS

excluding references to pages 85–6 and 245–54, but noted whether or not the *Oxford* number appears in the text).